"In his new book, *Jesus and the Shamanic Tradition of Same-Sex Love*, Will Roscoe lives up to the archetype of consciousness scout: going first and pushing boundaries, taking the reader on an intriguing, insightful and illuminating journey from Plato to the Gnostic Gospels to Siberian shamanism to AIDS. I found the book engaging, well-written and thought-provoking."
—Christian de la Huerta, author of *Coming Out Spiritually*

"Wonderfully readable...a real contribution to the field of gay spirituality, in part because of the in-depth research and academic excellence... Roscoe has indeed managed to synthesize a coherent spirituality that places same-sex love and modern gay consciousness at the heart of humankind's religious/spiritual quest."
—Toby Johnson, author of *Gay Perspective: Things Our Homosexuality Tells Us About the Nature of God and the Universe*

"Will Roscoe's gift has always been the ability to see the seemingly familiar with a new eye, a queer eye that leads him off in unexplored directions. Before we know it, we're seeing with a new eye as well, reimagining everything, even Jesus."
—Carol Queen, author of *The Leather Daddy and the Femme*

"Will Roscoe always takes us places we never thought we'd go. By delving into the sacred heart of the Jesus myth, he opens gateways of revelation that both astound and inspire. Precise, political, and deeply personal, Roscoe's work moves the discussion about the role of same-sex love in the evolution of human consciousness ahead by a quantum leap."
—Mark Thompson, author of the *Gay Spirit, Gay Soul, Gay Body* trilogy

Jesus and the Shamanic Tradition of Same-Sex Love

by Will Roscoe
Illustrations by Winfield Coleman

suspect thoughts press
www.suspectthoughtspress.com

Cover image by Stevee Postman
Author photo by Doug Rasmussen
Cover design by Shane Luitjens/Torquere Creative
Book design by Ian Philips with miracle assists from Kathleen Pratt
Print management by Jackie Cuneo/Little Jackie Paper

First Edition: December 2004
ISBN 0-9746388-3-8
10 9 8 7 6 5 4 3 2 1

Library of Congress Cataloging-in-Publication Data

Roscoe, Will.
Jesus and the shamanic tradition of same-sex love / by Will Roscoe.
    p. cm.
 Includes bibliographical references.
 ISBN 0-9746388-3-8 (pbk.)
1.   Homosexuality--Religious   aspects--Christianity--History   of
doctrines--Early church, ca. 30-600. 2.   Love--Religious aspects--
Christianity--History of doctrines--Early church, ca. 30-600. 3. Secret
Gospel according to Mark--Criticism, interpretation, etc. 4.
Homosexuality--Religious aspects. 5.   Love--Religious aspects. 6.
Shamanism. I. Title.

BR115.H6R67 2004
270.1'086'64--dc22

                                    2004023377

Suspect Thoughts Press
2215-R Market Street, PMB #544
San Francisco, CA 94114-1612
www.suspectthoughtspress.com.

For all the boys flying above the clouds...*I love you guyz!*

TABLE OF CONTENTS

ILLUSTRATIONS

PREFACE

When the opening of Terrence McNally's play, *Corpus Christi*, was announced in New York City in 1998, it was greeted with outcries from Catholics, Muslim fatwas and random threats of violence. In response, the theater canceled the production. It took a published letter of protest from leading playwrights to bring about its premiere. At the end of a long century of shocking experiments in the arts, McNally had managed to find a subject still capable of provoking outrage: love between persons of the same sex.

The premise of McNally's play is not so different from that of *Jesus Christ Superstar*, the popular 1970 rock opera. Although *Superstar's* very human portrayal of Jesus offended the orthodox, its premise was consistent with a basic article of Christian faith—that the Bible's narratives are relevant to all people in all times. McNally's offense was to use this premise to relate the "greatest story ever told" to the lives of contemporary gay people. But as he later explained, "If a divinity does not belong to all people, if He is not created in our image as much as we are created in His, then He is less a true divinity for all men to believe in.... Such a God is no God at all because He is exclusive to His members."

Although critics dwelled on McNally's gay Jesus, the underlying message of *Corpus Christi*—that gays, like Jesus, have been misunderstood and persecuted—has merit whatever the sexuality of Christianity's founder might have been. This message was brought home tragically only days after the play's opening, when a college student in Wyoming named Matthew Shepard was brutally murdered by antigay attackers, his body left dangling from a barbed wire fence. Those who saw the staging of the crucifixion in *Corpus Christi* could not fail to make the connection to Shepard's horrifying death. Suddenly, what was shocking about McNally's play was not what it claimed about Jesus, but what it revealed about society today.

Jesus and the Shamanic Tradition of Same-Sex Love will likely trigger similar reactions, although one hopes on a less dramatic scale. It will be characterized as claiming that Jesus was gay, and this will elicit varying reactions along the spectrum from revulsion to incomprehension. An explanation will be sought for such a perverse idea, and for some it will be found in the fact that the author "admits" to being gay himself. For many, this will be enough to dismiss the book out of hand as a product of wishful thinking.

In point of fact, I do not claim that Jesus was gay, although this has been done recently, and rather convincingly, by Theodore W. Jennings Jr. in *The Man Jesus Loved: Homoerotic Narratives from the New Testament.*

11

Jesus and the Shamanic Tradition of Same-Sex Love

Drawing on some of the same material used here, Jennings suggests that the mysterious beloved disciple of the Gospel of John was Jesus' lover. At least, that is how Greek-speaking readers of John would have understood the gospel's references to a male follower of Jesus identified merely as "the one whom he loved." But here Jennings' questions stop. That Jesus had a male lover does not lead him to revise anything else in the conventional account of Christianity's origins.

Jesus and the Shamanic Tradition of Same-Sex Love offers a more radical re-envisioning of the past. It suggests that same-sex love was the chrysalis in which Christianity's revolutionary ideal of a universal and redeeming form of love was forged, and it suggests that this concept of love was derived from its rituals (not the other way around)—in particular, a secret ritual whose symbols and gestures are shown to have an ancient history. This moves same-sex love from the margins of Western religious history to its center.

Some will say this amounts to claiming a special status for homosexuality, which will be declared elitist and offensive. Robert Graves once dismissed Plato's idealization of male homosexuality on these grounds, calling it, "A moral aberrancy...the male intellect trying to make itself spiritually self-sufficient." Today's critics will likely challenge me along theoretical lines. Since all generalizations about homosexuals (and anything else for that matter) can be shown to be false by citing exceptions, they will say, then none can be made, and heterosexuals and homosexuals have no meaningful differences. This objection, however, betrays an assumption that what is different must be better or worse; that difference is inimical to equality. But as we will see, one of Jesus' most profound teachings is that different people are to be equally loved, and that we should love not because of the value of the other but because of the value of loving.

Yet others will say that my conclusions are false because they do not accept the premises on which they are based: that there is such a thing as a history of ideas and religion, and that past and present forms of same-sex love, intimacy, and relationships can be compared. Some will find errors here or there and dismiss the book on these grounds: if the author made this mistake, then undoubtedly there are others. At least a few diligent souls will consider the overall body of evidence offered on a point by point basis. These are the criticisms authors appreciate most because they show the way to improvement.

But ultimately all these criticisms miss their mark. My goal is to tell a story, and I hope it will be judged as such. Is it engaging and vivid? Does it draw its readers into actively imagining the unknown, in identifying with the Other? Or perhaps it offers useful lessons. Viewed from this perspective, my quotations of historical sources and discursions into context and background are merely literary devices, equivalent to the kind of random detail characteristic of novels which serves to produce what Roland Barthes called "the reality effect."

I do believe, however, that the account that follows is plausible — and given the fragmentary nature of the evidence, plausibility is the strongest claim any history of Christianity's origins can make. But even if the Secret Gospel, upon which much of this story depends, should be proven a forgery, I still think the story is worth reading. It offers new and challenging perspectives on religious history and sexuality. It has helped me as a gay man make sense of what I witnessed in the course of an epidemic that decimated my generation.

But if this story is plausible, then why has it not been told before? The answer has partly to do with the conspiracy of silence that still surrounds the subject of homosexuality and marginalizes its study, and also with the fact that until quite recently much of the evidence that makes it possible to tell this story simply has not been available. Our understanding of early Christianity is being revolutionized as a result of ancient texts discovered in the past century at Nag Hammadi, Qumran, and elsewhere, some of which are still in the process of being translated and published. The single most important piece of evidence on which this book is based, the Secret Gospel of Mark, was only discovered in 1958. As a result of these discoveries — and a greater willingness on the part of scholars to draw on noncanonical Christian writings, the so-called apocrypha — a new picture of early Christianity is emerging. The movement that became the official religion of the Roman Empire and remains the dominant moral system of Western civilization began as an apocalyptic and messianic Jewish sect that drew on both mysticism and magic. And it arose in a cultural milieu far stranger that we have ever imagined.

The story of people and places told here is set within a metanarrative that traces the history of the images and symbols — the archetypes — associated with same-sex love. In the course of this history, two of these archetypes were synthesized to produce a new primal image, that of Divine Twins, representing the ideal of reciprocal love between equals. The symbols and mythical motifs associated with this archetype informed the teachings of Jesus and others, as I discuss. (It should be noted, however, that my use of the term "archetype" does not follow the strict Jungian definition, but has the looser meaning of a core set of images and themes that can be traced across cultures and in the psychology of individuals.)

Until recently, history has been written with the assumption that individuals in the past are heterosexual unless proven otherwise. If men and women in other times married, few historians would question that they were heterosexual. But in fact throughout much of history practices of arranged marriage and female subordination have made heterosexuality compulsory. Is it valid to assume that individuals preferred to do things that they were, in fact, required to do?

In contrast, the historian who wishes to characterize an individual in the past as gay must meet a high standard of proof. One cannot call Emily Dickinson lesbian, for example, even though she never married and maintained intimate relationships with other women, because there is no evidence that she ever had sex with a woman. Even in the case of individuals known to have engaged in same-sex intercourse, the conclusion that they were homosexual is often challenged on the grounds that "heterosexuals"—that is, people who conform to heterosexual social roles—are known to sometimes engage in homosexual acts. For gay historians, this double standard effectively places us back into the closet. We are expected to do something rarely asked of heterosexual historians—when writing of the past, to ignore our intuitions and insights—to, in effect, pretend that we are not gay.

In writing this book, I have chosen not to ignore my intuitions and insights. When I read Plato's description of what a lover feels at the sight of his beloved, it is understandable to me because it reminds me of my own experiences of love, which have occurred within same-sex relationships. When Jesus tells his disciples that laying down one's life for one's friends is the greatest love, I think of the acts of devotion I have witnessed between lovers and friends who are gay. And when I read of passionate expressions of love between men, I don't need to know whether or not they had sex. I identify with the expressions because I have made and received them, too, in both sexual and nonsexual relationships.

Of course, simply because something in the past seems familiar today does not justify claiming it as gay or as relevant to contemporary homosexuals. But these reactions can be used as working hypotheses. By questioning them—why does this seem familiar? how is it not familiar? what social and cultural factors are these similarities and differences based on?—we gain valid insights into both past and present.

In the final analysis, I believe we can only understand the past to the extent that we can relate at least some part of it to the present. Being a mother in the past is not the same as that role today, but it is "like" it. In attempting to understand the otherness of the past, the familiar provides a base camp for forays into the unknown. As Morton Smith, a scholar who figures prominently in this book, once observed, "History is a work of the imagination within limits set by the imagination." These qualifications, however, will probably not satisfy those who find any comparisons between contemporary gay people and the past anachronistic. Theorists today argue that gay identity is a social construction, a consequence of labeling and social factors that did not exist until the late nineteenth century. Being a recent invention, it has no history and cannot be compared to anything in history.

These points ought to be made when past forms of heterosexuality are assumed to be relevant to the present, as well. Today's small nuclear families, single-parent households, dual-career couples, and high divorce rates could hardly be more different from the families of the polygamous, patriarchal Hebrews of the Old Testament. Yet millions believe, whether Jewish, Christian, or agnostic, that because their orientation is heterosexual they stand on the side of the patriarchs, while lesbian, gay, bisexual, and transgendered people do not. Rather than abandon this ground altogether, however, I counter the heterosexual reading of the past with an alternative queer reading of the same.

Actually, I only rarely use the words "gay" or "homosexual." This is because my subject is not sex but love. This is the second important feature of this book. *Jesus and the Shamanic Tradition of Same-Sex Love* offers an alternative way of looking at intimacy between members of the same sex than that afforded by the concept of homosexuality.

The practice of categorizing people based on sexual object choice originated less than a century and a half ago, when European medical doctors and other authorities became aware of a population of men and women who preferred intimacy with members of their own sex. Initially, these people were defined as being gender-different—they were men and women who did not conform, sexually or otherwise, with expectations for their sex. But it was their sexual behavior that most violated the laws and sensibilities of society, and ultimately it was on the basis of this that they were defined. What made them different from the majority was not their personalities or talents, not their emotions, not the qualities of the relationships they formed, but simply their sexual object choice. They were homosexuals. What else they had in common was rarely considered.

But the heterosexual/homosexual dichotomy is a lopsided one. Homosexuals are not viewed as a distinct kind of people, who consistently vary from heterosexuals. Rather, it is only when they act on their sexual desires that they break ranks with the majority. When they love friends or relatives they do so no differently than others. What this means practically is that whatever does *not* involve sexual desire for the same sex remains by default heterosexual. Homosexuality is a subset of a heterosexual universe.

Labeling people in terms of sex has various implications. It implies that a clear line can be drawn between love that involves sexual desire and love that does not, despite what Freud discovered about the role of sexual motives in all love relationships, even within the family. It also implies that relationships between members of the same sex involving sexual desire are categorically different from same-sex relationships that

15

are nonsexual.

In the course of researching and reflecting on the subject of this book, it became clear to me how limiting these categories are. The recurring theme I uncover has to do with same-sex relationships, but their emotional, not their sexual, aspects. In today's world, passionate love between individuals of the same sex is rarely expressed except by those who are willing to be labeled gay. But this was not always the case. For many ancient Greeks, the devotion of male lovers could serve as a model for all relationships, same-sex and opposite-sex, sexual and nonsexual.

As an alternative to sexual labels, I use the term "same-sex love." This is not a synonym for "homosexuality." That remains essentially a psychological term, referring to the inner motivation of some individuals. Rather, "same-sex love" refers to a kind of relationship with certain sociological features, namely, the relative sameness and equality of the partners. The dynamics of such relationships are different from those of opposite-sex relationships, especially in societies where women have less status and autonomy than men. Further, these dynamics are present regardless of whether the individuals involved have sex or desire sex with each other, although they are especially likely to be present in intimate relationships. It is on this basis that Jesus' teaching on the love of friends is linked to Plato's philosophy. Both were concerned with a kind of love that is particular to the dynamics of relationships between equals and sames.

Finally, three technical notes. Since readers may not have special knowledge of ancient history, I try to provide essential background on people, times, and places in the main body of the text. In other cases, however, I have placed detailed background and topics that are of interest but not central to the narrative in appendices. At the same time, although this book is based on extensive research, I have chosen not to use footnotes; instead, key sources are summarized in a bibliographic essay. Conversely, at the risk of putting off the general reader, I have left certain key terms in Greek and other languages, when their nuances might be lost in translation or because their recurring use reveals connections that otherwise might be missed. Finally, note that all comments within quotations enclosed in brackets are my own.

PROLOGUE
I Desire to See

When a young man or woman wishes to become a shaman, the first thing to do is to make a present to the shaman under whom one wishes to study.... The young aspirant, when applying to a shaman should always use the following formula:

    "I come to you because I desire to see."

    The gift would then be placed outside the tent, or the house, according as it was summer or winter, and would remain there for some time as a present to the helping spirits that would in time be at the pupil's command....

    The evening after a shaman has received and set out a gift of this nature, he must...invoke and interrogate his helping spirits in order to "remove all obstacles," that is, to eliminate from the pupil's body and mind all that might hinder him from becoming a good shaman. Then the pupil and his parents, if he have any, must confess any break of taboo or other offence they have committed, and purify themselves by confession in face of the spirits....

    The first thing a shaman has to do when he has called up his helping spirits is to withdraw the soul from his pupil's eyes, brain and entrails. This is effected in a manner which cannot be explained, but every capable instructor must have the power of liberating the soul of eyes, brain and entrails from the pupil's body and handing it over to those helping spirits which will be at the disposal of the pupil himself when fully trained. Thus the helping spirits in question become familiarised with what is highest and noblest in the shaman-to-be; they get used to the sight of him, and will not be afraid when he afterwards invokes them himself.

    The next thing an old shaman has to do for his pupil is to procure him an angak'ua, *i.e. the altogether special and particular element which makes this man a shaman. It is also called his "lighting" or "enlightenment," for* angak'ua *consists of a mysterious light which the shaman suddenly feels in his body, inside his head, within the brain, an inexplicable searchlight, a luminous fire, which enables him to see in the dark, both literally and metaphorically speaking, for he can now, even with closed eyes, see through darkness and perceive things and coming events which are hidden from others: thus they look into the future and into the secrets of others.*

    The first time a young shaman experiences this light, while sitting up on the bench invoking his helping spirits, it is as if the house in which he is suddenly rises; he sees far ahead of him, through mountains, exactly as if the earth were one great plain, and his eyes could reach to the end of the earth.

Jesus and the Shamanic Tradition of Same-Sex Love

Nothing is hidden from him any longer; not only can he see things far, far away, but he can also discover souls, stolen souls, which are either kept concealed in far, strange lands or have been taken up or down to the Land of the Dead....

Knud Rasmussen, *Intellectual Culture of the Iglulik Eskimos*

CHAPTER ONE
He Fled from Them Naked

This story begins on a spring night in ancient Jerusalem two thousand years ago. Jesus and his closest followers have just finished their Passover meal—their last supper together—and Jesus has foretold his betrayal and death. With a group of his disciples, he steps out into the night and proceeds up the Kidron Valley to the garden of Gethsemane on the Mount of Olives. Instructing three followers to serve as guards, he goes into the garden alone to pray. Actually, he throws himself on the ground and pleads, "Father,...remove this cup from me." He returns to the guards three times only to find them asleep. Then Judas arrives at the head of a crowd armed with clubs and swords. He addresses Jesus as "Teacher," and he kisses him.

The four gospels agree on what happens next: Jesus is seized, his followers flee. But then comes the mystery—two verses in the Gospel of Mark that no commentator has ever been able to adequately explain. In fact, they provide a clue to a side of early Christianity that has remained hidden for eighteen centuries: The religion so often cited today as mandating the condemnation of homosexuality and gay people originated as a mystery cult in which same-sex love was not only idealized, it was an integral element of its oldest rite.

According to the New Revised Standard Version translation: "A certain young man [*neaniskos*] was following him, wearing nothing but a linen cloth [*sindōn*]. They caught hold of him, but he left the linen cloth and ran off" (Mark 14:51-52). The King James version is even more explicit, and in this regard follows the original Greek more closely: "A certain young man was following him, having thrown a linen cloth around his naked body. And the young men caught him. But he, leaving behind the linen cloth, fled from them naked."

Who was this young man? What was he doing at Gethsemane that fateful night, wearing only a towel around his waist, "following" Jesus? One commentator has suggested he was a hapless bystander walking in his sleep. Others argue that he is none other than the author of the Gospel of Mark, who, following ancient literary conventions, identifies himself indirectly. But this only increases the mystery—the author of a gospel, fleeing the scene of Jesus' arrest, naked? It is easy to understand why the other gospels do not have these verses. Harder to explain is why they were kept in Mark at all. Either "Mark" (the true authorship of the gospels is unknown) was a poor writer or perhaps his readers had a point of reference for understanding these verses that we lack.

Or, perhaps, text that explained the presence of this young man that was once part of Mark has been removed.

Jesus and the Shamanic Tradition of Same-Sex Love

UNSPEAKABLE TEACHINGS

Given the loss of nearly all Christian writings from the first century except for the New Testament, it seemed likely that the young man of Mark 14, would remain forever a mystery. But in 1958, an American scholar, Morton Smith, made a discovery that not only explains his presence, it offers a radically new view of Jesus and the movement he launched.

In that year, Smith received permission to catalog the library of the Greek Orthodox monastery of Mar Saba in the Judean desert southeast of Jerusalem. Many of the monastery's oldest books had been destroyed in a fire in the early 1700s. But as Smith browsed the shelves he found that pages from damaged books had been glued together to make covers for other books. Prying the layers apart, he could read lines from ancient manuscripts. In other cases, passages from lost books had been preserved by copying them into the margins and end papers of surviving books. Nonetheless, Smith was in despair of finding anything significant, when he happened to notice three pages of handwriting in the back of a 1646 edition of letters by St. Ignatius. As he later recalled:

> One afternoon near the end of my stay, I found myself in my cell, staring incredulously at a text written in a tiny scrawl I had not even tried to read in the tower when I picked out the book containing it. But now that I came to puzzle it out, it began "From the letters of the most holy Clement, the author of the Stromateis, to Theodore."

The text apparently came from a collection of correspondence by the early church father, Clement of Alexandria (ca. 150-215 C.E.). Its contents were nothing less than sensational.

In Clement's time—a century and a half after the death of Jesus— Christian communities were proliferating from Mesopotamia to Spain. But as Christianity had spread it had also grown more diverse. Its doctrines and rites had yet to take the forms we recognize today. Some Christians were libertines whose sacraments included *agapai* or "love feasts"—orgies, apparently, in which all conventions of matrimony, gender, and kinship were suspended. Yet others pursued the opposite extreme. Retreating to remote deserts and mountain fastnesses, they devised torturous regimes of self-denial, some walling themselves inside their cells until they died buried in their own refuse. In some churches, sexual abstinence, even virginity, was required for baptism. Not a few Christian men sought to transcend sexuality altogether by castrating themselves, while Christian women sought the same end by cross-dressing as men.

Nowhere was this diversity greater than in Clement's Egypt. Whereas the Gospel of Luke (written around 80-85 C.E.) emerged as the preferred text for churches in Asia Minor, and Matthew (written about the same time) in Syria and Palestine, in Egypt numerous sects all had their own versions of scripture. Church fathers like Clement waged battles on two fronts: against polytheism, still the official religion of the Roman Empire, and against competing versions of Christianity. Clement's treatise, *Exhortation to the Greeks*, is a withering assault on paganism, which he accuses of every imaginable abomination, while his rambling dissertation, *Miscellanies*, takes on Gnosticism, an influential branch of early Christianity that emphasized the acquisition of esoteric knowledge, or *gnōsis*, over faith, and held that only an elect could attain salvation through rigorous efforts to free spirit from matter.

Among the Gnostics, the followers of Carpocrates were particularly active. According to Irenaeus, a contemporary of Clement, the Carpocratians believed that for the soul to escape an endless chain of reincarnations it was necessary to experience "every kind of life as well as every kind of action," including what Irenaeus calls "those things which we dare not either speak or hear of, nay, which we must not even conceive in our thoughts." (Expanding on this, Epiphanius, the late-fourth-century heresy hunter, claimed that the Carpocratians practiced "every kind of homosexual act and carnal intercourse with women, with every member of the body" [27.4.6].) The Carpocratians, however, believed that "things are good or evil simply in virtue of human opinion"—a common Gnostic tenet. Interestingly, Irenaeus quotes from a Carpocratian book that refers to secret teachings of Jesus (*Against Heresies* 1.25.1-5).

Clement despised the Carpocratians above all other heretics. In *Miscellanies* he accuses them of practicing economic and sexual communism, including orgiastic "love feasts" (3.2). It is not surprising, therefore, that the letter Morton Smith discovered is concerned with precisely this group. The Carpocratians, Clement tells his correspondent, are "wandering stars," "slaves of servile desires." Their teachings are "unspeakable."

Before he refutes them, however, he makes some surprising admissions. The church at Alexandria, he states, was in possession of a Secret Gospel of Mark—a *mustikou euaggeliou*—which was read "only to those who are being initiated into the great mysteries [*megala mustēria*]." It consisted of the original gospel of Mark plus additional material, which, according to Clement, Mark himself added, based on his notes and those of the apostle Peter. In this way, Mark created a second, "more spiritual" gospel. Clement next admits that the Carpocratians have a copy of this Secret Gospel, which they obtained through "deceitful arts."

Jesus and the Shamanic Tradition of Same-Sex Love

In the end, Clement's dispute with the Carpocratians boils down to differences in the interpretation of the Secret Gospel, not in its existence or contents—they pollute it, he complains, "mixing with the spotless and holy words utterly shameless lies."

To refute them, Clement quotes directly from the Secret Gospel— a passage missing from the Gospel of Mark as we know it today:

> To you, therefore, I shall not be slow in answering your questions, refuting falsifications by proclaiming the very words of the Gospel. For instance, after "And they were in the road going up to Jerusalem," and the following, up to "After three days he shall arise," the Secret Gospel counters word for word: "And they came to Bethany. And there was in that place a woman whose brother had died. And coming forward she prostrated herself before Jesus and said to him, 'Son of David, be merciful to me.' But the disciples admonished her.
>
> "And being angered, Jesus went with her into the garden where the tomb was, and immediately a great cry was heard from the tomb. And coming near, Jesus rolled back the stone from the door of the tomb and entering immediately where the young man [*neaniskos*] was he extended his hand and raised him up, holding his hand. But the young man, looking at him, loved him and began to implore that he might be with him and going away from the tomb they came into the house of the young man, for he was rich. And after six days, Jesus instructed him. When evening arrived, the young man comes to him, having wrapped a linen cloth around his naked body, and he remained with him that night. Jesus taught him the mystery of the kingdom of God. Rising from that place, he returned to the other side of the Jordan." [my translation]

Only at this point does Clement respond to Carpocratian claims: "But 'naked man with naked man' [*gumnos gumnō*] and the other things you wrote are not found."

The letter quotes one more line from the Secret Gospel before the transcription abruptly ends:

> And after the words, "And he comes into Jericho," the Secret Gospel adds only, "And the sister of the youth whom Jesus loved and his mother and Salome were there, and Jesus did not receive them."

Before examining this material more closely, let us review all that Clement has revealed. There is a Secret Gospel of Mark used in mystery rites. It contains "sayings" whose interpretation leads acolytes "into the innermost sanctuary of that truth hidden by seven veils," and it includes an account of Jesus performing a private, nocturnal ritual with a young man he has raised from the dead. Finally, the Carpocratians have a copy of this Secret Gospel, which they claim as their authority for libertine practices involving something called *gumnos gumnō*. Of all this Clement denies only the reference to *gumnos gumnō*.

Smith concluded that the letter was written sometime in the 190s and sent to a destination in Palestine. In the early 200s, when the persecution of Christians unleashed by Septimius Severus forced Clement and other church leaders to flee Alexandria, the church there and its possessions—and likely the Secret Gospel—were destroyed. Clement's letter, however, was somehow preserved in Palestine and eventually included in a manuscript collection of his letters. There is no indication that anyone besides the scribe who copied it in the mid-1700s, and Morton Smith who found it in 1958, ever read it. In any case, the manuscript collection has not survived. The preservation of this one letter and its quotation from the Secret Gospel of Mark appears to be one of the great accidents of history.

As New Testament scholar Geza Vermes observes, "Mark's Gospel brings us nearer the Jesus of history than any other New Testament writing."

If so, then the passage Clement cites from an early version of Mark brings us that much closer to the historical Jesus. For today's churches, of course, the discovery of a competing version of a gospel is a scandal, not the least because of the questions it raises about the status of the writings that are, according to Christian doctrine, the original and authentic speech of God (see the appendices, "God's Word or Human Handiwork?" and "Spell-Checking the Word of God"). Of course, at this late date the churches are not likely to change the contents of the New Testament. Discoveries like Smith's, no matter how strong the evidence for their authenticity, will never be more than footnotes to writings long since declared canonical. Even so, Clement's letter raises a tantalizing question. Is it possible that a secret gospel of Mark really existed, with contents that have been removed from the version we know today?

All the weight comes down on the side of summarily dismissing Smith's discovery. Indeed, everything about Clement's letter, including its authenticity (Smith is the only scholar who has examined it directly), has been questioned. If not the letter itself, then surely the Secret Gospel quotation is fake. Some critics have hinted that Smith himself forged it. For many, the phrase *gumnos gumnō* and the implication that Jesus was, in the words of John Crossan, "a possibly homosexual baptizer," is sufficient to brand the document and Smith's conclusions as fantastic, and, on that basis, foreclose further discussion. Meanwhile, the seventeenth-century book in which Smith found the letter copied has disappeared. There are rumors that the Greek Orthodox Church may have destroyed it for this very reason: because it "implies" that Jesus was homosexual.

For the record, I do not believe that this text provides any evidence regarding Jesus' emotional or sexual orientation. At the same time, I do believe it provides compelling evidence that the first Christians, including Jesus, engaged in mystical practices involving intimate same-sex contact. This leads me to conclude that the earliest circles of Christianity were homophilic, not homophobic. In the final analysis, however, the real significance of the Secret Gospel is not what it suggests about Jesus but what it shows us about Jesus' teachings and the place of same-sex love in those teachings.

The discovery of Clement's letter coincides with an historical epoch in which questions concerning sexuality, and especially homosexuality, have produced deep fissures in Christian churches and within society as a whole. For the faithful, it represents a challenge to orthodoxy, but at the same time an opportunity to renew their understanding of Christianity's origins. For gay people—Christian and non-Christian—it presents an opportunity to read themselves into the heritage of Western religion and spirituality as a whole.

Smith devoted over a decade to the study of his discovery and published two books on the subject—a comprehensive, technical monograph, *Clement of Alexandria and a Secret Gospel of Mark* (1973), and a popular account, *The Secret Gospel: The Discovery and Interpretation of the Secret Gospel According to Mark* (1973, 1982). He concluded that the letter was indeed in the style and language of Clement, and that the Secret Gospel passage it quotes was consistent with the writing and vocabulary of canonical Mark.

The passage, in which Jesus raises a man from the dead, is clearly a simple version of the Lazarus story told in the Gospel of John. This is interesting because John is otherwise quite different from Mark in most respects. It was written at least twenty years after Mark, in the late 90s, by a Greek-speaking Christian living outside Palestine for a community of Jewish converts to Christianity, who had formed a church after being expelled from their synagogue. The gospel provides ample evidence of the conflicts they were involved in, and it takes pains to show that Jesus was really the Jewish messiah. It is the only gospel with the miracle of water turned into wine and the story of the raising of Lazarus.

The significant differences in content and style between John and Mark have led most scholars to conclude that John's author was unaware of Mark. John's account of Jesus' trial and crucifixion, however, follows Mark's closely, and some scholars take this as evidence that John had at least some familiarity with Mark. The close parallel of the Lazarus story with the Secret Gospel passage is additional evidence that John drew on early Markan sources.

In fact, as Smith shows, the part of Mark in which the Secret Gospel passage likely belonged is also paralleled by John. This leads him to conclude that the Lazarus story is not only older than John, it is older than John's sources. In other words, behind both Mark and John is an original text—"proto-Mark"—probably written around the year 50, probably in Jesus' language, Aramaic. It included some version of the Lazarus story. The Aramaic text was then translated into Greek twice. One translation was used by the author of Mark, the other by the author of John.

The Lazarus story, however, was not included in canonical Mark. Was it originally part of the gospel but removed? In that case the Secret Gospel represents an earlier, more complete version of Mark. Or was the Secret Gospel derived from canonical Mark, and the story of the young man raised from the dead a later addition? Or, yet another possibility, was material that had been removed from Mark put back in to produce the Secret Gospel?

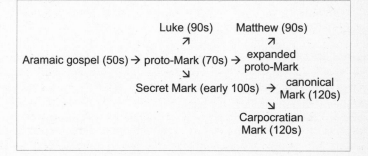

Fig. 1. Development of the Gospel of Mark.

Smith considered all these scenarios at length. Ultimately, he concluded that, based on style, the Secret Gospel was written by someone imitating Mark, but drawing on an original Aramaic gospel. The Secret Gospel, in this case, is *later* than canonical Mark. Thus, "Mark" was reworked at least four times: by Matthew and Luke, by the author of the Secret Gospel, and by the Carpocratians. Given that Carpocrates is known to have been active in Alexandria between 125 and 130, Smith believes that the earliest date for the writing of the Secret Gospel is around 100 C.E.

Smith, however, admitted that this theory does not account for all of the facts. Clement had every reason to portray the Secret Gospel as derivative, when in fact it may have been an original text that the church was at pains to disown because of its libertine elements. This is the conclusion of Helmut Koester: canonical Mark is based on the Secret Gospel, not the other way around.

Drawing on Smith's and Koester's suggestions, the history of the Gospel of Mark looks something like the sequence outlined in Figure 1.

Those eager to discount the Secret Gospel and its disturbing implications, on the other hand, have argued that it is merely a pastiche of phrases borrowed from canonical Mark plus some additions, the idiosyncratic product of a single, unorthodox church. It would be easier to conclude so if it were not for the uncanny way in which the Secret Gospel helps resolve several outstanding questions in New Testament studies, among them the presence of the naked youth at Gethsemane. As Smith asked at the conclusion of his exhaustive study, "Will the reader please offer another explanation for all these problems?"

CHAPTER TWO
The Mystery of the Kingdom of God

To appreciate what the Secret Gospel reveals about early Christianity we need to examine the meaning of a key phrase in it. What was the "mystery of the kingdom of God" that Jesus teaches the young man who comes to him after six days and remains for the night? This phrase also occurs in canonical Mark, chapter 4, where Jesus refers to the mystery of the kingdom of God as a teaching he has given only to his disciples (4:11). In parallel passages in Matthew (13:11) and Luke (8:10) it appears in the plural, as the "*mysteries* of the kingdom of God."

In Jesus' time, the Greek word *mustērion* typically referred to ceremonies in which religious secrets were revealed to an elect. A "mystery" was a "mystery rite." Such rites were common in the ancient world—the cults of Isis, Cybele, Dionysus, and others all had secret ceremonies in addition to their public worship. Clement's letter, however, offers the only evidence we have of Jesus performing such a rite.

What could this have been?

The first clue is the *sindōn*, or white linen cloth, which the young man is described as having wrapped around his waist. This is the same garment worn by the anonymous youth in Mark's account of Jesus' arrest. In fact, the wording is identical—*peribeblēmenos sindona epi gumnou*, literally, "having thrown a linen cloth about his naked body." In ancient Judaism, the *sindōn* was a ritual garment, worn during circumcisions and on other religious occasions. It was also the garment in which the dead were buried. When Jesus was taken down from the cross, his body was wrapped in a *sindōn*.

Sources from a later date indicate that Christians adopted the use of white linen for ritual purposes as well. In the apocryphal Acts of the Holy Apostle Thomas, from the first half of the third century, a *sindōn* is wrapped around the naked body of a convert undergoing baptism (121). Other texts describe the miraculous appearance during baptisms of a youth dressed in white linen. According to the narrator of the Acts of Barnabas, during his baptism, "a certain man standing clothed in white raiment" appeared, who revealed to him "the mysteries of God." (The Acts of the Holy Apostle Thomas just cited has a youth appear during one baptism, who holds a burning torch [27].)

This motif can be traced back to the Gospel of Mark. The three women who come to anoint Jesus' body encounter a young man (*neaniskos*) sitting in the tomb dressed in a white robe (16:5, *peribeblēmenos stolēn leukēn*, the same wording used to describe the *sindōn* worn by the naked youth). In Revelation this phrase is used to describe the dress of the saints in heaven. As the similarity of the language in all these instances suggests, the white linen cloth and white robes were symbolically linked in the minds of early Christians—one was the garment of death, the other the garment of resurrection.

Given the historical and symbolic use of the *sindōn*, its occurrence in the Secret Gospel is strong evidence that the rite being performed was none other than baptism.

Jesus, of course, did not invent baptism. It was introduced by John the Baptist, who had begun preaching the imminent end of the world around 28 C.E. In so doing, he joined a long line of Jewish prophets reaching back eight centuries. He differed from his predecessors, however, by offering a way to prepare for the end. Ritual immersion in flowing water, he claimed, could cleanse them of their sins. This was a significant break with Jewish tradition. Although bathing for purification was a common procedure, the atonement of sins required repentance as well as sacrifices that could only be performed at the temple in Jerusalem by priests who charged fees for their services. Needless to say, these religious authorities took a dim view of John and his movement.

When Jesus was baptized by John, however, he seems to have experienced something more than a symbolic cleansing. According to Mark, "Just as he was coming up out of the water, he saw the heavens torn apart and the Spirit descending like a dove upon him" (1:10). In other words, he had a vision, and he was possessed. The gospels, however, provide little evidence that Jesus himself baptized. Neither Matthew, Mark, nor Luke (the so-called "synoptic" gospels because they closely parallel each other) refer to him baptizing, while John is ambiguous. In chapter 4, the Pharisees accuse Jesus of "baptizing more disciples than John [the Baptist]" (4:1), but in this context the charge is implicitly denied. Later, however, John describes Jesus performing a ritual foot washing, which, as we will see, has all the characteristics of baptism.

The gospels' silence on the origins of baptism stands in contrast to their ample testimony concerning Christianity's other signature rite, communion. This silence seems even stranger when we consider the evidence from Christianity's oldest records—the letters of the apostle Paul.

CHRIST WITHIN YOU

Writing in the 50s, two or more decades before the composition of the first gospel, Paul provides us with the earliest glimpse we have into the religious movement that Jesus is credited with founding. Even so, twenty years had elapsed since Jesus' death. Already, the leadership of the Jerusalem church had passed to individuals who were not among the first disciples, such as James, presumably Jesus' brother, while its first missions outside Judea—to the Samaritans and to gentiles in Antioch—were undertaken by Greek-speaking Jewish Christians, the "Hellenists," as Acts calls them, similarly unrepresented in Jesus' original following.

Paul asserted that God had commissioned him to convert gentiles to Christianity. Prior to this, "Christianity" was essentially a Jewish sect. Many of its leaders—those "of the circumcision," as Paul calls them, or "Hebroi" as they called themselves—continued to observe Jewish religious laws and festivals. Paul, however, maintained that God's forgiveness of sins canceled these obligations (Col. 2:14). Gentiles did not have to become Jews to follow Jesus. This put him at odds with the Jerusalem church, including some of the original disciples, such as Peter. Paul, however, claimed to have greater authority than even those who had known Jesus personally. He was possessed by Jesus' spirit, an entity he refers to as "the Christ." As he claims in his Letter to the Galatians, "Christ lives in me" (2:20).

Paul nonetheless represents the middle ground of early Christianity. On one side were the traditionalists in Jerusalem, like James, whose missionaries openly competed with him. On the other were libertines, who believed that not only Jewish laws but all laws and conventions were nullified by Jesus' resurrection. In fact, libertines appear to have been well-represented in Paul's own churches. In his Letter to the Romans, he complains that they cite his teachings to justify their practices: "Some people slander us by saying that we say, 'Let us do evil so that good may come'" (3:8; cf. Acts 20:30). These Christians believed that having been united with Jesus and filled with his spirit they were holy. In such a state they could do no wrong. Indeed, they might even "do evil so that good may come." Despite their doctrinal differences, however, all these parties—traditionalists, libertines, and Paul himself—appear to have engaged in esoteric practices and to have made competing claims about the spiritual powers this gave them.

Paul's situation, therefore, is quite interesting. To defend his outreach to gentiles, he argues that the arrival of Christ means that heaven has broken through to earth and the end days have arrived. This canceled Jewish religious laws, even as it fulfilled Jewish messianic prophecies. At the same time, Paul had to foreclose the mystical and libertine implications of his teachings, which threatened to radicalize his mission and undermine his leadership (see "Sex and Spirit in Corinth").

Paul himself was baptized two or three years after Jesus' death. His comments about the rite show that it was a well-established procedure, and, indeed, the focus of intense theological speculation. From this we can infer an outline of what it involved. In the Letter to the

Romans, he writes:

> Do you not know that all of us who have been baptized into
> Christ Jesus were baptized into his death? Therefore we have
> been buried with him by baptism into death, so that, just as
> Christ was raised from the dead by the glory of the Father, so
> we too might walk in newness of life. For if we have been
> united with him in a death like his, we will certainly be
> united with him in a resurrection like his. (Rom. 6:3-5).

He uses similar language in the Letter to the Colossians: "When
you were buried with him in baptism, you were also raised with him
through faith in the power of God.... So if you have been raised with
Christ, seek the things that are above, where Christ is, seated at the right
hand of God" (2:12; 3:1).

Obviously, baptism had acquired a rich symbolism, which served
to foster a profound experience for those undergoing it. The baptismal
pool symbolized Jesus' tomb. To be immersed in it was to die a death
"like his" and be buried "with him." Re-emerging from the waters, one
experienced Jesus' resurrection as well—or had a vision of it, as Jesus
did when he was baptized. The implication of all this is that the
proselyte and Christ were somehow joined together. However this was
effected, it must have occurred prior to the immersion, for it was *as*
Christ that proselytes died and *as* Christ that they were buried and
resurrected. (Morton Smith suggested that the death and resurrection
themes were added after Jesus died—unless he really did have
foreknowledge of his death—and that the rite as he performed it
centered on possession by a spirit and an experience of heaven. But
given the prevalence of death and rebirth themes in rites of passage
generally, they very well could have been part of Jesus' procedure
without referring specifically to his own fate.) Clearly, undergoing
baptism in Paul's time involved more than repeating formulas and
making ritual gestures. United with Christ, proselytes became Christ. At
the same time, they were united with their fellow Christians as well into
a single "body," Paul's metaphor for the church.

That union with Christ entailed what is otherwise referred to as
spirit possession is evident from Paul's references to Christ entering the
proselyte and the proselyte's body becoming Christ's. The baptized, he
writes in Letter to the Galatians, are "clothed" in Christ (3:27). In
Romans (8:9) and the First Letter to the Corinthians (3:16), he says that
the Holy Spirit "dwells" within them. The Letter to the Ephesians
(attributed to Paul but believed to have been written by one of his
followers) even employs sexual metaphors to describe this union:
proselytes become members of Christ's body, just as in marriage men

and women become "one flesh" (Eph. 5:30-31). In Galatians, the implications of this are made clear: when bodies are merged, social differences are erased, including those of gender: "There is no longer Jew or Greek, there is no longer slave or free, there is no longer male and female; for all of you are one in Christ Jesus" (3:28; for more on this formula, see "Hetero-androgyny in Early Christianity"). No wonder Ephesians calls this a "great mystery" (5:32)! As such, only a few of Paul's followers received it (1 Cor. 1:14-17).

The dramatic enactment of an individual's death and rebirth turns out to be a common element of what anthropologists refer to as "rites of passage"—ceremonies that serve to conduct, and actively transform, individuals from one social status to another. As Arnold van Gennep showed some time ago, these rites typically have three phases. First, initiates are separated from everyday life. This is accomplished through periods of seclusion, all-night vigils, nudity, exorcisms, and so forth. Next is a transitional period, characterized by what Victor Turner termed liminality or marginality. Normal social conventions are suspended, constraints are lifted, high and low are reversed, and social differences, including those of gender, are erased. These procedures recreate the conditions of chaos at the beginning of the cosmos, in the course of which initiates symbolically die. In the third and final phase, rites of reincorporation mark the initiates' reintegration into the community. These typically entail the bestowal of symbols representing their new identities and roles.

All three phases can be discerned in Paul's statements on baptism. His description of the rite as "this mystery, which is Christ within you" (Col. 1:27) and the fact that only a select few received it, indicates it was conducted in private. Thus, it necessarily entailed the separation and seclusion of the participant. If during the proceedings the initiate was "clothed" in Christ, then he likely disrobed in preparation. This would have inaugurated a liminal phase, during which the union with Christ was effected and the proselyte experienced death, burial, and resurrection. Being "clothed" in Christ may be a reference to the reincorpation phase of the rite, when the naked initiate was given new clothing to don. All this appears to have been accompanied by a liturgy, which Paul occasionally paraphrases in his letters, one example being the formula in Galatians, "There is no longer Jew or Greek, free or slave, male or female…" (3:28).

Unfortunately, this is the extent to which we can reconstruct baptism from Paul's letters. His reticence in reporting its details, however, is consistent with Smith's hypothesis that it began as a secret rite. When the gospels were written, in the last quarter of the first century, it was still secret, hence their silence. Nonetheless, the evidence Paul provides supports the conclusion that the rite outlined in the Secret

Gospel was baptism. Like baptism in Paul's references, it is described as a mystery and like baptism it is performed in private and it involved nudity. It appears to have had the same goal as well—to impart knowledge and experience of heaven. Whether the Secret Gospel rite centered on the themes of death and rebirth is not clear from the brief description in Clement's letter. They appear to have been the dominant themes of baptism in Paul's time. But Paul refers to baptism typically in the context of his theological discussions, to illustrate points about his doctrine of resurrection. Between the lines, however, we can begin to see another dimension of the rite, equally important: the unification of the initiate with the spirit being, Christ. This preceded and, indeed, was the means for, the experiences of death and resurrection central in Paul's account.

THE KINGDOM OF GOD

If the "mystery" Jesus teaches in the Secret Gospel was a mystery rite, what was the "kingdom of God" that it conveyed mystical knowledge and experience of?

The phrase "kingdom of God" appears frequently in the gospels of Mark and Luke, and in parallel passages in Matthew in the form "kingdom of heaven" or "kingdom of the heavens." The "kingdom" was the preeminent topic of Jesus' teachings. Scholars believe that references to it were present in the earliest writings of Christianity, which the gospels' authors drew on. It is, first and foremost, the domain in which God resides, that is, heaven. By extension, it refers to God's rule and to any domain where that rule prevailed—in the words of the Lord's Prayer, "Thy kingdom come, thy will be done." But what could it mean to be "taught" this kingdom in a mystery rite? Clearly, something more than acquiring information was involved.

The gospels refer to "entering" the kingdom of God or heaven in several places. In Mark, Jesus tells his disciples that, as insiders, they have been "given the secret [*mustērion*] of the kingdom of God," while those "outside" are given only ambiguous parables (4:11). Today, we read these passages metaphorically. The "kingdom of God" is a metaphor for the new age that will dawn when God's rule is established on earth. One can enter this kingdom now by adopting a lifestyle in accordance with this rule. But as we will see, in the first century, references to entering the kingdom of God were sometimes meant literally by many who believed that traveling to heaven was a real possibility. To understand this belief, we need to look at the way Jews and others in the ancient world conceived of heaven.

Among the peoples of the ancient Near East, the Egyptians, Mesopotamians, and Israelites shared similar conceptions of the universe. The cosmos was believed to have a tripartite structure. Somewhere beyond the visible sky, surrounding or encircling the earth, was heaven, the home of the gods or celestial bodies thought of as gods. These figures were typically depicted as living in temple-like structures or palaces, which were organized like royal courts with a supreme deity enthroned and ruling over the other heavenly personnel. Beneath heaven was earth, the domain of humans, and beneath the earth was the underworld, the abode of the dead and inferior or malignant gods. Human existence was confined to earth, but supernatural beings could traverse all three levels.

Over time this model became more complex. In the late second millennium, Babylonian and Assyrian texts begin to refer to multiple heavens—three or seven—organized one above the other. Earlier, but more ambiguously, Sumerian incantations refer to seven heavens and seven earths. Among the Israelites, concepts of heaven began to change following developments in the period of Hosea. Prior to this, they were still largely polytheistic, worshiping figures like Baal and Asherah, as well as Yahweh. But in the mid-eighth century B.C.E., a party centered in Jerusalem began to demand the exclusive worship of Yahweh. Although this party eventually succeeded in suppressing the worship of other gods, belief in spirit beings, from the eerie *hayyoth* and *cherubim* in Ezekiel's vision to the "messengers" (Hebrew, *malakh*; Greek, *aggelos*), who appear throughout the Bible, continued.

From belief in a supreme deity who rules heaven it follows that other supernatural beings occupy subordinate realms, and thus there is not one heaven but several. Jews likely encountered this idea first among the Babylonians, but it was Greek concepts of the cosmos that had the greatest influence on them, due to the predominance of Greek language and culture throughout the Near East following Alexander's conquests in the late fourth century. Ancient Greeks, like the peoples of the Near East, originally envisioned the cosmos as having three levels: heaven, earth, and an underworld. Heaven was the exclusive domain of the gods. The only human to join to their ranks (interestingly enough) was the hapless shepherd Ganymede, abducted by a sex-crazed Zeus in the guise of an eagle and borne aloft to Olympus.

Beginning in the seventh century, however, the influence of Persian and Mesopotamian astrology led the Greeks to refine their astronomical observations. As they gained a better understanding of the movements of the planets, philosophers began to speculate that the celestial bodies were fixed to a sphere that rotated around the earth. This eventually gave rise to the idea that each planet (and the moon and sun) was attached to its own sphere, and that these spheres circled the earth in a series. Socrates outlines such a model in *Phaedo*, describing the earth as a sphere with the moon, sun, planets, and fixed stars revolving around it, each in its own orbit.

By the first century B.C.E., the idea that the earth was encircled by a hierarchical series of spheres—multiple heavens—had become commonplace. This is how the cosmos is described in Book 6 of Cicero's dialogue, *The Republic*, in an account given by Scipio Africanus of a dream in which his grandfather, Africanus the Elder, appeared. In the dream, Africanus elevates Scipio above the earth and reveals to him the structure of the universe. According to Scipio:

> And as long as I continued to observe the earth with great attention, How long, I pray you, said Africanus, will your mind be fixed on that object; why don't you rather take a view of the magnificent temples among which you have arrived? The universe is composed of nine circles, or rather spheres, one of which is the heavenly one, and is exterior to all the rest, which it embraces; being itself the Supreme God, and bounding and containing the whole. In it are fixed those stars which revolve with never-varying courses. Below this are seven other spheres, which revolve in a contrary direction to that of the heavens. One of these is occupied by the globe which on earth they call Saturn. Next to that is the star of Jupiter, so benign and salutary to mankind. The third in order, is that fiery and terrible planet called Mars. Below this again, almost in the middle region, is the Sun—the leader, governor, the prince of the other luminaries; the soul of the world, which it regulates and illumines, being of such vast size that it pervades and gives light to all places. Then follow Venus and Mercury, which attend, as it were, on the Sun. Lastly, the Moon, which shines only in the reflected beams of the Sun, moves in the lowest sphere of all. Below this, if we except that gift of the gods, the soul, which has been given by the liberality of the gods to the human race, every thing is mortal, and tends to dissolution, but above the moon all is eternal. For the Earth, which is in the ninth globe, and occupies the center, is immoveable, and being the lowest, all others gravitate towards it. (6.17)

This scheme was systematically formulated in the mid-second century C.E. by Claudius Ptolemy of Alexandria. In the Ptolemaic model, eight spheres encircle earth, one for each of the seven planets (which, in turn, represented various gods) and one for the fixed stars. Beyond that is a formless realm of pure ether (see fig. 2).

This conception of the heavens reflected Hellenistic beliefs about

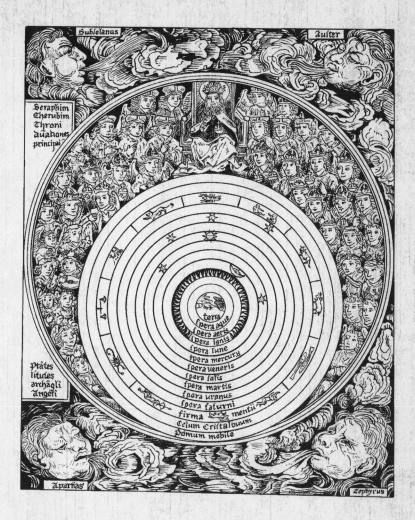

Fig. 2. *The Ptolemaic model of the heavenly spheres as depicted in a late-fifteenth-century engraving. In addition to seven planetary spheres, inner spheres are assigned to the four elements and outer rings to the firmament, Milky Way, and the ineffable "first principle." Superimposed on this Hellenic model is the Christian kingdom of the heavens with its hierarchical levels and celestial personnel (the seraphim, cherubim, "thrones," "dominations," "principalities," "powers," "virtues," archangels, and angels). After Hartmann Schedel,* Liber chronicarum *[Nuremberg Chronicle] (Nuremberg: Antonius Koberger, 1493).*

life after death—in particular the idea that the human soul was immortal. The Egyptians were the first to articulate this belief in their sacred texts. According to The Book of the Dead, when individuals died their spirit or soul escaped their bodies and began an arduous journey through the netherworld eventually followed by an ascent to the stars. In Egyptian art, the soul was depicted as a human-headed bird or as a hawk that could fly to heaven; or it was said to enter heaven by climbing a ladder—the "Ladder of God" as inscriptions at one pyramid describe it. Initially, it was believed that only the souls of pharaohs could achieve this, but over time the idea developed that anyone's soul could enter heaven, if one lived a righteous life.

In *Ancient Philosophy, Mystery, and Magic*, Peter Kingsley shows how these Egyptian beliefs, beginning in the sixth century, influenced the followers of the Greek philosopher Pythagoras and those of the legendary figure, Orpheus. Orpheus and Pythagoras were credited with founding mystery rites and establishing a distinct religious lifestyle. Their followers believed that the soul represented a spark of divinity within humans. Because it originated in heaven, it was immortal. When individuals died, their souls were released from their bodies and sought to return to their celestial home. In Sicily and Italy, Orphics painstakingly etched poems describing this journey onto precious leaves of gold, which they buried with the deceased. These describe a perilous passage that began with a descent to the underworld, where the soul was purified by fire, then an ascent to heaven, during which it shed all connection to matter. Finally, it reached the highest heaven where it existed as being without form, that is, as pure energy. The Pythagoreans instituted rites re-enacting this journey in which they confined themselves inside caves or sealed chambers.

Thus, to Egyptian ideas about death, descent, and regeneration, the Orphics and Pythagoreans added their speculations concerning the soul's journey after death. As Socrates explains in the *Meno*, "They [the Orphics] say that the human soul is immortal. At one time it comes to an end, which they call dying, at another time it is reborn, but it never perishes; therefore one must live one's life as piously as possible" (81b). The fate of the soul, in other words, depends on how well individuals conduct themselves in their lifetimes—whether they preserve the purity of the divine spark within them. Over time, this belief gave rise to another. If a pure soul could enter heaven, then why not a living person who was pure?

The model of multiple heavens was linked to another development in ancient religion—the spread of monotheism. Increasingly, pagans joined Jews and Christians in recognizing a supreme deity. For some, this figure was paternal, typically Zeus; for others, maternal, such as Isis or Cybele, the Phrygian Mother of the Gods whose worship was imported by the Romans. With the rise of a supreme deity enthroned in the highest heaven, the other gods and goddesses of the Greco-Roman pantheon were relegated to the realms beneath this domain—that is, to the region of the planetary spheres which encircled the earth. Thus, each planet was assigned to a god (or thought of as being the god). Over time, however, the gods of Olympus came to be viewed less as deities with distinct personalities and more as generic spirits and demons.

The Hellenistic model of the cosmos proved to have many uses. For the Romans, it provided a way of imagining how the diverse societies they had annexed into their empire could be integrated into a coherent system. Their subject peoples could retain their cultural distinctiveness, but cultures were ranked in a hierarchy that recognized Roman society as supreme. Early Christians projected their beliefs onto Hellenistic cosmology as well. The highest heaven was God's exclusive kingdom, but there were other supernatural domains, as the frequent references to plural heavens in the New Testament imply. The Lord's Prayer, literally translated, begins, "Our father who art in the *heavens*." Matthew even speaks of "the kingdom of the heavens" (2:1), which only makes sense if one imagines two or more heavens under the dominion of a superior realm. Ephesians is even more explicit, referring to the "heavenly places" (*epouraniois*), and describing Christ as he "who ascended far above all the heavens" (4:10).

For Christians, the image of a superior heaven ruling over all others was compatible with their belief that the risen Christ would conquer the nations of the world and bring them under a single spiritual regime. The church itself came to be organized in this way—in a vertical chain of authority that linked God, popes, priests, and congregations in an orderly sequence. Ultimately, however, the image of multiple heavens was transitional. It enabled pagans to embrace a supreme deity without necessarily abandoning belief in other gods. For Jews, it served to preserve Yahweh's supremacy while making allowance for popular belief in spirits.

Indeed, monotheism goes hand in hand with belief in spirits. For when the supreme deity resides in the heaven furthest from earth, intermediaries must be found to bridge the gap. Spirits, who occupy the region between heaven and earth, can communicate with both, and thereby bear the prayers of humans to God and God's blessings to humans. As E. R. Dodds observed of the Hellenistic era, "Virtually every one, pagan, Jewish, Christian or Gnostic, believed in the existence of these beings and in their function as mediators."

This is not to say that spirits were viewed without ambivalence. They could communicate with the supreme deity in heaven, and they had supernatural power, but they were not gods. They had the weaknesses and compulsions of humans, and when these were combined with their powers, the results could be truly malevolent. At the same time, their capacity to bridge opposites gave them the potential to establish lines of communication between humans and God.

In the Jewish version of this cosmology, the supernatural beings who occupy the lower heavens originally served God in his domain, but, as narratives like 1 Enoch relate, they revolted against his rule (sin in Judaism being viewed as a form of revolt against God), and they were expelled from the highest heaven. As a result, parts of creation no longer fell within God's rule. The realms between the highest heaven and earth, and the underworld beneath earth, were now under the authority of these renegade spirits. It was the role of the Messiah, according to prophecies in the Tanakh, or Hebrew Bible, to re-establish God's rule, the kingdom of heaven, by defeating these spiritual "powers." Christians, too, believed that they were engaged in a war with hostile spirits. In the New Testament they are referred to variously as "rulers" and "powers" (*archons*), "authorities" (*ezousia*), "demons" (*daimōnes*), "spirits" (*pneuma*), and "messengers" or angels (*aggelos*). These, in the words of Ephesians, are the "rulers and authorities in the heavenly places" (1:21; 3:10).

If the Secret Gospel and Paul's letters were all the evidence we had concerning the origins of Christian baptism, we still might conclude that references to death, rebirth, and ascent in relation to baptism were merely metaphorical language. But these are not the only sources from this era that talk about entering heaven. Jews and pagans sought this goal as well, and the evidence they left shows that underlying the metaphors and literary conventions used by Paul and other New Testament authors was not only a belief in the possibility of entering heaven but a definite body of techniques for doing so.

CHAPTER THREE
To Gaze Upon the Throne of God

In the oldest writings from the Near East, there is no reference to humans entering the domain of the gods. The ancient Israelites considered the very desire to do so evidence of wickedness and pride. For this, the prophet Isaiah railed against the king of Babylon:

> Once you thought in your heart,
> "I will climb to the sky;
> Higher than the stars of God
> I will set my throne.
> I will sit in the mount of assembly,
> On the summit of Zaphon [an abode of the gods]:
> I will mount the back of a cloud—
> I will match the Most High."
> Instead, you are brought down to Sheol [hell],
> To the bottom of the Pit. (Isa. 14:13-15)

Still, there were exceptions. In a Mesopotamian myth from the late third millennium B.C.E., the king Etana is born aloft through the gates of heaven by an eagle; but then, overcome with fear, begs to be returned to earth (see fig. 3). A list of Sumerian kings refers to Etana as "the shepherd who ascended to heaven," which immediately calls to mind Ganymede, the Phrygian shepherd, carried to heaven by Zeus in the guise of an eagle (see "The Boy Who Became a God" and fig. 4). The Hebrew Bible also credits a few notable individuals with entering heaven—the patriarch Enoch, whom God "took," the prophet Elijah, and, above all, Ezekiel.

Ezekiel's first vision occurred in the year 593 B.C.E, as he stood along the banks of the Chebar River in Babylon. Suddenly, "the heavens opened," and he witnessed an apparition of four monstrous creatures he calls *hayyoth*, or "living beings" emerging from clouds of flame:

> They had the figures of human beings. However, each had four faces, and each of them had four wings; the legs of each were (fused into) a single rigid leg, and the feet of each were like a single calf's hoof; and their sparkle was like the luster of burnished bronze.... Each of them had a human face (at the front); each of the four had the face of a lion on the right; each of the four had the face of an ox on the left; each of the four had the face of an eagle (at the back). (Ezek. 1:5-10)

On the heads of these fabulous creatures rested the firmament, the color of "terrible ice." Finally, above the firmament itself, Ezekiel sees:

> ...the semblance of a throne in appearance like sapphire; and on top, upon this semblance of a throne, there was the semblance of a human form. From what appeared as his loins up, I saw a gleam as of amber—what looked like a fire encased in a frame; and from what appeared as his loins down, I saw what looked like fire. There was a radiance all about him. Like the appearance of the bow which shines in the clouds on a day of rain, such was the appearance of the surrounding radiance. That was the appearance of the semblance of the Presence of the Lord. When I beheld, it, I flung myself down on my face. And I heard the voice of someone speaking. (1:26-29)

(Other descriptions of God's throne appear in 1 Kings 22:19; Isaiah 6; and Daniel 7:9.)

Ezekiel witnesses all this from his vantage point on earth. But later in the Book of Ezekiel another occasion is related when the "hand of God" falls upon the prophet as he sits before the elders of Judah. A fiery spirit appears who grabs him by the hair and lifts him to a place "between heaven and earth" (8:3). Here he witnesses the destiny of Jerusalem played out before him in a vision in which an etheral figure "clothed in linen" plays an important role.

Attempts by later generations to explain and expand on Ezekiel's visions gave rise to a distinct body of writings. Known as the Merkavah literature because of its detailed descriptions of God's throne, or *merkavah*, the authorship of these texts is typically attributed to biblical figures, such as Isaiah, Abraham, and even Moses. Although inspired by the Book of Ezekiel, the accounts of heavenly ascent found in Merkavah texts differ in an important respect. Ezekiel's ascent stops short of heaven itself, but in the Merkavah literature protagonists routinely enter heaven and, indeed, the presence of God himself.

One of the earliest examples is 1 Enoch or the Book of Enoch, parts of which are believed to have been written before 175 B.C.E. When the first complete manuscript of Enoch was brought to Europe in 1773, after being discovered in Ethiopia, it created a sensation. Christians were confronted with a text older than any gospel that described the heavenly ascent and deification of a human. At the same time, Jews were faced with an ancient Hebrew text filled with elements, including anthropomorphism, at odds with Judaism as it had developed under the rabbis. Eventually, more Merkavah texts were identified, and it became evident that the desire for direct contact with the divine, which typifies

Fig. 3. Etana ascending to heaven on the back of an eagle on a Sumerian cylinder seal from the late third millennium B.C.E. After Henri Frankfort, Cylinder Seals: A Documentary Essay on Art and Religion of the Ancient Near East (London: MacMillan, 1939), pl. XXDIVh.

religious feeling in the Hellenistic era in general, was shared by Jews as well.

Over time, the influence of Hellenistic cosmology on Merkavah literature becomes apparent. Multiple heavens are first mentioned in the Testament of Levi, an Aramaic text originally written in the second century B.C.E., and later translated into Greek, with a section added describing Levi's ascent through seven heavens. The Parables of Enoch, written in the first century C.E. and added to the Book of Enoch, also alludes to multiple heavens. In rabbinic literature, both three and seven heavens are mentioned (see "Paul's Ascent to the Garden"). The number seven, however, had special significance—the sanctuary of the temple of Israel in Ezekiel's vision was entered by climbing seven steps. In either case, whether three or seven, the highest heaven was Yahweh's domain—his kingdom—while the heavens below were populated by angels and other celestial beings.

In the earliest Merkavah narratives, ascent to heaven is sudden and involuntary—a rapture—not something actively sought. The protagonist is literally abducted, grabbed by the hair and lifted to heaven like Ezekiel or swept up in a whirlwind like Elijah (2 Kings 2:11). Hellenistic cosmology, however, requires a more tortuous trajectory. A series of celestial levels must be traversed. Instantaneous transport gives way to an ascent in stages, an episodic journey that becomes a spiritual adventure in which repeated obstacles and challenges must overcome, resulting in the spiritual growth of the protagonist.

The most elaborate narratives of this type are found in a body of texts considered the successor to the Merkavah tradition. Written between 100 and 800 C.E., they are referred to as Hekhalot texts because of their subdivision of the highest heaven into seven halls or palaces (*hekhalot*) each of which must be breached before the protagonist reaches God's throne. These writings are also notable for their detailed descriptions of the heavens and heavenly palaces, and meticulous lists of names and ranks of angels and other celestial beings. They diverge from Mekavah narratives in that their protagonists are no longer legendary figures from the Hebrew Bible but individuals said to be historical rabbis. They are typically aided in their journeys by one or more angels, who function as psychopomps or spirit guides. In 2 Enoch, the protagonist is borne to heaven on the wings of two angels (reminiscent of the eagle-borne flights of Etana and Ganymede). Other angels, sometimes hostile, guard the gates of the heavens and must be appeased or overpowered.

The Hekhalot Rabbati, composed in the third century C.E. (although Morton Smith and Gershom Scholem believed that it drew on sources from first-century Palestine), provides a dramatic description of these figures:

Fig. 4. The abduction of Ganymede by Zeus as an eagle as depicted in a sixteenth-century engraving. After Achille Bocchi, Symbolicarum Quaestionum, *Emblem LXXIX.*

> At the gate of the seventh palace, they stand angry and war-like, strong, harsh, fearful, terrifying, taller than mountains and sharper than peaks. Their bows are strung and stand before them. Their swords are sharpened and in their hands. Bolts of lightning flow and issue forth from the balls of their eyes, and balls of fire (issue) from their nostrils, and torches of fiery coals from their mouths. They are equipped with helmets and with coats of mail, and javelins and spears are hung upon their arms. (17.8)

When the protagonist enters God's presence, he collapses in a faint or trance. God or his emissary raises him up (that is, resurrects him) and reveals to him visions and secret knowledge. He may be shown the fate of the righteous in the afterlife and that of the wicked in Sheol. In these texts, the morally neutral underworld of the Hebrew Bible becomes the site of horrific punishment. (In Plato's *Republic*, the hero Er similarly witnesses the judging of the righteous and the unjust when his soul travels to a "mysterious region" where earth and heaven meet [10.614].) Finally, the subject returns to earth and uses the knowledge he has gained to instruct or guide his people. In a few accounts, he is deified and remains among the heavenly hosts. All this corresponds to the mythical pattern Joseph Campbell described as the hero's journey.

Then Open Your Eyes

Pagan pursuit of heavenly ascents is documented in a body of writings known as the *Greek Magical Papyri* (*Papyri Graecae Magicae*, or PGM). Produced in Egypt between the second century B.C.E. and the fifth century C.E., the magical papyri are compendiums of spells and rituals for nearly every imaginable purpose, from the mundane (to obtain luck or sexual favors) to the transcendental. Among the latter are spells whose express purpose is ascending to heaven. As in Hekhalot narratives, the agency by which this journey occurs is not God (or a god) nor his emissary, but rather that of the individual who seeks mystical experience for the benefits it conveys.

The leading example comes from the great papyrus book of the Bibliothèque Nationale in Paris. Known as the Mithras Liturgy (after a god named in its opening lines), it was written around 300 C.E. The "liturgy" consists of detailed instructions for a private rite enabling those who perform it to "ascend into heaven as an inquirer and behold the universe." It begins with the invocation of a spirit so that, as the "inquirer" is told to say, "I might be born again…and the sacred spirit may breathe in me" (or "into" me). The subject then feels himself being lifted up to a height somewhere in midair (like Ezekiel). From this vantage point he sees the "divine order of the skies: the presiding gods rising into heaven, and others setting"—in the words, the celestial spheres, the heavens, encircling the earth. He is told to repeat secret names and formulas, and "then open your eyes, and you will see the doors open and the world of the gods which is within the doors, so that from the pleasure and joy of the sight your spirit runs ahead and ascends."

Next, the inquirer sees a "youthful god, beautiful in appearance, with fiery hair, and in a white tunic and scarlet cloak, and wearing a fiery crown" (recall the radiant youths who appear in early accounts of baptism; a similar figure occurs the Hekhalot literature as well). Later, he sees seven gods wearing *sindōn*, whom he is told to greet with their secret names. Finally, he sees a god who is "immensely great, having a bright appearance, youthful, golden-haired, with a white tunic and a golden crown and trousers." Lightning bolts leap from his eyes and stars from his body. The inquirer is instructed to repeat an incantation in which he proclaims, "While being born from a life-generating birth, I am passing on, released to death." Following this, he receives a revelation from the god. The liturgy goes on to provide instructions for ascending with a "fellow initiate"—the scenario of the Secret Gospel.

These spells often call for an assistant, typically a youth. One charm for producing an ecstatic trance instructs the magician and his assistant to prepare by abstaining from intercourse for three days. The magician begins the rite by repeating a formula consisting of "holy names" seven times to summon a spirit. Then he utters the formula into the ear of the assistant seven more times. "Right away," the instructions explain, "he will fall down. But you sit down on the bricks and make your inquiry, and he will describe everything with truth." The spell ends with the magician crowning himself and his assistant with a garland and dismissing the lord or spirit. Finally, the magician is instructed to waken the assistant by "having your palms spread on your buttocks, your feet together on the ground" and reciting another formula. Many spells call for use of a *sindōn*. The magician may be instructed to lie naked on a white linen cloth or to wear clean white garments. One spell instructs the magician to "wrap a naked boy in linen."

As Fritz Graf shows in *Magic and the Ancient World*, spells have a ritual structure similar to that of baptism and other initiation rites. They begin with procedures that separate and isolate the participants from normal social contact through the observance of preparatory periods, fasting, sexual abstinence, and other restrictions. The spell itself is typically performed at night, an appropriate time for liminal proceedings. The variety of formulas, recipes, and paraphernalia employed is almost bewildering, but most have the same purpose: to summon and obtain the assistance of a spirit helper, or "god" or "lord." Once the *parhedros*, or spirit helper, has been summoned and its assistance secured, the spell concludes with procedures equivalent to a reincorporation phase—dismissal of the spirit, donning of new clothes, and formal withdrawal from the ritual space.

Magic fell outside the scope of conventional religion in the ancient world. Whereas priests used rituals to honor and appease the gods, *magoi*, or magicians, sought to manipulate the gods and appropriate their powers for their own ends—for wealth, sexual favors, cures, and so forth. Obviously, anyone who could do this would have little need for formal religion with its priesthoods, temples, and public ceremonies. Not surprisingly, magic was denounced throughout ancient history; its practice remained an underground tradition.

Historians have portrayed the rise of Greek philosophy as a triumph of rationality over superstition and magic, while decrying the renewed fascination with magic in the Hellenistic era as evidence of cultural decline. In fact, magic has played a vital role in Western cultural and intellectual history. As Kingsley points out, both Empedocles and Pythagoras, founding figures of Greek philosophy, were acknowledged healers as well as theoreticians. Furthermore, he adds, "It is clear that the type of healing and medicine involved had a great deal to do with the world of incantation, magic, and ritual."

Indeed, the distinction between magicians and socially approved prophets and healers in the ancient world is not always easy to make. *Magoi* and their commonplace counterparts, *goētēs* (peddlers of charms and cures), often performed rites in aid of others, sometimes for payment, sometimes not. The author of the Mithras Liturgy claimed to "write these mysteries…not for gain but for instruction." Others, like Apollonius of Tyana, a contemporary of Jesus, sought contact with the gods and their powers but were not labeled *magoi*. (Apollonius' career actually parallels that of Jesus in several aspects: he was credited with performing miracles, raising the dead, healing the sick, and ascending bodily to heaven.)

Jewish law prohibited magic. Although the prophets Elijah and Elisha performed feats similar to those achieved by spells—stopping and starting rain, purifying polluted water, curing the sick, reviving the dead, and, in Elijah's case, ascending to heaven—they did so without the rigmarole of spells and as public, not secret, acts. In the course of the Hellenistic era, however, Jewish mysticism was deeply influenced by magic. The Hekhalot literature provides extensive evidence of this. Indeed, Peter Schäffer, a leading authority on the subject, characterizes the entire body of Hekhalot writings as "eminently magical texts." Some of the procedures they describe have direct parallels in the magical papyri, including preparatory periods of fasting and continence, incantations, streams of names or words with no apparent meaning, water divination, and the use of secret names or "seals."

The Hekhalot Zutarti, for example, relates a technique for securing a special blessing intended for those who endure "the suffering of descending and ascending to the *merkavah*" (on the substitution of "descent" for "ascent," see below). To do this, the individual "must sit fasting for forty days. He must put his head between his knees until the fast gets control of him. He must whisper toward earth and not toward heaven, so that earth may hear and not heaven. If he is an adolescent, he may say it as long as he does not have an emission. If he is married, he must be prepared [that is, continent] three days in advance."

Other elements common to both the Hekhalot literature and magical papyri include multiple heavens, ascent with companions or assistants, pantheons of celestial beings—some friendly, some hostile—and a radiant youth who appears at a key moment. If further evidence were needed of the extent of the interaction between Jewish mysticism and pagan magic, one need only consider the Greek names for heavenly personnel found in Hekhalot texts and the Hebrew names frequently invoked in spells. (Of course, this influence extended beyond the realm of mysticism. In the Hellenistic era, many synagogues had gentile members, while Jews were widely exposed to Greek culture in Palestine and throughout the Mediterranean.)

Hekhalot texts, like the Mithras Liturgy and other spells, take for granted that others can be taught how to ascend to heaven—what the Secret Gospel implies when it says that Jesus "taught" the youth the mystery of heaven. The Hekhalot Rabbati opens with the question, "What are those songs that a person should utter if he wants to gaze at the sight of the *merkavah*, to descend safely and to ascend safely?" It goes on to report how Rabbi Nehuniah convened a college of scholars and, while in a trance, related the details of how to undertake the journey, including how those who make the "descent" can take companions with them: "Cause them [the companions] to stand over them or seat them before them, and say to them: 'Watch and look and listen, and write down everything that we say and everything that we hear from before the throne of glory'" (20.4). In another text, Rabbi Ishmael returns from an ecstatic journey to heaven with an instruction manual for "descending" to the *merkavah* and gazing "at the king and at his beauty." "I did it," he says. "But I still could not believe, until the least of the students in our college also did it."

(According to David J. Halperin, the substitution of "descent" for "ascent" in Hekhalot texts derives from a literary tradition in which the horses of the Egyptians who pursued Moses and his followers are said to have seen the celestial heights reflected in the waters of the Red Sea.

Similarly, the Visions of Ezekiel, a Hekhalot text of the fourth or fifth century, relates how "Ezekiel" sees the seven firmaments by peering into the waters of the Chebar River. Visiting the throne of God in this case entails a descent into the waters. Hence, Hekhalot texts refer to *yorede merkavah*, "those who go down in the chariot." Perhaps this concept reflects as well the practice of water divination known to have been used by Jewish mystics, magicians, and Gnostics alike.)

It is important to note that the supernatural outcomes related in the magical papyri and the Hekhalot literature are not the direct result of the procedures employed. Rather, the procedures are directed at gaining the aid of spirits. It is they who accomplish the desired outcomes by exercising their powers on behalf of the individual. The Mithras Liturgy, for example, provides instructions for obtaining the assistance of the sun god. After following the prescribed procedures, the inquirer can "ask the god for what you want, and he will give to you" (PGM IV.778).

Often spirits must be compelled to aid the magician, or hostile spirits must be overcome. In the Mithras Liturgy, the gods rush at the inquirer as he stands on the threshold of their domain. He withstands their assault by uttering commands, peculiar sounds, and strings of untranslatable gibberish. In other cases, the magician gains mastery over spirits and gods by using their secret names, which are often referred to as the "keys" to heaven, or by bearing symbols or "seals." In the Hekhalot literature, these efforts are directed at angels in the form of adjurations. The goal, however, is the same—in Schäffer's words, "to bring the angel down to earth...to carry out the mystic's wishes."

Another method of obtaining the aid of a spirit was by uniting with it. This could be done by eating a symbolic meal with it, consuming a potion made from objects symbolic of it (the idea behind Christian communion), or simply inhaling its essence into oneself. In a spell from Egypt, the magician addresses the spirit as "lord of life, King of the heavens" and appeals to it to "come into my mind and my understanding for all the time of my life and accomplish for me all the desires of my soul. For you are I, and I, you" (PGM XIII.790-95). Once possessed by the spirit, the Mithras Liturgy explains, "You speak as if prophesying in ecstasy" (PGM IV.736-39).

Christianity arose in the same period in which Hellenistic magic and Jewish mysticism were converging. Key Merkavah texts such as 2 Enoch, the Ascension of Isaiah, and the Apocalypse of Abraham were written contemporaneously (more or less) with the books of the New Testament. Paul may have been familiar with the Book of Enoch; the Letter of Jude cites it by name. Some Merkavah texts, such as the Ascension of Isaiah, originally written by Jewish authors, were rewritten

Fig. 5. Jesus reviving Lazarus using a magician's rod on a gold glass plate from the fourth century C.E. *After C. Morey,* Catalogo del Museo Sacro *(Vatican City, 1959), no. 31 in IV, p. 9 and pl. V.*

for Christian audiences.

The influence of magical ideas and practices on Christianity is evident in the New Testament. Indeed, the gospels provide an almost embarrassing number of examples: curing by touch and manipulation; looking upward; sighing or groaning; use of Aramaic phrases and magical words; use of spittle; touching the tongue; using "the finger of God"; directing commands and banishments at demons, and demanding they reveal their names; demanding faith or trust from patients; praying and fasting; secrecy; preparatory periods; and, of course, use of the white linen ritual garment. Even the phenomenon of speaking in tongues, or glossolalia, reported by Paul and in Acts (see "Sex and Spirit in Corinth") has parallels in the incantations consisting of strings of nonreferential sounds found in magical papyri. Indeed, the association between the supernatural feats of Jesus and the practices of magicians was so entrenched that conventional depictions of the raising of Lazarus show him using a magician's rod (see fig. 5).

In fact, all the gospels portray Jesus as either commanding a spirit or being possessed by one. This was the source of his power. In the words of Acts, "God anointed Jesus of Nazareth with the Holy Spirit and with power" (10:38). His followers, too, were possessed by a spirit. As Jesus explains in Matthew, "It is not you who speak, but the Spirit of your Father speaking through you" (10:20). In Jesus' case, however, this union was so complete that he was, for all purposes, a spirit himself. This is how he wanted to be seen, anyway. Being united with a spirit meant that he was the "son of (a) god."

As far as outsiders were concerned, however, it looked like magic. In John, hostile Jews are made to say, "He has a demon" (8:48; 10:19). That is, he controlled a spirit, the standard modus operandi of the magician. Pagans made the same assumption, and invoked the names "Jesus," "Mary," "God" and others in their spells. All these similarities led Morton Smith to produce a study titled *Jesus the Magician*. Although Jews may have seen Jesus as following in the footsteps of the wonder-working prophets of the Hebrew Bible, his frequent resort to ritual gestures and formulas was unprecedented for Judaism.

For early Christians, controlling spirits was central to their goal of establishing the kingdom of God on earth. This required that the world be rid of malevolent spirits, the "authorities" and "rulers" referred to in the New Testament, so that God's rule once again extended to the entirety of creation. Thus, Jesus' battle with Satan and his exorcisms were central to his mission. His triumph over "the principalities and powers" opened the heavens and made his subsequent resurrection possible.

This idea may lie behind certain ambiguous verses in Luke (16:16) and Matthew (11:12) that speak of entering the kingdom of heaven by "force." Perhaps this is a reference to the kind of procedures magicians and Hekhalot mystics used for overcoming hostile spirits on their journeys to heaven. If so, the "force" involved probably took the form of commands and adjurations, use of secret names, and possession of "keys" or "seals." Passages in Luke and Matthew that refer to the disciples subjecting demons "in your name" and doing mighty works "in your name" hint at these practices as well.

The similarity between the role of spirits in pagan magic and early Christianity has been obscured by the way in which key terms in the New Testament are translated. In English, the word "angel" has only positive connotations; it is the antonym of "demon." But in Greek, *aggelos* had the more general sense of "spirit" or "spiritual messenger." Paul used it to refer not only to messengers of God, but emanations of Satan as well (2 Cor. 12:7). In this usage, *aggelos* is a synonym of *daimōn*, or "demon," not its opposite.

Paul's references to angels are consistent with general Hellenistic beliefs concerning spirits. In his Second Letter to the Corinthians, he implies that they occupy a realm near enough to humans to observe them and intefere in their affairs (4:9; 11:10). In the First Letter to the Corinthians, he claims to have power over them. "Do you not know that we are to judge angels?" (1 Cor. 6:3), and he boasts about his ability to "speak in the tongues of mortals and of angels" (1 Cor. 13:1).

Elsewhere, however, he distances himself from such practices:

> And when you were dead in trespasses and in the uncircumcision of your flesh, God made you alive together with him, when he forgave us all our trespasses, erasing the record that stood against us with its legal demands [i.e., Jewish religious laws]. He set this aside, nailing it to the cross. He disarmed the rulers [*arkhas*] and authorities [*ezousias*] and made a public example of them, triumphing over them in it. Therefore do not let anyone condemn you in matters of food and drink or of observing festivals, new moons, or Sabbaths. These are only a shadow of what is to come, but the substance belongs to Christ. Do not let anyone disqualify you, insisting on self-abasement and worship of angels, dwelling on visions, puffed up without cause by a human way of thinking. (Col. 2:13-18)

Here Paul is trying to counter opponents to his mission, who seem to be Gnostic Jewish Christians, observant of Jewish religious laws, but engaging in esoteric practices. They "worship angels" (that is, seek to control or influence them) and "dwell on visions." Paul's response is not to deny the efficacy of such practices, but simply to remind his followers that Christ has dominated these "rulers" and "authorities." In his Letter to the Romans, he writes, "Neither death, nor life, nor angels, nor rulers, nor powers…will be able to separate us from the love of God in Christ Jesus our Lord" (8:38). In other words, his opponents overvalue their interactions with angels and undervalue the significance of Christ's death. This history-changing event has nullified angelic powers as well as the laws of man. Nonetheless, long after Paul, Gnostic Christians continued to seek contact with angels and some, like Clement's rivals, the Carpocratians, claimed the ability to dominate or control them for magical operations.

Of course, the "Christ" Paul writes of is a spirit, too. It differed from "angels," "demons," and other "rulers" only in the extent of its power. But in the context of baptismal rites, the "Christ" had the same function as the lords and spirits invoked in spells. It was summoned. It united with the proselyte. And in that state, the proselyte experienced death, resurrection, and ascent to heaven.

The first Christians, whether from Jewish or gentile backgrounds, shared the assumptions of their time. They lived in a complex, segmented universe, populated with both human and supernatural beings. Far above was a realm of pure spirit, energy without form, ruled over by a supreme deity. Closer—indeed, hovering just above them—were lesser but still powerful spirits who could intervene in their affairs. It was possible, however, for humans to influence these spirits and even command them. Further, some humans could spiritualize themselves enough—through right living, purification, and magic—to enter spiritual realms directly and behold the supreme deity in the highest heaven.

But what evidence is there, aside from the Secret Gospel, that Christians actively sought to enter heaven this way? The best evidence comes from none other than Paul. In his Second Letter to the Corinthians, he writes, referring to himself in the third person:

> It is necessary to boast; nothing is to be gained by it, but I will go on to visions and revelations of the Lord. I know a person in Christ who fourteen years ago was caught up to the third heaven…. And I know that such a person—whether in the body or out of the body I do not know; God knows—was caught up into Paradise and heard things that are not to be told, that no mortal is permitted to repeat. (12:1-4)

Here, as in Colossians, Paul is responding to the claims of competing missionaries. But in this case, rather than downplay the importance of their spiritual feats, he competes with them, "boasting" that whatever they can do, he can do better.

But did Paul attain this experience by employing esoteric techniques, such as those found in Hekhalot texts and magical papyri, or did he experience a rapture? His language is open to interpretation. The word translated as "caught up," *harpazō*, also has the meanings "to be seized, to be captured," which recalls how Ezekiel was seized and lifted up toward heaven. At the same time, he uses the passive voice—"was caught up"—without identifying the agency by which it occurred, God's or his own. Another difference between Paul's report and others is that his experience seems to have been auditory rather than visual. In the end, however, these differences make sense if we see Paul's experience as transitional, representing a point in the evolution from Merkavah texts, in which the subject is instantaneously transported to heaven, to the Hekhalot literature, in which the subject actively seeks access to heaven.

With the examples provided by Jewish mystical writings and Greek magical papyri before us, we can now return to the Secret Gospel and imagine what happened that night when the young man Jesus raised from the dead came to him to learn the mysteries of the kingdom of heaven.

CHAPTER FOUR
The Rites of Heaven

Those who accept the Bible on faith do not need rational explanations for the miracles and supernatural feats it reports. Historians, on the other hand, are constrained to explain the past in terms of normal human capacities and the known laws of nature. Faced with reports of miraculous events, many have felt compelled to treat them as myths— or propaganda, depending on one's point of view (see "Uprising to Heaven"). More recently, historians influenced by postmodernist theories have adopted the view that such documents are literary productions whose form and content are determined not by their authors (whether individuals or institutions) but by the rules of the genre (or discourse) they belong to. Neither view, however, takes seriously the possibility that such accounts are attempts to relate real experiences.

Modern medicine and psychology provide many examples of phenomena that, in a different time or culture, might very well be understood as supernatural—from spontaneous healing to multiple personality disorder to various conditions, physiological and environmental, that can trigger hallucinations. Understanding accounts of heavenly ascent this way—as narrativized reports of psychological experiences—provides an alternative to either accepting them at face value or dismissing them out of hand. In fact, the writings we have been considering often provide clues to the actual nature of the experiences they report.

Paul, for example, allows that his ascent to heaven was a subjective experience when he twice equivocates, "whether in the body or out of the body I do not know; God knows." The protagonist in the Ascension of Isaiah, on the other hand, is clearly in a trance state:

And while he [Isaiah] was speaking with the Holy Spirit in the hearing of them all, he became silent, and his mind was taken up from him, and he did not see the men who were standing before him. His eyes indeed were open, but his mouth was silent, and the mind in his body was taken up from him. But his breath was (still) in him, for he was seeing a vision. (6.6-16)

Yet another mode by which experiences of heaven could be attained is related in the Testament of Levi. According to the narrator, a "spirit of understanding from the Lord" came over him: then "sleep fell upon me, and I beheld a high mountain." The journey to heaven was a dream.

If the experiences underlying accounts of heavenly ascent were largely psychological—that is, dreams or visions (or hallucinations)—we need to take another look at the methods described in the magical papyri and Hekhalot literature. What was their role in producing such experiences? In fact, many of these procedures, including fasting, sensory deprivation, isolation, the narrowing of attention, formulaic language, and breath control—are known to foster altered states of consciousness. Examples can be found throughout the world, from shamanic séances in tribal societies to contemporary Pentecostal churches to New Age groups that use guided meditation and hypnotic induction. This is how spells and rituals "worked"—by altering the consciousness of those who used them, allowing them to "be" the spirit, to give spirit material form.

Paul credited the experiences of death and resurrection central to baptism to possession by "a spirit of God." As he explains in the Second Letter to the Corinthians, "the lord"—that is, Jesus—"is that spirit" (3:17). In Jesus' version of the rite, the spirit would have been an angel or other emissary of God. It was "Jesus' spirit" in the sense of belonging to him or being under his control. After his death, it came to be understood as Jesus' spirit in the sense of emanating from him or being sent by him from heaven.

The Secret Gospel and Paul's letters provide the outline of what occurred when Jesus "taught" the "mystery of the kingdom of God." It was done at night. Jesus and the initiate were alone, the initiate naked except for a linen towel. The proceedings must have been lengthy, since we are told that the initiate "remained" with Jesus the entire night. But here the outline ends. The magical papyri and Jewish mystical texts, however, make it possible to fill in the blanks.

Much of what occurred would have been directed at summoning and interacting with a "lord," or spirit. First, it was invoked—probably through repetitive prayers, hymns, and incantations. Then it was brought under control through the use of secret names or by bonding with it. This would have culminated with Jesus entering a trance state in which the spirit spoke and acted through him. A third step entailed the transfer of the spirit to the initiate. Here, consciousness-altering techniques were used to induce a hypnotic state in the initiate who, like the assistant in the Mithras Liturgy, immediately faints. The spirit was now in him; the two were one. In this state, the initiate saw what the spirit saw: heaven in all its glory. Perhaps the spirit spoke through him, offering prophecies or speaking in tongues, or even providing a narrative of the visions unfolding in the subject's unconscious mind. The proceeding ended when Jesus dismissed the spirit, awakened the initiate, and gave him clothing to don.

Jesus and the Shamanic Tradition of Same-Sex Love

NAKED MAN...WITH NAKED MAN?

How, exactly, was the spirit transferred from Jesus to the young man? In the Mithras Liturgy, the magician whispers into the assistant's ear, and he immediately faints. In the Hekhalot Rabbati, the rabbi stands behind the assistants he wishes to take with him on the journey to the *merkavah* and chants prescribed "songs." But Clement's letter raises the possibility that Jesus used a much more intimate method.

Here is where we must seriously consider the reference to *gumnos gumnō*, "naked man with naked man." Although Clement says this phrase was not present in Mark's Secret Gospel, the Carpocratians claimed it was, and Clement admits that their copy was taken from his own church. Further, it seems to have been the basis for some practice in which the Carpocratians engaged, apparently in connection with baptism. If so, it was likely an element of the third and final step of invoking a spirit: transferring it from one body to another.

That early baptism involved nudity is not shocking. Even Jewish rites required undressing. Paul's language implies as much in the Letter to the Galatians, where he writes, "As many of you as were baptized into Christ have clothed yourselves with Christ" (Gal. 3:26). Similar language occurs in the Letter to the Colossians, where he speaks of "putting off the body of the flesh" (2:11; see also, 1 Cor. 15:33ff, 2 Cor. 5:2).

References to nudity occur as well in the Gospel of Thomas, one of the Gnostic texts discovered in 1945 at the Egyptian site of Nag Hammadi. Probably written in the early second century, it includes sayings that some scholars believe originated with Jesus himself. In one *logion*, or saying, Jesus announces, "When you disrobe without being ashamed and take up your garments and place them under your feet like little children and tread on them, then [will you see] the son of the living one" (37). This probably refers to baptismal procedures that involved initiates disrobing and then "seeing" or "receiving" Jesus. (That Jesus may have disrobed when performing baptism is not far-fetched either, considering the scene in the Gospel of John, where he strips and then washes the feet of his disciples before their Passover meal.)

One of the earliest surviving church handbooks, the Apostolic Tradition, compiled in Rome in the early 200s, required both the initiate and the deacon to disrobe for baptism (21.3). The rite was performed in a tank filled with "living" (that is, flowing) water after an all-night vigil. The instructions directed, "Let the candidates stand in the water, naked" (21.11). Perhaps the Carpocratian version of Secret Mark simply read, "They stood in the water, naked man with naked man." If so, it merely makes explicit what is implied in these early church orders. Indeed, Clement himself uses the term *gumnos* to describe the state in which the

56

soul must approach God. The fact that he does not accuse the Carpocratians of sexual offenses in connection with *gumnos gumnō* is revealing. Perhaps the phrase was, after all, in Clement's copy of the Secret Gospel. Or, if it was missing, perhaps Clement himself edited it out. If so, what was the problem with it, if nude baptism was commonplace? Could this phrase had meant something more after all?

Smith cites a variety of sources to suggest that *gumnos gumnō* involved physical contact, and that it was a recognized magical technique. The most tantalizing parallel comes from a treatise by Aelian, a contemporary of Clement, titled *On Animals*. It describes a method used by the Libyans (neighbors to Clement's Egypt) to cure victims of snake bites. A man lies next to the one who is sick, *gumnos gumnō*, "naked man with naked man," and through friction imparts "the innate power of his own skin" to the sufferer (16.28).

Something similar is found in Egyptian mythology, where the goddess Isis restores Osiris by laying upon his lifeless body. In the Hebrew Bible, the prophet Elisha revives a dead child by lying on him and putting "his mouth on its mouth, his eyes on its eyes, and his hands on its hands.... And the body of the child became warm" (2 Kings 4:34). Perhaps this was a form of artificial resuscitation. Elijah also "stretched out over" a child three times and restored him to life (1 Kings 17:21). Similarly, in the late fourth century, Saint Martin is described as "stretching himself out over the lifeless limbs" of the dead to revive them (Sulpicius Severus, *Vita s. Martini*, 7.3; 8.2). Something similar also can be found in love spells. One reads: "She puts what is in her hand into my hand, what is in her mouth into my mouth, what is in her belly onto my belly, what is in her female parts onto my male parts" (PGM IV:117-121; see also PGM IV:400-1).

The final precedent Smith cites is a passage in Plato's *Symposium* — the subject of chapter 6 — where Agathon asks Socrates for permission to recline next to him in order to absorb his wisdom by pressing their bodies together.

The image evoked by these examples is that of two males, unclothed, standing in the baptismal pool (or something representing that), embracing — an intimate procedure to be sure, but not necessarily sexual. In fact, something quite close to this occurs in accounts from Syria. The Syriac Acts of John, composed in the late fourth or early fifth century, relates a baptism that begins with a repetition of Christian doctrine, followed by the consecration of water and oil, the singing of angelic hymns (a common motif in Hekhalot texts), and a confession of faith. Then the initiate disrobes and his entire body is anointed with oil. A series of immersions follows. At the conclusion, the initiate is clothed in white garments, given a kiss, and hailed as a bridegroom and youth.

Similar procedures are alluded to in a baptismal liturgy from fifth-century Edessa in northern Syria:

> As a babe from the midst of the womb he looks forth from the water; and instead of garments the priest receives and embraces him. He resembles a babe when he is lifted up from the midst of the water; and as a babe every one embraces and kisses him. Instead of swaddling-clothes they cast garments upon his limbs, and adorn him as a bridegroom.... By the beauty of his garments he proclaims the beauty that is to be.... Mystically he dies and is raised and is adorned; mystically he imitates the life immortal. His birth (in Baptism) is a symbol of that birth which is to be at the end, and the conduct of his life of that conversation which is (to be) in the Kingdom on high. (Narsai, Homily 21)

Here rebirth is resurrection: "He that is baptized is baptized (and buried) as in a tomb; and they call and raise him up from his death." Once again we see all the elements of the secret rite: disrobing, anointing, immersion, white garments, metaphorical resurrection and ascent, and an embrace in which the naked initiate is symbolically "clothed," much as Paul refers to proselytes clothing themselves with Christ.

A naked embrace, *gumnos gumnō*, at the climax of the rite would have been an immediate and dramatic method of enacting the transference of spirit from one body to another.

One other form of physical contact is mentioned in these accounts: kissing. In fact, early Christians frequently kissed. Paul urged both his male and female followers to "greet one another with a holy kiss" (Rom. 16:16). By Clement's time, however, the practice had become the source of scandal. In *The Instructor*, he complains of congregations "that do nothing but make the churches resound with a kiss," causing "foul suspicions and evil reports" about Christians in general (3.11). The proper expression of affection, he insists, is a kiss with a "chaste and closed mouth," not an "unholy kiss, full of poison"—that is, one in which the tongue is used.

In some circles, however, the kiss seems to have had a deeper significance. According to the Gospel of Philip, another Gnostic text from the collection at Nag Hammadi, "It is by a kiss that the perfect conceive and give birth. For this reason we also kiss one another. We receive conception from the grace which is in one another" (59.2-5).

Kissing is prominently featured in two other Nag Hammadi texts, along with other baptismal motifs. Both bear the title "Apocalypse of James"—scholars have dubbed them the First and Second Apocalypses to distinguish them. They come from a period when Jewish, Christian, and Gnostic ideas frequently intersected. Some Gnostic circles, as these texts show, cited James as an authority. (The historic James is known to have been a leader of the early Jerusalem church and a representative of that party of early Christianity that was both Jewish and observant of Jewish laws. Nonetheless, the Jamesian party seems to have been no less interested in esoteric experiences than Paul.) In both apocalypses, Jesus and James are described as embracing and kissing.

The First Apocalypse relates the secret teachings Jesus gives to James prior to his ascent to heaven, including instructions for defeating the archons who block his way. The text is especially concerned with the subject of "femaleness" and a figure called Achamoth, daughter of Wisdom or Sophia, with whom Jesus identifies himself. (It also refers to female disciples of Jesus, including Salome, one of the women who observed Jesus' crucifixion, and an authority cited by the Carpocratians and others.) James is described as embracing and kissing Jesus in two places (31.5; 32.5).

The Second Apocalypse of James may be even earlier, since it draws on Jewish Christian ideas but shows little knowledge of the New Testament. Here, James refers to himself as "he who stripped himself and went about naked, he who was found in a perishable state, though he was about to be brought up into imperishability [that is, ascend to heaven]" (46.15), and it has Jesus say to him, "For just as you are first, having clothed yourself, you are also the first who will strip himself." Immediately following this, according to James, "He kissed my mouth. He took hold of me…"(56.15).

Mouth-to-mouth contact underlies language in the Gospel of Thomas as well. Here, Jesus says: "He who will drink of my mouth will become like me. I myself shall become he, and the things that are hidden will be revealed to him" (108). Indeed, Paul writes in a similar vein in the First Letter to the Corinthians: "We were all given one spirit to drink" (12:13).

The Christian practice of kissing echoes procedures found in spells in which magicians blow on or exchange breath with an assistant or subject. One spell instructs the magician to blow on his subject "from the tips of the feet up to the face." More to the point, the Gospel of John describes Jesus imparting the Holy Spirit to his disciples by breathing on them (or, as the Greek term suggests, *into* them). In fact, the idea that an exchange of breath could transfer a spirit from one person to another is the logical complement of the way that exorcism was understood in Jesus' time—as the extraction of an unwanted spirit. One method for this, according to a case related by the Jewish historian Josephus, involved drawing a spirit out through the victim's nostrils.

Before concluding the exploration of the meaning of *gumnos gumnō*, the possibility that it indeed involved sexual contact has to be seriously considered. If a nude embrace was a method of transferring a spirit from oneself to another, intercourse or an exchange of bodily fluids as part of that embrace would have made the symbolism even more powerful. It is important to keep in mind, however, that such contact would not have been thought of as occurring between two human males. Rather, since the initiator (Jesus) was possessed by a spirit, any sexual exchange would have been between the initiate and that being. In this case there would be no need for the spirit to leave Jesus to be transferred to the initiate—the initiate went to the spirit, as it were, by uniting with the body it possessed. And if the spirit was God or an emanation from God, then so the initiate became, at that moment, God.

The idea that heavenly beings could have sex with humans was well-established in Jewish tradition. Genesis, chapter 6, relates how the "sons of God came in unto the daughters of men" and conceived monstrous offspring. The "sons of God" has long been understood as referring to angels. In 1 Enoch, where the story is retold and elaborated, they are referred to as the "Watchers."

This may have been the inspiration behind the Jewish, Christian, and Gnostic mystics who sought erotic encounters with angels. In the New Testament, both Jude and 2 Peter attack Christian leaders described as "dreaming ones" (that is, vision seekers) who "defile the flesh," reject "dominion, lordship" (*kuristēta*), and slander "the glorious ones" (*doxas*) (Jude 1:8). The words used here are technical terms for grades of angels. The "dreaming ones," it would seem, were having erotic encounters in their visions, and this was connected to their denigration or surmounting of angelic powers. That Jude has something like this in mind seems likely considering that he cites the Book of Enoch by name (1:14).

Gnostics like the Valentians and Naasenes often employed sexual images and metaphors in describing union with Christ and with angelic spirits. The Gospel of Philip, probably written in Syria in the late third century, is especially rich in this kind of imagery. It refers to a sacramental rite called the "Bridal Chamber" in the course of which initiates were "united" with their angelic counterparts, and it quotes Jesus as praying, "You who have joined the perfect light with the holy spirit, unite the angels with us also" (58.11-12). It also speaks of malevolent male and female spirits who seek to "unite" with the souls of humans of the opposite sex. Those who have undergone the Bridal Chamber rite, however, are immune from these spirits, because they are already married to a spirit.

BACK TO THE GARDEN

Reconstructing the Secret Gospel rite gives us the solution to the mystery posed at the beginning of this book: the presence of the naked youth at the scene of Jesus' arrest.

Arriving at night, like the youth in the Secret Gospel, and wearing only a *sindōn*, he must have been there for the same reason—to be baptized by Jesus. One other detail in Mark's account links this scene to baptism as well: Judas' kiss. This gesture, which served to identify Jesus to the authorities, is usually explained as the traditional greeting between a student and his rabbi. The language of Mark, however, is suggestive. Judas does not merely kiss Jesus (*phileō*), he "ardently" kisses him (*katephileō*). In light of the evidence we have just reviewed, we might wonder whether Judas' kiss was merely a traditional greeting or whether he meant to expose not only Jesus but the secret of his mystery rite as well. His kiss, in that case, amounted to a double betrayal.

Let us return now to that night and re-imagine it with all the details we have at hand.

According to the Gospel of John, after their final meal, Jesus "went out with his disciples across the Kidron Valley to a place where there was a garden, which he and his disciples entered" (18:1). The Kidron Valley was Jerusalem's cemetery. To this day it is lined with ancient tombs and gravestones. By taking this route, Jesus made a symbolic journey to the land of the dead followed by an ascent to heaven—the "garden," as it is often described in apocalyptic literature. Gethsemane was a perfect setting for baptism—a ritual of death, rebirth, and ascent.

Jesus posted guards and entered the garden. The young man awaited him, naked except for a linen towel wrapped around his waist. Like the youth in the Secret Gospel, he had prepared for six days and no doubt awaited the proceedings with anticipation. But that night Jesus was distracted. He left three times to check on his guards, only to find them asleep each time. At one point, he threw himself on the ground and pleaded pathetically for his father to "let this cup pass from me" (Matt. 26:39). Finally, he began.

As at the last supper, Jesus disrobed. The youth removed his towel. Jesus anointed his body with oil (or, perhaps, with water from the stream trickling through the garden). He prayed continuously, using repetitive and formulaic language. As the rite unfolded, he summoned a spirit, and it possessed him. (An echo of this occurs in Luke 22:43, which has an angel appearing at this point.) Then he embraced the youth, "naked man with naked man." As he placed his mouth upon his to breathe his spirit into him, perhaps he spoke words like those in the Second Apocalypse of James:

My beloved! Behold, I shall reveal to you those (things) that

(neither) the heavens nor their archons have known....
Behold, I shall reveal to you him who is hidden. But now,
stretch out your hand. Now, take hold of me. (56.15-57.15)

This was the gesture of resurrection. In the Secret Gospel, Jesus takes hold of the youth's hand and brings him back to life. Now, with the same gesture, he would lead another youth to heaven.

But that night something went terribly wrong. The secret rite was interrupted. Instead of the kiss of mystical union, there was the bitter kiss of Judas's betrayal. Jesus was seized. When the young man tried to flee, some of the men in Judas's crowd grabbed hold of his *sindōn*. It slipped from his waist. Naked, he disappeared into the night – and from the pages of history.

Gospel accounts of the episode at Gethsemane dwell on two points: Jesus' anguish at the foreknowledge of his death and his disciples' inconstancy – not only Judas's betrayal but the failure of the guards as well. One would think that the gospel authors would have avoided both topics if they could, since neither Jesus nor the disciples come off looking holy or heroic. Unflattering stories about that night must have circulated widely in the years following Jesus' death, so widely that the gospel authors found it necessary to acknowledge them, even as they attempted to give them the best possible "spin."

The Secret Gospel represents another problem – not what outsiders were saying, but what they might say if they knew the details of the ritual it outlines. So rather than adding explanations, the troublesome material was removed. Why the brief reference to the naked youth at Gethsemane was allowed to remain, however, is not clear. Like a band-aid, it both covers and draws attention to what is missing. Although John restored (or retained) the Lazarus story, all traces of a secret rite with a naked youth were removed.

Whether *gumnos gumnō* involved sexual intimacy or simply a chaste embrace, such a practice, at least in its origination, presumes a homophilic milieu. Could those who found such intimacy repellant think up such a thing, let alone carry it out? It seems reasonable to imagine that any group of individuals employing such practices, whatever their sexual orientations might have been, viewed same-sex intimacy as something other than an "abomination."

Although *gumnos gumnō* may not have entailed sexual arousal, outsiders undoubtedly would have assumed that it did. Even the purest intentions and chastity of the participants would not make such a practice acceptable to those determined to denounce and regulate same-sex desire – then or now. That such accusations were made regarding Jesus is hinted in the Gospel of John, where Jesus weeps at the news of

Lazarus's death, and the Jews are made to exclaim sarcastically, "See how he loved him!" (11:36).

Two thousand years later a predilection for private rituals with naked youths would still land even a messiah in jail.

FORGETTING THE SECRET RITE

Palestine in the first century was a social and political powder keg. Harsh Roman rule and interference with Jewish religious institutions provoked a series of violent incidents and uprisings, and created bitter dissent among Jews. In his epic narrative, *The Jewish War*, the ancient historian Josephus chronicles the numerous radical movements, deeply religious and fiercely nationalistic, that challenged Roman authority. In those tumultuous times, many Jews, from John the Baptist to Jesus and Paul, were convinced that the arrival of the "kingdom" was imminent.

Whereas John's baptism was controversial, Jesus' secret version of it was an even greater break with tradition. In the words of Acts, John baptized with mere water, but Jesus baptized with the "holy spirit" (11:16). He "poured out" this spirit, and it filled his followers until they, too, were possessed. And whereas John's rite was performed in public, Jesus performed his in secret, in the dark of night. Further, it did more than just prepare the individual who received it for the coming kingdom. In Jesus' words, the initiate was "baptized with the baptism that I am baptized with" (Mark 10:38); presumably, the initiate had the same vision of heaven opening that Jesus had coming up from the waters of the Jordan River. All this, and above all the claim that heaven could be experienced by those on earth, being closely tied to Jewish messianic expectations, was politically charged.

It is not surprising, therefore, that Jesus' private ceremony, with its magical trappings and naked embrace, was kept secret after his death, and that baptism is hardly mentioned in the gospels. Paul, however, underwent some version of this rite and learned its liturgy; some of these traditions seem to have been transmitted to Christian communities in Syria and Egypt as well. By the time the Gospel of John was written, however, seven decades after Jesus' death, baptism was no longer secret, and any magical elements in it had been eliminated.

The compatibility of Paul's theology with Gnosticism made it necessary to adjust this as well. In Paul's letters, the coming of the spirit is always linked to baptism, but in Acts it occurs independently of this rite. By the end of the second century, the doctrine of baptism as a supernatural experience that conveyed power was being replaced with the less radical idea that it conveyed merely a promise of future life. Although Clement's letter hints that teachings and rituals for the "perfected" persisted in Alexandria, these "higher mysteries" were probably abandoned after the persecution of 202 C.E.

Even so, as we have seen, traces of the Secret Gospel rite can be found in many early Christian writings. Clement quotes an Egyptian Gnostic of the mid-second century who stated that Jesus taught "at first by examples and by stories with hidden meanings, then by parables and by enigmas, but in the third state, clearly and nakedly, in private." The Acts of John (or John's Preaching of the Gospel), an apocryphal text probably written in the early second century, imaginatively reconstructs the scene at Gethsemane as a collective initiation rite: the disciples hold hands in a circle and dance (§94)! In the Second Book of Jeu, a Gnostic text from the fourth century, Jesus provides instructions for a series of baptisms preparatory to an ascent through the heavens.

Although the secret rite was forgotten (or suppressed), early Christians continued to have visionary experiences of heavenly ascent. Accounts can be found in the Odes of Solomon, the Shepherd of Hermas, the Vision of Paul, and the Passion of Perpetua. Following the pattern found in the Merkavah literature, the subject experiences a rapture, a sudden, involuntary vision in which they enter heaven.

Clement and his student Origen often used the imagery of heavenly ascent in their writings. Both believed that some Christians could enter heaven in the present by acquiring *gnōsis*, or knowledge, an idea the Church eventually rejected. As Clement wrote, "And, perchance, such an one has already attained the condition of 'being equal to the angels.' Accordingly, after the highest excellence in the flesh, changing always duly to the better, he urges his flight to the ancestral hall, through the holy septenniad [the seven heavenly abodes] to the Lord's own mansion; to be a light, steady, and continuing eternally, entirely, and in every part immutable" (*Miscellanies* 7.10). Here the imagery of heavenly ascent is seamlessly interwoven with Hellenistic cosmology and the platonic idea of essential forms. Origen uses similar language in his treatise, *Against Celsus* (7.46). There is a key difference, however, between these allusions to heavenly ascent and what we find in magical spells and Jewish mystical writings. Clement and Origen do not refer to specific experiences of ascending to heaven. Rather, they use the language of heavenly ascent metaphorically. What was once a goal achieved through psychological and ritual techniques has become an abstract ideal.

The symbols associated with heavenly ascent have an even longer history. The image of a ladder to heaven can be traced back to ancient Egypt, where inscriptions refer to "coming forth into heaven by the Ladder of God" and entering heaven "by means of the two fingers of the god who is the Lord of the Ladder." Aphraates, an early Mesopotamian Christian, described the ladder to heaven in Jacob's vision as the "mystery" instituted by Christ (*Demonstratio* 4.5). In her vision, the martyr Perpetua (d. 203) sees "a golden ladder of great size stretching up to heaven" (1.3). Finally, we find this symbolism in the Hekhalot literature in descriptions of "the path of the heavenly ladder whose one end is on earth and whose other end is in heaven at the right foot of the Throne of Glory" (Hekhalot Rabbati 16.1).

Another long-standing motif associated with heavenly ascent is that of "nakedness." As we saw, Paul used the metaphor of nakedness not only to describe the state of humility and purity required to enter the kingdom of heaven, but to allude as well to the "stripping off" of the old personality in preparation for being "clothed" in a new one, which was the function of baptism. Gnostics and neoplatonists like Plotinus, who wrote in the mid-third century, used this metaphor as well. What was "stripped off," however, was more abstractly defined as "matter"—or, rather, materiality broadly defined to include not only the physical body that restrains the soul but all social conventions and relationships that keep individuals entangled with the mundane world. All this must be stripped away, Plotinus explains, before the soul can fulfill its yearning to "ascend again towards the Good":

> So, to those that approach the Holy Celebrations of the Mysteries, there are appointed purifications and the laying aside of the garments worn before, and the entry in nakedness—until, passing, on the upward way, all that is other than the God, each in the solitude of himself shall behold that solitary-dwelling Existence, the Apart, the Unmingled, the Pure, that from Which all things depend, for Which all look and live and act and know, the Source of Life and of Intellection and of Being.
>
> And one that shall know this vision—with what passion of love shall he not be seized, with what pang of desire, what longing to be molten into one with This, what wondering delight! (6.7)

> To any vision must be brought an eye adapted to what is to be seen, and having some likeness to it. Never did eye see the sun unless it had first become sunlike, and never can the soul have vision of the First Beauty unless itself be beautiful.
>
> Therefore, first let each become godlike and each beautiful who cares to see God and Beauty. (6.9)

Traditions of baptism as a mystery rite are an integral part of the legacy of early Christianity. The Pistis Sophia, a Gnostic text compiled in the third century from earlier materials, illustrates the longevity of the themes originating with the Secret Gospel. Here we find a communion (another mode of union with a spirit), baptism, white linen garments, magical formulas, mystical instruction, androgyny, and, finally, entry into the kingdom of heaven. (Baptism by fire, referred to here and in other Gnostic and magical texts, is alluded to in the Gospel of Matthew, where John the Baptist announces the coming of one who will "baptize you with the Holy Spirit and fire" [3:11].)

Jesus said to them, "Bring me fire and vine branches." They brought them to him. He laid out the offering and placed on it two wine jugs, one on the right and the other on the left of the offering. He placed the offering before them. He placed a goblet of water before the wine jug on the left. And he set bread, according to the number of the disciples, in the middle between wine goblets and he placed a goblet of water behind the bread. Jesus stood before the offering; he placed the disciples behind him, all garbed in linen garments. In their hands was the number of the names of the father of the light-treasure. He cried out, saying, "Hear me, Father, father of all fatherhood, unlimited light. *Eeaoh, eeaoh, eeaoh, aohee, oheea, pseenother, thernopseen, nopseether, hepthomaoth, marachachtha, marmachachtha, ee-ay-ahnah, menaman, amanayee too ooranoo, eesrahee ohmayn, ahmayn soobaheebahee, apahahp, hahmayn, hahmayn, derhahrahee hahpahoo, ahmayn, ahmayn, boobiahmeen, meeahee, amen, amayn, etc....*" (The incantations and prayers continue. Be cautious when repeating these.) Then Jesus spoke to them, "This is the method and this is the mystery which you shall celebrate for men who will believe in you...but hide this mystery and do not give it to all men, only to him who does all things which I have said to you in my commandments. This, therefore, is the true mystery of baptism for those whose sins are forgiven and whose misdeeds are blotted out. This is the baptism of the first offerings, which leads forth to the true place and to the place of light."

Then the disciples said to him, "Rabbi, reveal to us the mystery of the light of your Father, since we heard you say, 'There is a baptism of fire, and a baptism of the Holy Spirit of light, and there is a spiritual anointing which leads the souls to the light-treasure.' Speak to us now of their mystery, so that we may inherit the Kingdom of God."

Jesus said to them, "These mysteries about which you ask, there is no mystery higher, which will lead your soul to the light of lights, to the places of truth and the good, to the place of the holy of all holies, to the place in which there is neither female nor male, nor form in that place, but a continuing, indescribable light." (4.142-43)

CHAPTER FIVE

No One Has Greater Love Than This

By definition, Jesus' secret baptism was not for the masses. On what basis did he select those whom he baptized? What were the qualifications for receiving this mystery?

Morton Smith argued that the section of Mark, chapter 10, from verses 13 to 45, when the Secret Gospel material is added to it, forms a complete set of baptismal instructions. It begins by describing the prerequisite for being baptized: become like little children. Then specific requirements are related, followed by a prophecy of the passion and resurrection — the central themes of Paul's references to baptism. This is where Smith would insert the Secret Gospel, which provides a liturgy for the service. The section ends with post-baptismal instruction in verses 35-45.

The specific requirements for receiving baptism are contained in the story that begins at verse 17. A man approaches Jesus and kneels (in Matthew he is a *neaniskos*, or young man [19:20]). "Good Teacher," he asks, "what must I do to inherit eternal life?" Jesus tells him that he must practice monotheism and obey the commandments. The man replies, "Teacher, I have kept all these since my youth." Then the text reads: "Jesus, looking at him, loved him and said, 'You lack one thing; go, sell what you own, and give the money to the poor, and you will have treasure in heaven; then come, follow me'" (10:21). Apparently, qualifying for baptism from Jesus required the renunciation of property. (In fact, voluntary poverty is known to have been practiced by the Jerusalem church and later by the Carpocratians and others.) The man in Mark is unwilling to give away his possessions, so he does not receive baptism. If the Secret Gospel material is added back into this chapter, however, we read of another man, also rich, who *does* receive baptism. The difference? Presumably, he was willing to give up his wealth.

The two Greek words for love, *agapē* and *phileō*, appear repeatedly in passages dealing with baptism and with those followers to whom Jesus seems to have been especially close. The formula, "...and looking at him, loved him [*ēgapēsen*, from *agapē*], and said...follow me" appears not only in Mark 10:21, but in the Secret Gospel as well, where the young man "looked on him and loved him [*ēgapēsen*], and began to beseech him that he might be with him." In the Gospel of John, Jesus loves Lazarus (11:3), but here the stronger word, *phileō*, is used, which, like *agapaō*, can mean "love" in the sense of care and respect toward another, but is also used to denote the feeling of a man for his wife. *Phileō* has the additional meaning "to kiss." The only other use of *phileō* to describe Jesus' feeling toward another is in reference to the mysterious beloved disciple mentioned in the Gospel of John.

Although he is present in several episodes and is the authority for the writing of John—if not its author (see 21:24)—he is never named. Rather, in each episode he appears he is identified only as "the disciple whom Jesus loved" (13:23; 19:26; 20:2; 21:7, 21:20-25). At the last supper, he "reclines" on Jesus' breast. In the course of Jesus' crucifixion and burial, his actions are contrasted favorably to those of Peter, Mary, and Thomas. In *The Community of the Beloved Disciple*, Raymond Brown argues that he was an idealized but historical figure, perhaps the follower of John the Baptist mentioned in the first chapter of John. In the early second century, a religious community, probably in Syria, cited the gospel attributed to John in defending their version of Christianity against followers of other disciples. Thus, the Gospel of John contrasts the beloved disciple to Simon Peter in five of the six passages in which he is mentioned. At some point in the second century, however, the Johannine community divided. A larger group became Gnostic, while a smaller group merged with the greater church. Both continued to use the Gospel of John, but its popularity among Gnostics made orthodox churches more reluctant to cite it.

The true identity of the beloved disciple can never be known for certain now, but among the more plausible guesses is that he was Lazarus. Both figures are described as being loved by Jesus, and given John's report that Lazarus accompanied Jesus in public and inspired others to become followers, he, too, was a disciple. Significantly, just as Lazarus exits from John's narrative, after being a key figure in chapters 11 and 12 (the latter opens with a feast at which Lazarus reclines upon Jesus' breast), the beloved disciple enters, in chapter 13, reclining upon Jesus' breast at the last supper. For whatever reason, perhaps because the historical Lazarus had become controversial, John hereafter refers to him only as "the disciple whom Jesus loved."

The identification of Lazarus with the beloved disciple helps explain the exchange near the end of John between Peter and the resurrected Jesus. Some of Jesus' disciples, it appears, had claimed that the beloved disciple was immortal. Apparently he wasn't, leading the author (or authors) of John to insert an aside at this point explaining that Jesus never said he was (21:20-25). But if the beloved disciple was Lazarus, it is easy to understand how such a belief developed. He had been raised from the dead; surely he could not die again.

There are only a few allusions to the beloved disciple outside of John. One apocryphal text mentions "the disciple whom Jesus loved and whom he instructed in his mysteries" (*Iohannis Evangelium Apocryphum Arabice* 53.8), which suggests that the author was familiar with the Secret Gospel material. The Second Apocalypse of James explicitly invokes the beloved disciple by having Jesus refer to both himself and to James as "the beloved"—and, as we have seen, he kisses and embraces his beloved. (Apparently aware of the incongruence of identifying James as both the brother of Jesus and his beloved, the author has a passage in which Mary describes their relationship as that of *step*brothers.) The Second Apocalypse of James is a crucial document because it reunites the beloved disciple tradition of John with the Markan tradition of a secret rite with a youth, both ultimately derived from the Secret Gospel.

Lazarus, of course, corresponds to the youth of the Secret Gospel who, according to the passage Clement quotes, takes Jesus to his home immediately following his resurrection, "for he was rich." Lazarus, too, seems to have been well-to-do, given that he owned a home as well and was able to host a feast for Jesus and his entourage. Given this, a second look at the rich youth of Mark 10:17 and Matthew 19:16 may be in order. It was suggested earlier that he stood in contrast to the Secret Gospel youth: because he does not give up his wealth he fails to qualify for "treasure in heaven." The Secret Gospel youth, on the other hand, is taught the mysteries of heaven because, presumably, he gave up his riches. This makes sense given that voluntary poverty is among the earliest traditions of Christianity.

But it seems equally possible now that the rich youth of canonical Mark and the resurrected youth of Secret Mark were the same. All that is missing from the narrative to establish this is an aside explaining that when the rich youth (Lazarus) returned home he suddenly fell ill. John picks up the story at precisely this point: "A certain man was ill, Lazarus of Bethany, the village of Mary and his sister Martha" (11:1). His family, apparently known to Jesus already, sends him an urgent message: "Lord, he whom you love is ill." Jesus, however, delays his arrival even though, as John reiterates, he loves Lazarus. When he finally arrives at Bethany, Lazarus has been dead four days. Jesus orders the tomb opened, and Lazarus emerges swathed in the traditional Jewish burial shroud—white linen cloth. Turning back to the Secret Gospel, we then read how Jesus initiated the resurrected youth, who arrived for a ritual of death and rebirth appropriately dressed in the same burial garment. So, in the end, the rich youth receives "treasure in heaven," the mystery of the kingdom of God, after all.

The story's message in this case is more nuanced than a simple exhortation to give up wealth. The youth who fails to live up to Jesus' standards nonetheless receives the highest mystery and becomes a disciple. Why? Because Jesus loves him, and Jesus' love is unconditional. It is for sinners as well as the devout. All he requires, as we will see, is that his love be returned. And in the larger Markan narrative it is. The same formula—"looking at him, loved him"—describes the youth's love for Jesus that earlier describes Jesus' love for the rich youth.

Who, then, was the young man at Gethsemane, also wearing white linen wrapped around his naked body? Is he the same youth in the Secret Gospel or a different individual altogether? It seems unlikely that the same person would undergo baptism twice, given what we know about the rite. If he was a different youth, on the other hand, he still may have been an important figure in the early movement, despite the suppression of his name. Earlier it was noted that some scholars speculated that the naked youth was "Mark" himself. Although it seems improbable that a gospel author and disciple would portray himself as fleeing from the scene of Jesus' arrest, it makes sense if his intention was to establish himself as being among the few baptized by Jesus and therefore a member of his inner circle. One other clue supports this. According to canonical Mark, Jesus is alone at Gethsemane when he pleads for his father to spare him from his pending death. Yet, Mark relates both his prayers and actions. Did someone, in fact, overhear his words and later report them, so that they became part of the stories told about that night, stories that the actual authors of the gospels a generation later drew on to create their narratives?

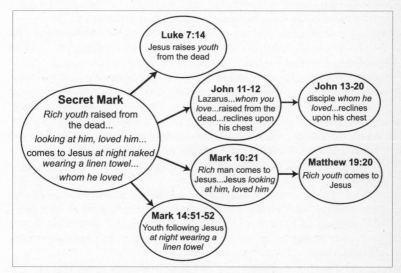

Fig. 6. Relationship between the Secret Gospel youth and figures in Mark, Matthew, John, and Luke.

Figure 6 illustrates the relationships between all these figures. Above all, it is the use of the term *neaniskos* that ties these pieces of evidence together. It is a uniquely Markan term; its only occurrences outside Mark are in Matthew's account of the rich young man and Luke's variation on the Lazarus story, in which Jesus resurrects a young man by exclaiming, "*Neaniskos*, I say to you, rise!" (7:14)—episodes all derived from the Secret Gospel of Mark.

Although the identities of these figures may never be known for certain, it is clear that love had a central role in Jesus' secret rite. Indeed, it was a prerequisite for receiving it. In addition to obeying the commandments and forsaking riches, there must be love. And this love is spontaneous and unconditional. It is love at first sight—instantaneous because it results from the recognition of oneself in another—the love of equals and sames. Thus, it is mutual and reciprocal. Jesus expresses this love toward men, and men express it toward Jesus—and in the Secret Gospel, the source of these memories, Jesus and his beloved each express it toward the other.

THE LAST SUPPER

The Gospel of John includes the most extensive exposition on love in the New Testament, in the chapters relating the occasion of Jesus' last meal with his disciples.

According to John, the meal has begun when Jesus suddenly rises, throws off his robes, and stands naked before his disciples. He wraps himself in a linen cloth (*lention*, John's synonym for *sindōn*) and proceeds to wash the feet of each disciple, using the cloth to dry them. Simon Peter protests, but Jesus continues. The lesson, he tells them, is that they must maintain perfect reciprocity amongst them, they must be a brotherhood of equals: "If I, your Lord and Teacher, have washed your feet, you also ought to wash one another's feet.... Servants are not greater than their master" (13:14-16). Although this leaves the roles of teacher and disciple, master and servant in place, it places them on equal footing. Some may be leaders and some followers, but all are equally valued.

In Luke's account, Jesus goes further. The disciples begin to dispute which of them should be regarded as the "greatest," and Jesus rebukes them all. "The greatest among you," he says, "must become like the youngest, and the leader like one who serves.... I am among you as one who serves" (22:26-27).

John goes on to relate Jesus' prediction of his own betrayal. Here is where the unnamed disciple—"whom Jesus loved"—enters the picture. He has been reclining, Greek-style, on Jesus' chest. Simon Peter signals to him to ask Jesus who the betrayer is. Whispering, the beloved disciple inquires, "Lord, who is it?" "It is the one to whom I give this piece of bread," Jesus says (13:23-30), handing the bread to Judas, who promptly flees. The other disciples are mystified.

Now Jesus delivers his sermon on love.

He begins by exhorting the disciples to love him and to love one another, using the word *agapē* (with the exception of verse 16:27, where he uses the stronger term *phileō* to refer to God's love for the disciples). He tells them, "They who have my commandments and keep them are those who love me, and those who love me will be loved by my father, and I will love them and reveal myself to them" (14:21). Following him, in other words, is not a matter of obedience or submission—it is an expression of love. And this love is reciprocal: the disciples who love Jesus will be loved in turn by him and his father. Indeed, it is by displaying their love toward each other—through, presumably, such symbolic acts as washing each others' feet—that they will distinguish themselves in the eyes of the larger world.

It becomes apparent that what Jesus means by "love" is something more than a congenial sentiment. It is the means by which his followers unite with him. As he tells the disciples, he will be "in" them, and they "in" him. And in his absence, a spirit will come, an "advocate" or "helper"—the Holy Spirit—whom the disciples will know because, like Jesus, "he abides with you, and he will be in you" (14:17). *Menō*, the Greek term translated here and elsewhere as "abide," also has the sense of "to dwell," and by extension its connotations of "occupy," "live inside," "possess." The language here suggests assimilation and absorption, the metaphors underlying communion, in which the flesh and blood of Jesus are absorbed by consuming bread and wine. To "love" Jesus is to be filled—possessed—by him, that is, by his spirit.

To describe this union, Jesus uses metaphors of fertility and procreation. He is the vine; his disciples its fruit-bearing branches. "Abide in me as I abide in you. Just as the branch cannot bear fruit by itself unless it abides in the vine," he says, "neither can you unless you abide in me.... My Father is glorified by this, that you bear much fruit and become my disciples" (15:1-8), and he exhorts them, "Go and bear fruit" (15:16). Later, he compares their pain over his coming death to that of a woman in labor: "When her child is born, she no longer remembers the anguish because of the joy of having brought a human being into the world" (16:21). Loving Jesus and uniting with him is creative—like the vine and its branches, like the union of man and woman—something new is produced, whether "fruit" or "offspring."

But when he goes on to cite an exemplar of love it is not the love of husbands and wives, nor that of kin. It is the love of friends:

> I have said these things to you so that my joy may be in you, and that your joy may be complete. This is my commandment, that you love one another as I have loved you. No one has greater love than this, to lay down one's life for one's friends. (15:11-13)

Jesus and the Shamanic Tradition of Same-Sex Love

That Jesus considered the love of comrades qualitatively different from that of other relationships is evident in statements attributed to him in Mark, Matthew, and Luke in which he denies his own family. Indeed, in Luke and Matthew, he announces that it is his intention to divide families: "Whoever comes to me and does not hate father and mother, wife and children, brothers and sisters, yes, and even life itself cannot be my disciple" (Luke 14:26; cf. Luke 12:51-53; Matt. 10:34-37; Gospel of Thomas 55.1-2a, 101). He even expresses hostility toward motherhood. When a woman in a crowd shouts, "Blessed is the womb that bore you and the breasts that nursed you!," he replies, "Blessed rather are those who hear the word of God and obey it!'" (Luke 11:27-28; Gospel of Thomas 79:1-2). In the Gospel of Thomas the language is even blunter: "Whoever knows the father and the mother will be called the child of a whore" (105). (Paul mollifies this hostility to the family significantly—see "Paul's Love.") As Jesus declares in all three synoptic gospels, "Whoever does the will of God is my brother and sister and mother" (Mark 3:35; Matt. 12:50; Luke 8:21).

The presence of these statements in all three synoptic gospels is strong evidence that they were part of the source documents they drew on. They are, in other words, about as close to something Jesus actually might have said as we are likely to get—notwithstanding the claims of modern moralizers regarding Christianity's so-called family values.

But could Jesus really have been this hostile to family and marriage? John Crossan, pointing to the social disruption visited upon peasant Jews by the Romans, argues that he was not trying to destroy families that were viable but replace ones that were not. William Countryman, however, concludes in his study, *Dirt, Greed, and Sex*, that Jesus did indeed have a radical goal in mind: nothing less than the elimination of the hierarchical patriarchal family. All the gospels provide evidence of this, he argues, but chapter 10 of Mark in particular (the same chapter with the baptismal material discussed earlier) outlines reforms that effectively strip the family of its "unquestioned centrality." The most significant of these, Countryman suggests, is Jesus' prohibition of divorce in verses 11-12.

Taken out of context, this prohibition sounds ultraconservative. In fact, no major denomination today adheres to it. But in Jesus' time it represented a revolutionary reform. Jewish laws permitted men to divorce their wives for various reasons, including barrenness and adultery, and it permitted them to have sexual relations with other wives and slaves. Jewish women, on the other hand, had no comparable rights, a reflection of their status as sexual property in a patriarchal society. By asserting that neither husband nor wife may divorce, Jesus placed them on equal footing. Instead of a sexual double standard, the same standards of adultery are applied to both, and while women are

74

not allowed to divorce their husbands, neither are husbands allowed to divorce their wives. The traditional sexual property rights of men is annulled.

In first-century Palestine, this would have been a notable improvement in a woman's status. In Countryman's words, it took her "out of the realm of disposable property and made her equal to her husband." Similarly, Jesus' welcoming of the children and his insistence that only those who can receive the kingdom of God "as a little child" will enter it (10:15) takes children "from the bottom of the family hierarchy and makes them persons in their own right." These verses are immediately followed by the story of the rich (young) man who wishes to be a disciple. Jesus' advice to him—give up both family and property—follows from his teachings on the status of women and children. Men must give up their dominant place in the family, including their property rights, sexual and other, in women and children. Jesus meant nothing less, Countryman concludes, than "the end of the entire hierarchical institution called family."

In place of stratified social relations, Jesus holds up the ideal of comradely love. This way of loving suspends existing hierarchies and transforms unequal relationships into egalitarian ones. Thus, after commanding his disciples to love each other, "as I have loved you" (John 15:12), Jesus announces, "I do not call you servants any longer, because the servant does not know what the master is doing; but I have called you friends, because I have made known to you everything that I have heard from my Father" (15:15). Love has erased differences; it is the primary instrument of the movement Jesus wishes to found: "I am giving you these commands so that you may love one another" (15:17).

Continuing his discourse, Jesus again refers to the coming of a "spirit" who will testify on his behalf (15:26). Finally, he reveals that he himself "came from the Father" (16:28) and brings his sermon to a close with a long prayer, ending with the words, "I made your name known to them, and I will make it known, so that the love with which you have loved me may be in them, and I in them" (17:26)—again, the themes of love and union.

The next chapter opens with Jesus and his disciples crossing the Kidron Valley.

Reconstructing the Secret Gospel rite has led us through some historically marginal terrain. Beginning with the accidental discovery of a forgotten gospel, we turned to miscellaneous Christian, Jewish, and pagan sources to unlock its meaning and to fill in the erasures of the New Testament. Yet we have ended up affirming the centrality of a theme in Jesus' teachings about which there is little disagreement—the importance of love.

Given all this, it is not surprising that love should have a significant role in Jesus' rite of baptism. But to understand how the magical operations of an hallucinatory ascent to heaven and Jesus' ethical and philosophical teachings are linked we need to look beyond the New Testament, to the social and cultural milieu in which Christianity arose. What did "love" mean in the Greek-speaking world of the first century?

Christian theologians claim that Jesus' teachings on love are what makes Christianity so different from previous religions. The commandment to love one's enemies (Matt. 5:44; Luke 6:27, 6:35) and the assertion that God loves sinners were, indeed, new ideas in the ancient world. Even so, those who received these teachings would have understood them in terms of what they already knew and believed about love.

The Hebrew Bible includes important teachings on love and altruism, above all the commandment to love one's neighbor (Lev. 19:18). Many Jewish customs harkened back to the values of an egalitarian society, such as requirements to care for the poor and widowed, to give workers and slaves a day of rest, and to periodically cancel debts and adjust property-holding. Jewish tradition was no less concerned with intimate love, as the Song of Songs attests. Love has an important role in the Hekhalot literature as well. According to Peter Schäffer, the ascent of the Hekhalot mystic was an expression of the "special love between God and Israel," and he quotes a text in which God says:

> For no time is like this time,
> Since my soul looks forward to seeing you (pl.).
> No time is like this time,
> Since your love clings closely to my heart.

Jewish values and traditions are inherent in Jesus' teachings on love. At the same time, Jesus transformed these ideas. "Neighbor" was extended to included everyone, not only other Jews. Further, his love and that of his father is unmotivated and unconditional — they even love sinners. And it is spontaneous. Jesus and his young male followers declare their love immediately upon seeing each other. In Jewish tradition, God's love is, first of all, specifically for Jews, but even then it is conditional upon their righteousness within the framework of religious law. Christian agape, in contrast, overrides established religious and social frameworks.

Considering this, we need to ask what other sources of ideas about love might have influenced Jesus and his circle. The answer lies in the intensely multicultural milieu of the Middle East in the first century. In

Galilee, a dozen Greek cities lay within twenty-five miles of Nazareth; Palestine was home to over thirty-five. The basic institutions of Greek civic culture were represented in each of these cities, from theaters to schools to gymnasia. Many Jews adopted Hellenized lifestyles and abandoned or modified their observance of religious laws. Like Paul, if they read the Tanakh, they did so in a Greek translation known as the Septuagint. Even in Jerusalem, Jews were as likely to speak Greek as Aramaic.

Although it is unlikely that Jesus himself read Greek, he may have spoken some, and some of his earliest followers undoubtedly could read and write Greek. Scholars have pointed out similarities between Jesus and the movement he inspired, and the Greek Cynics, beggar philosophers whose lifestyle and ethical anecdotes parallel those of Jesus. As Burton Mack observes, "Jesus' genius was to let the sparks fly between two different cultural sensibilities, the Greek and the Semitic." The result was a synthesis of Greek ideals of individual virtue and Jewish traditions of utopian communalism that was the crowning achievement of Hellenistic civilization. The "kingdom of God," in the minds of early Christians, was a social vision—an alternative society—as well as a mystical experience of redemption and perfection.

Early Christians who could read Greek literature would have found many references to love, its nature, and its significance in plays, poetry, speeches, and philosophy. And in all these kinds of writings they would have found one authority cited above all others: Plato. Indeed, Plato's writings were the wellsprings for nearly all speculative and ethical thinking in the Hellenistic era. Today Plato is viewed as the father of Western philosophy—in the words of one scholar "that thinker without whom there would be no European culture." Among his many contributions to Western civilization was a theory of love as a spiritual practice. Although Plato lived centuries before Jesus, his works were receiving renewed interest in the period that Christianity arose. Under the influence of this philosophical movement, known as neoplatonism, early Christian fathers such as Clement and Origen synthesized Christian beliefs with Plato's philosophy.

This is why, to fully understand what Jesus taught about love, we need to consider what Plato said four hundred years before. We need to sit in on another dinner, this one in Athens about the year 416 B.C.E. For it is Plato's account of this gathering that contains the fullest exposition of his ideas about love, heaven, and union with the divine.

CHAPTER SIX
To Be Made One Out of Two

Like the last supper, the *Symposium* involves a gathering of disciples dominated by the personality of a charismatic leader—in this case, Socrates. It, too, begins with a formal washing. Then the participants eat and, following that, drink wine, the same sequence as at the last supper. Next, like the disciples in the Gospel of Luke, they engage in a "dispute." Their subject is God—or, in this case, a god—Eros, the patron of love. Throughout these proceedings, Socrates' disciple, Agathon, reclines upon him just as the beloved disciple reclined on Jesus. (Agathon says he wants to absorb his teacher's wisdom by pressing their bodies together.)

Phaedrus gives the first of seven speeches. Eros is a mighty god, he says, eldest of all, since he has no parents, and he is the source of great benefits. One such benefit is the desire of lovers to maintain honor in each other's eyes, which fosters acts of heroism. Phaedrus cites the case of Alcestis, an Athenian woman who died for her husband. Then he mentions a pair of male lovers—Achilles and Patroclus. In holding up a homosexual relationship as an ideal, Phaedrus was entirely within the norms of his time. Male homosexuality was to a remarkable extent institutionalized in classical Athens. Nonetheless, Greek same-sex practices differed in important ways from contemporary gay lifestyles. Few Greek men were exclusively homosexual. Most conformed to expectations to marry and produce children, especially sons. But one prerogative of Greek men, at least those who were freeborn citizens, was to have affairs outside of marriage and, as long as these did not preclude marriage, it was unimportant if they were affairs with women or other men.

Actually, most homosexual relationships in classical Greece were not between men as such, but men and youths in their early to late teens. This was in keeping with a fundamental feature of societies throughout the ancient Mediterranean, which was their stratified and hierarchical nature. Each class and social group was ranked in relation to others, higher or lower. Many groups were internally hierarchical as well, including families. In all cases, men held a superior position, with adult male citizens holding the highest status of all. This principle was extended to sex as well. Sexual partners in the ancient world were never equals. The man who took the active, penetrative role always had higher status than those, whether women, boys, or slaves of either sex, who were penetrated.

Greek beliefs about love reflect this. *Erōs* was the emotion men felt toward the objects of their desire. Sexual objects, however, were presumed not to feel desire, unless they were debauched women or prostitutes. Lovers did not love "each other." Rather, men's desire was directed toward their partners, and their partners received it. Indeed, different words were used to identify lovers in homosexual relationships. The "active," older man was the *erastēs*, the "passive," younger man the *erōmenos*.

All this seems a far cry from Jesus' teachings on comradely love, which emphasize reciprocity and the revaluation of social differences. Yet, if we attend closely to the way Plato develops his argument in the *Symposium*, we will see that his ideas are not only related to those of Jesus, they shed light on the link between Jesus' theory (his doctrine of love) and his practice (ritual ascent to heaven). Much as Jesus defined the love of comrades by pointing to what it is *not*—familial and conjugal love—Plato distinguishes his definition of eros indirectly, by having each speaker undermine one or more of the assumptions behind conventional views of love and sexuality, until, by the end of the *Symposium*, an entirely new understanding emerges.

The first speaker, Phaedrus, expresses the most conventional views. The roles of lover and beloved, as he describes them, are asymmetrical. The *erastēs* feels passion toward his *erōmenos*, but the *erōmenos* is not expected to return his love to the same degree. Because the lover is under the inspiration of a god, Eros, he is more divine than the beloved. If the beloved does return his passion it is notable, as in the case of Achilles, who gave his life for Patroclus. But here Phaedrus makes a revealing aside, acknowledging the existence of a debate on whether Achilles was the beloved or the lover. Phaedrus argues that since Achilles was beardless he was undoubtedly younger than Patroclus and, therefore, the beloved. Nonetheless, the very possibility of such a debate suggests that the roles of lover and beloved in classical Greece were not always clear-cut or fixed. Already, Plato is undermining the distinction between the two.

The next speaker, Pausanius, offers an important clarification. There are two forms of love, he declares—one inspired by the Younger Aphrodite, daughter of Zeus and the female Titan, Dione; the other inspired by Heavenly Aphrodite. The love of the Younger Aphrodite, he explains, is common and indiscriminate. Because she was born of a man and woman and has qualities of both sexes, this Aphrodite's love can be directed at either women or boys. The love of Heavenly Aphrodite, however, is spiritual. Born from the foam that formed around Uranus' severed genitals when Chronos flung them into the sea, she has only a father. Her love, therefore, is only for males. It is the love of men for boys and youths.

Pausanius dwells on the distinction between honorable and dishonorable love. The issue at stake relates to a central contradiction in

Jesus and the Shamanic Tradition of Same-Sex Love

Greek male homosexuality—the incompatibility of sexual submission on the part of youths with their future role as adult citizens and civic leaders. Pausanius proposes a compromise: the beloved may allow his lover sexual favors when given in return for wisdom and other virtues he receives from him. Pausanius refers to this as "voluntary servitude" and "voluntary slavery" (184c). In assuming that sex always involves dominant and submissive roles, and that sexual submission is antithetical to male status, Pausanius expresses common Greek biases.

The next speaker, the physician Eryximachus, counters with a different perspective. There are healthy and unhealthy forms of both common and spiritual, heterosexual and homosexual love, he declares. Examples can be found in animals as well as humans. Healthy love has the power to heal, he argues, because, like medicine and music, it effects a reconciliation of opposites. Uranian love—"the noble Love, the heavenly Love of the Muse Urania"—is healthy because it is temperate (187d-e). Common love, however, must be used carefully because pleasure can lead to licentiousness. With this, Eryximachus effectively redefines the terms of the debate, offsetting Pausanius' grim view of sex as slavery for the beloved with the possibility that desires can be healthy and, in being fulfilled, have healthful benefits.

Now, Aristophanes, presumably the famous comic playwright, rises to speak. To illustrate the power of Eros, he proposes to tell a myth concerning humankind's "original nature." Aristophanes' myth (which seems to be Plato's invention) turns Greek ideas about sexuality on their head.

The first humans, Aristophanes begins, were doubled front-to-back, and there were three sexes instead of two: double males, double females, and male-females, or androgynes. They were, respectively, the children of the sun, the earth, and the moon. These doubled beings could walk upright, either backwards or forwards as they pleased, and they could roll over and over at a great pace, turning on their four hands and feet like tumbleweeds. In fact, they were so strong they dared to challenge the gods. The gods, under Zeus, decided to split them in half.

After this, Aristophanes says, humans were forever seeking their lost halves—women from the doubled female seeking women, men from the doubled male seeking men, and men and women from the androgyne seeking the opposite sex. Whenever they found their other halves, they threw their arms around each other and yearned to grow into one. Seeing this, Zeus felt sorry for them, so he rearranged their genitals to enable them to have intercourse. This made it possible for men and women to have children, while men who had sex with other males "would get some satisfaction from their union and they would take a break, then return to their work and attend to the rest of life" (191c). Thus, Aristophanes defines three categories of people based on sexual orientation—heterosexuals, male homosexuals, and lesbians. This scheme is much closer to modern categories of sexual preference than it is to those of Plato's own time, which did not define individuals on the basis of sexual object choice.

Much of Aristophanes' speech up to this point has been tongue-in-cheek, in the style of the real Aristophanes' comic plays. But now his tone becomes more serious. At the same time, his focus shifts to same-sex love exclusively.

"Whenever a lover of boys [*paiderastēs*], or anyone else," he says, "happens to encounter the person who is their other half, they are overcome with amazement at their friendship, intimacy, and love, and do not want to be severed, so to speak, from each other even for a moment" (192b-c). This ardent desire is for more than sex. It is something the soul itself longs for but does not apprehend or understand. Aristophanes explains:

> If Hephaestus were holding his tools and standing over the pair lying there together, he might say: "What do you people want from each other?" If they had no answer, he might continue: "Is this what you desire, to be together as much as possible, so that you would not leave each other day and night? If you desire that, I am willing to weld and forge you into one and the same being, so that from being two you will have become one and can henceforth live as one being, both of you sharing a single life in common. When you die, you will share a death in common, there in Hades, as one being instead of two. Consider whether you would like this and would be satisfied should this happen." We know that when they heard this, not a one would refuse, nor would they appear to want anything other than that. On the contrary, they would think they had discovered what they had really desired all along, namely, to be made one out of two by being joined and welded together with their beloved. (192d-e)

With this, Aristophanes draws his speech to a close:

> So, the name "love" is given to the desire for wholeness.... While he benefits us most in the present moment by leading us into relationships that suit us, he provides us great hope for the future: if we show proper reverence for the gods, he will restore us to our original nature and, by healing us, will make us happy and blessed. (193a; 193d)

At this point, distinctions of age and status have been reduced to a vanishing point. After all, the two halves produced by splitting a doubled male being are, logically, twins, and therefore indistinguishable. Although Aristophanes employs the language of age-based relationships, his *erastēs* and *erōmenos* occupy points on a continuum of same-sex desire, not fixed roles. As he explains, those who are halves of the male-male figure pursue males from the time they are young, hanging about men and "becoming entwined with them" (191e). When they grow up, the object of their love shifts to younger men, but their fundamental orientation remains the same, that is, same-sex. Such men, Aristophanes says, often become statesmen and "are not interested in marriage and having children" (192b). But when he goes on to describe the bond between same-sex lovers, he makes no reference to age differences. Instead, he evokes a powerful image of equality and mutuality: two lovers being welded into one by the god of fire.

Agathon, whose victory in a playwriting contest is the occasion for the gathering, speaks next. He proposes to praise Eros himself, not merely the benefits he confers. Eros is fair, young, tender, flexible of form, graceful, and lives among flowers. He is just because he never uses force—men serve him of their own free will. Being the master of all pleasures, he is temperate (how could he rule if he was not?). He is courageous, having conquered the god of war himself. He is a poet and responsible for inspiring music, art, divination, archery, medicine, and other boons. Agathon continues in this vein then glibly concludes, "That is my speech. Let it be dedicated to the god. It's partly playful and partly serious, and as good a job as I am capable of" (197e).

Now, finally, it is Socrates' turn to speak. He begins by claiming to have been struck dumb by the beauty of Agathon's speech. However, he understood the goal of the symposium to be the offering of praise that was true, not to attribute to Eros all sorts of greatness and glory, whether deserved or not. So he proposes to offer the truth in his speech. He begins by asking Agathon a question: Is love the love of something? Yes, says Agathon, it is love of something one lacks—namely, beauty and good. With this premise, Socrates begins his exposition on *erōtika*, or "love matters."

Instead of expounding ideas of his own, however, he credits his account of love to a woman named Diotima (201d). Whether Diotima was an historical person or a figure invented by Plato has long been the subject of debate (see "Why Was Diotima a Woman?"). Socrates says she was a seer "who was wise and skillful in this and many other things," and that she was his teacher in the matters of love. By citing a woman and a priestess as his authority, Socrates removes the discussion of love from the discourse of philosophy and places it in the realm of religion and mysticism. Indeed, his speech dwells as much on describing the subjective dimension of eros as it does on propounding theories about it.

According to Socrates, Diotima began her lesson by explaining that Eros is a great *daimōn*, or spirit, whose nature is intermediate between divine and mortal. He conveys the prayers of mortals to the gods, and bears the commands of the gods to mortals. As a mediator, he is connected to the arts of the prophet and the priest, and to sacrifices, mysteries, charms, prophecy, and incantation. He is neither mortal nor immortal, but always shifting between life and death, poverty and plenty. Diotima tells Socrates that he does not understand the nature of the god, because he has confused Eros with the beloved. The beloved is beautiful, not Eros, for Eros is desire for what one lacks, namely beauty.

Love, she explains, is the desire to possess the beautiful, which includes the good. Indeed, it is the desire for the everlasting possession of the beautiful, for possessing beauty bestows happiness. But why, she asks Socrates, is the pursuit of love accompanied with so much yearning and zeal? Because, answering her own question, lovers are seeking "birth in beauty both in body and in soul" (206b). It is human nature to want to procreate through male-female union, and especially to procreate what is beautiful or perfect. Generation represents a means of attaining eternity and immortality. It naturally follows from the desire for the everlasting possession of the good.

The desire for immortality manifests itself not only in procreation, however. Ambitious men, for example, seek to perpetuate memory of themselves by gaining fame. In fact, Diotima explains, there are two kinds of desire for generation:

> Those who are pregnant in body are more oriented toward women and are lovers in that way, providing immortality, remembrance, and happiness for themselves for all time, as they believe, by producing children. Those who are pregnant in soul however—for there are people who are even more pregnant in their souls than in their bodies...are pregnant with and give birth to what is appropriate for the soul. What, then is it that is appropriate for the soul to bring forth? Good sense and the rest of virtue, of which all poets are procreators, as well as those artisans who are said to be inventors. (208e)

The desire to possess beauty is linked to the urge to create. This is just as true in the case of men who form relationships with other males, as it is with those who marry women and beget offspring. If the seeds of wisdom have been implanted in them in their youth, Diotima explains, such men will seek beauty and good as adults, and their souls will be pregnant with creative endeavors. When one of these men finds another who has a noble soul, he is inspired:

When he attaches himself to someone beautiful, I believe, and associates with him, he gives birth and brings forth what he was pregnant with before, both while in that person's presence and while remembering him when he's absent. Together with him he nurtures the offspring produced, so that such men have much more to share with each other and a stronger friendship than that which comes from rearing children, since they share in the rearing of children who are more beautiful and more immortal.

Everyone would prefer to bring forth this sort of children rather than human offspring. People are envious of Homer, Hesiod, and the other good poets because of the offspring they left behind, since these are the sort of offspring that, being immortal themselves, provide their procreators with an immortal glory and an immortal remembrance. (209c-d)

Up to this point, Diotima tells Socrates, she has related only those mysteries of *erōtika* into which he might qualify to be initiated. She doubts whether he could approach the higher mysteries (*epoptikos*) and rites (*telea*), however. Nonetheless, she continues, admonishing Socrates to do his best to follow along.

To approach *erōtika* correctly, an individual must begin to appreciate beautiful bodies while he is young. With guidance, he will come to love the body of one person and engage in beautiful conversations with him. Next he must learn that the beauty of any one body is the same as the beauty of every other body. This will lead him to abandon the love of a single body and become a lover of all beautiful bodies. Eventually, however, he will see that the beauty of souls is more valuable than that of bodies, and he will ally himself with a mentor who has such a soul without regard for his physical appearance. Under his lover's guidance, he learns that all forms of beauty are related, whether that of bodies or laws or routine pursuits. Now he begins to transcend the desire for beauty in its individual forms—whether bodies or objects or pursuits—and turns to "the great sea of beauty" and to acquiring knowledge of it by giving "birth" to beautiful conversations and philosophical thoughts.

"When someone moves through these various stages," Diotima explains, "from the correct love of young boys and begins to see this beauty, he has nearly reached the end" (211b). Now, suddenly, he sees something wondrous—a vision of "the beautiful itself, pure, clear, unmixed, and not contaminated with human flesh and color and a lot of other mortal silliness" (211e).

In summing up her lesson, Diotima employs the imagery of ascent:

In the activities of Love, this is what it is to proceed correctly, or be led by another: Beginning from beautiful things to move ever onwards for the sake of that beauty, as though using ascending steps [or rungs of a ladder], from one body to two and from two to all beautiful bodies, from beautiful bodies to beautiful practical endeavors, from practical endeavors to beautiful examples of understanding, from examples of understanding to come finally to that understanding which is none other than the understanding of that beauty itself, so that in the end he knows what beauty itself is. (211b-211c)

At this point, it should be noted, heterosexual love has dropped out of the discussion entirely. All the references in Socrates' exchange with Diotima are to same-sex love. This form of love transcends sensuality and produces a mystical experience that connects the lover to the divine. It is beneficial and healing. At the same time, it fosters practical outcomes in the real world by inspiring the creation of beautiful things. It is, as Jesus implies in the Gospel of John, a special mode of procreation.

With Diotima's sublime description of essential beauty, Socrates ends his speech. The other guests applaud, and the mood of the party once again becomes jocular.

The symposium is not over yet, however, for there is still one more speech. A drunken Alcibiades bursts in and delivers a mock tirade against his teacher, Socrates.

Like Marsyas, the flute-playing satyr whose songs bewitch those who hear them, Socrates' words possess the souls of his listeners. Whenever he hears him, Alcibiades complains, "My heart pounds and the tears flow—even more than among the Corybantes" (215e). To make matters worse, Socrates has resisted all of Alcibiades' attempts to seduce him—a reversal, it should be noted, of the usual roles, since the older man normally takes the initiative. In fact, Alcibiades accuses Socrates of "acting more like a darling than a lover" on several occasions, forcing the young men who would court him to assume the role of the *erastēs*, or older partner (222b). In the meantime, Socrates' philosophical arguments have bitten Alcibiades like a viper, taking hold of his soul and causing him to be possessed with the "madness and Bacchanalian frenzy of philosophy" (218b).

All this actually serves to illustrate, albeit humorously, the spiritual development Diotima outlined. Alcibiades is an impetuous and lusty youth who has come to find beauty in souls as well as bodies, and then finds himself caught up in a philosophical quest for beauty in its highest form.

His tirade over, Alcidiades vies with Agathon for the privilege of reclining next to Socrates. Then a crowd of drunken revelers invades the scene, and the party breaks up.

THE WING OF THE SOUL

Plato expands on his philosophy of love and his concept of the soul in the *Phaedrus*, a dialogue relating the conversation between Socrates and a youth named Phaedrus as they take a walk beyond the walls of Athens on a hot summer afternoon.

The soul, Socrates explains to his companion, is an animating, indwelling, vital force whose state is one of constant motion. It is being without form, hence immortal, and it is synonymous with consciousness and willpower. Those who have souls are actors rather than being acted on. The soul can take various forms, but most often it has the shape of a wing. That is the physical form most like the divine. Wings can soar aloft, carrying objects from the lower regions into the upper sky where the gods reside (246d-e). When perfect and fully winged, the soul "travels through the sky and takes part in the governance of the entire cosmos" (a role attributed to angels and spirits in Judeo-Christian belief, as we have seen) (246c). Imperfect souls, however, lose their "wings" and sink to the earth, taking up an abode within a human body.

The desire of the soul is to escape the body and behold Truth and Beauty in the highest heaven. This realm is above the domain of the gods, who come and go in their chariots. It is the heaven "beyond the heavens," where the gods themselves ascend when they die (247c). It lacks color, shape, or form. It is visible only to mind. It is absolute knowledge and existence—divine intelligence—purest, ultimate reality. Here, according to Socrates, all is "brilliant shining beauty," simple, calm, and blessed (250b-c).

Among humans, only the minds of philosophers ever acquire wings, Socrates says, because only they think about "what our soul saw when it was traveling with a god, looking down on the things we now say are and rising up into what really is" (249c). This remembering of beauty is none other than the form of madness inspired by Eros. Because madness serves to release the soul from the yoke of custom and convention, it is beneficial.

The love of physical beauty, Socrates suggests, reflects the soul's desire to return to the vision of supreme beauty it beheld before being imprisoned in a body. This is why the lover, at the very sight of beauty, reacts with amazement. A shudder runs through him; he is in awe; he wants to worship his beloved; he becomes heated and perspires. He is transported in a kind of rapture. In Socrates' words, "He longs to fly up, but he is unable to and gazes upward like a bird, not caring for the

Fig. 7. Abraham being carried to heaven on the wings of birds in a fourteenth-
century manuscript of the Apocalypse of Abraham, *a merkavah text from the
late first or early second century* C.E. After Obscestvo ljubitelej drevnej pis
'mennosti, *vol.99 (St. Petersburg, 1891).*

things below, and for this reason is regarded as mad" (249d-e). This apprehension of beauty is a blessed mystery. Of all the forms of possession, or madness, Socrates says, this is the best. The wing of the lover's soul moistens and warms. Slowly, it begins to grow, and here Socrates uses sexually suggestive language, alluding to erection, intercourse, and ejaculation. This is why, he concludes, Eros is called the winged one (251a-252c).

The parallels with Jewish and Christian patterns of celestial ascent are notable. In merkavah narratives such as the Ascension of Isaiah and the Apocalypse of Abraham, the protagonist is borne to heaven on the wings of angels or birds (see fig. 7). Equally intriguing, as we will see later, is the way that Socrates' account parallels shamanic motifs. Shamans frequently experience an elevation in body temperature when performing rites, while the looking upward Socrates mentions recalls the rolling back of the eyes that occurs when shamans enter trance states. (Jesus as well is described as rolling his eyes heavenward when performing healings.) Shamans also report bird-like flights to the realm of the gods.

The Greeks depicted the experience of being seized by love in both myth and art. A fifth-century bowl from Athens shows a young man being embraced by a winged Eros (*gumnos gumnō*, by the way), who lifts his yielding body heavenward (see fig. 8). The same imagery occurs in mythology, in the Greek account of the origin of same-sex love. Zeus, enflamed with passion, transforms himself into an eagle and seizes the Phrygian shepherd Ganymede, sweeping him away to Olympus (see fig. 4). Interestingly, the historian Strabo uses the same word "seized" in describing male initiation rites in ancient Crete, in which youths were seized in staged abductions by adult men who become their lovers and mentors during an extended period of separation from the community (10.4.21; see "The Boy Who Became a God").

Having characterized the subjective experience of love, Socrates next considers *who* we love. This, he tells Phaedrus, is determined by our particular "god" — the archetypal figure that each of us is "following." In Socrates' words, "Each person selects his love from the ranks of the beautiful according to his own style, and he fashions his own sacred statue, as it were, adorning it and holding ritual celebrations in its honor, as though the beloved were himself the god" (252e). In other words, we seek others in whom we perceive our ideal of beauty — our god. By becoming possessed of our beloved, we receive the character and temperament of that god. According to Socrates, lovers are inspired by the ones they love "and derive their customs and practices from him, insofar as it is possible for a human being to be like a god, and since they take the beloved to be the cause of all this, they cherish him even more. They draw refreshing drink from Zeus and, like the devotees of

Fig. 8. The embrace of Eros. After a fifth-century B.C.E. *Attic bowl (in Cecile Beurdeley, L'Amour Bleu [Hohenzollernring: Evergreen, 1994], p. 42).*

Bacchus, pour it into the soul of their beloved, making him as similar as possible to their god" (253a).

In a roundabout way, Socrates approves of sexual intimacy as long as the lover remains the master of his passions:

> As the relationship continues and he comes close to his lover and touches him at the gymnasium and in other places where they associate, then the flow of that stream which Zeus as the lover of Ganymede named "the flood of passion" surges in abundance upon his lover. Some of it enters into the lover, and when he is filled to the brim, some of it spills over; and as the wind or an echo rebounds from smooth, hard surfaces to the place from whence it originated, so the stream of beauty returns to the beautiful darling [*paidika*, a diminutive term for the beloved] through his eyes, which is the natural route to the soul. Arriving there and setting him all aflutter, it moistens the passages of the feathers and causes the wings to grow and in turn fills the soul of the beloved with love. (255c-d)

The beloved, for his part, "longs as he is longed for" — he returns the love of his lover, *anterōs* for *erōs*. In Socrates' words, "he is seeing himself in his lover as in a mirror" (255d). The relationship is equal and reciprocal.

Plato's writings became the wellspring for Western ideas about love. Two observations need to be made, however. Although his account of what it is like to fall in love may remind us of our own experiences of romance and passion, the underlying model is that of involuntary possession by a spirit. That is, to describe love between humans, Plato borrows the language used to describe contact between humans and supernatural beings. A second point is that if Plato's writings are indeed a source of Western ideals of love, then it must be acknowledged that same-sex love can not only fulfill these ideals, it can be the source of them as well.

EROS AND AGAPE

With the *Symposium* and *Phaedrus* we are a long way from the conventional same-sex affairs common in classical Greece. In the *Phaedrus*, the lover and beloved are no longer differentiated by age, status, or sexual role. They differ only in the particular psychic qualities they possess, qualities that each partner ultimately discovers in himself as a result of finding them in the other. Plato saw this as an inherent potential of homosexual relationships. If age and status differences recede into the background, as they do in the speeches of Aristophanes and Socrates, then the sameness of same-sex lovers can become the basis of a genuinely reciprocal relationship. Taking age and status out of heterosexual relationships, in contrast, still leaves gender difference as a hurdle to mutuality.

Jesus' teachings contain similar insights. In first-century Palestine, no less than in classical Athens, opportunities for individuals to form voluntary and reciprocal relationships were limited. Unlike Athens, however, Jesus' society lacked institutionalized same-sex relationships. His examples of reciprocal love were the (presumably) nonsexual relationships of friends and brothers. Even so, Plato's philosophy and Jesus' teachings are linked by their frequent reference to love between members of the same sex.

Jesus' negative statements on family relations are consistent with his idealization of same-sex love. For Jesus, the love of friends is the "greater love" because it is voluntary. Nothing demands or requires that friends love each other; they can love without conditions. In contrast, love in kinship and other social relations in both Jesus' and Plato's times was contingent upon fulfilling assigned roles. The parable of the prodigal son (Luke 15:11-32) is a striking lesson precisely because the father does *not* behave in the expected way—he loves his wayward son regardless of the son's failings. In Jesus' time, this would have been the exception, not the rule.

Theologians have long contended that Christianity represented a radical break from earlier religions, and that Christianity's differences with previous systems of belief are greater than any similarities. In the 1930s, Anders Nygren, a Swedish bishop and theologian, published a classic study titled *Agape and Eros*, arguing at length that the Christian concept of agape, or love, was distinct from Plato's understanding of eros.

The fact that Plato and the authors of the New Testament used different terms for "love" lends support to Nygren's thesis. *Erōs*, which appears throughout Plato's works, never appears in the New Testament, while *agapē* was used in Plato's time only as a verb, *agapaō*, with the meaning, "to treat with affection, to caress, love, be fond of" (in reference to people) and "to be well pleased or contented with" (in reference to things). The New Testament, however, uses *agapē* as a noun to refer not only to the feeling humans can have for each other, but to their feeling toward God and to God's feeling toward them. Further, whereas eros is fundamentally sexual desire (although it can be spiritualized), agape is only applied to nonsexual relationships.

Nonetheless, like Plato's spiritual eros, the foremost example of agape is love between people of the same sex. The term is typically translated as "brotherly love," and the verbal form, *agapaō*, as "to regard

91

with brotherly love." Pairs of brothers, of course, were among Jesus' first followers. At the same time, agape is never used in the gospels to refer to the feeling between husbands and wives. Nygren acknowledges, however, that the word agape is not unique to the New Testament, and it was not coined by Christians. It was the term used for "love" in the Greek translation of the Hebrew Bible known as the Septuagint, which was widely used by Jews in the first century. Paul seems to have been the first to use agape as the technical term for Christian love. Jesus, of course, would have used an Aramaic word.

If it were simply the case that eros was sexual love and agape nonsexual love, Bishop Nygren would have had no need to write his treatise. Christians must contend with Plato's theory of love, because it seems to make the same distinction between sexual love and "spiritual" love so important in Christian doctrine. Nygren's goal, therefore, was to prove that spiritual eros is *not*, in fact, agape under a different name.

Nygren focuses on two teachings attributed to Jesus: the commandment to love one's enemies (Matt. 5:44f) and his assertion that he has come to call "not the righteous but sinners" (Mark 2:17). These verses highlight two features of Christian love. First, it is selfless, unmotivated by the worthiness, value, or beauty of the object loved. Hence, it occurs spontaneously; there are no conditions to hold it back. Secondly, it is the love God feels for all humans, even sinners. In the Hebrew Bible, God's love is reserved for the righteous, while in Greek tradition the gods are not described as loving humans at all. But in the New Testament, Jesus and God not only express love toward humans, they make a gift of this capacity to them—the capacity to love even one's enemies.

Nygren contrasts this to Diotima's statements in the *Symposium*. Diotima defines eros as acquisitive love, desire for what one lacks. It is motivated by the value of the person or thing loved—his goodness, his beauty. Hence, it is inherently self-centered. Humans love the gods because the gods have what they lack. Nygren acknowledges that eros can lead humans in an upward, spiritual direction—toward Beauty and Good—as well as in a downward direction, toward physical beauty and sexual desire. But while love of a god can lead one on an ascent to heaven, gods loving humans is never mentioned by Plato. After all, gods lack nothing; by definition, they are complete. What benefit could a god gain by loving humans? Agape, in contrast, is first and foremost God's unconditional love for humans. When Christians love others it is with this love, *from* God, a capacity or gift he has bestowed on them.

This, Nygren concludes, is a qualitative difference between Plato's eros and Christianity's agape. Both can be directed toward God, but only agape is truly selfless, and this, Nygren contends, is what makes Christianity new and special.

A more recent study challenges Nygren's views, however. In *Eros Unveiled*, Catherine Osborne invokes the image of Eros as Cupid, the Roman version of the god of love. Cupid fires his arrows randomly. They land without regard to the worth or beauty of the beloved, sometimes with tragic, sometimes with humorous results. Similarly, Plato describes lovers as being enslaved to the young men they love. In that circumstance, who possesses whom? Osborne argues that although Plato's theory of love seems to presume that there *is* beauty in the beloved, the Greeks knew that "blind" Eros sometimes led individuals to see beauty in unlikely places. "Thus there may be a sense in which this classical eros is a desire for beauty," she concludes, "but if so it is a desire to see beauty created and brought to perfection in the beloved, not a desire to possess it on the part of the lover. In this sense, eros is a generous-spirited love, an attitude towards the beloved, not a mean and grasping desire."

Osborne challenges Nygren's reading of Plato. Although the *Phaedrus* and *Symposium* describe eros as acquisitive love, she points out that these dialogues are not Plato's complete or final word on the subject. Plato also discusses love in the *Lysis*, and what he says there significantly undermines Nygren's argument.

In the *Lysis*, as in the *Symposium*, Plato presupposes the conventional understanding of eros as the desire to possess or acquire something one lacks. In the *Symposium*, he undermines this convention by blurring age and status differences and focusing on psychic differences between lovers that are nonhierarchical. In the *Lysis*, he adopts a different strategy: irony. Here, Socrates discusses three examples of love that are either mutual or not based on the expectation of gaining some benefit from the loved one—the relationship between parent and child, between lovers, and between friends. Since the Greek understanding of love was that it is based on the desire for some benefit and, therefore, is not mutual, Socrates is led to conclude that parents, friends, and lovers do not really love their respective objects. He ends on a note of exasperation: "If neither the beloved, nor the lover, nor the like, nor the unlike, nor the good, nor the congenial, nor any other of whom we spoke—for there were such a number of them that I cannot remember all—if none of these are friends, I know not what remains to be said" (222e).

Of course, this is absurd. Plato is saying, in as many words, if your definition of eros cannot encompass the selfless love that parents, friends, and lovers have for each other, then there is something wrong with it. Osborne argues that the *Lysis*, in undermining the acquisitive model of love, contradicts the *Symposium*, but I believe both dialogues further Plato's project of criticizing his society's ideas about love and relationships. In neither case does Plato openly reject the conventions of his time. He is not a heretic nor a revolutionary. Instead, he begins by accepting their premises, then either rendering them irrelevant or carrying them out to absurd and illogical conclusions.

As Osborne remarks:

> If the *Lysis* is taken seriously, Plato is actually offering us precisely the material we need to establish that the conventional interpretation of Diotima's speech will not do as an analysis of love, and hence that either the account offered in the *Symposium* is not seriously to be adopted, or it must be read in another way.... It is plain that the conventions of Greek ideology were familiar with a less self-centred picture of the lover than is presented on the usual interpretation of the *Symposium*. We may reasonably suppose that the [Christian] Fathers had a choice of models, even within their Greek heritage, that they might adopt in seeking to analyse the love of God and humankind.

In fact, Origen, Clement's successor at Alexandria, considered the distinction between eros and agape unimportant and suggested that the words could be used interchangeably.

Thus, both agape and eros can be selfless and unselfless. Humans' love for God is not purely self-centered, and God's love for humans is not entirely selfless. After all, only humans can give God worship, offerings, acts of mercy and charity, and other things he values, and it would be illogical to imagine that God does not delight in receiving these things. In fact, as C. G. Jung argued in his essay, "Answer to Job," what God gains by loving humans is nothing less than humanity itself, something Jung believes is lacking in the Old Testament figure of Yahweh, but realized in the New Testament figure of Jesus. And so, Jesus cannot be credited with inventing selfless, unconditional love. Certainly there were new elements of his message, but it is more accurate to see Christianity as carrying forward Platonic ideas about love, not rejecting them. (In fact, Nygren acknowledges that the growing interest with personal salvation in pagan mystery religions paved the way for Christianity.)

Nor does it help Nygren's case that various books of the New Testament interpret agape differently. Paul, for example, consistently stresses agape as God's unmotivated and spontaneous love, while in the Gospel of John agape is what binds the community of believers and distinguishes them from outsiders. Paul's view of agape was undoubtedly based on his unique experience—a persecutor of Christians, God nonetheless loved him and by virtue of that love, he was converted. Consequently, Paul stresses God's love for Jews and pagans alike, worthy and unworthy. John, in contrast, stresses the disciples' love for each other. For him, this mystical union of comrades is the vehicle for realizing heaven on earth.

Paul and the Johannine community interpreted baptism differently as well. For Paul, it entailed possession by a spirit and heavenly ascent. For the community founded by the "beloved disciple" the important feature of Jesus' baptism was the reciprocated love between Jesus and the initiate, and their union as an expression of love. Paul's notion of agape was more radical in that it could be expressed toward anyone, including sinners and even persecutors of Christians. The agape of the Johannine community remained grounded in the circle of loving disciples.

In the debate over eros and agape, three important developments from Plato to Jesus are often overlooked. First is the elaboration of the motif of heavenly ascent. The idea that the souls of the dead (and sometimes the living) could ascend to heaven was common to Orphism and mystery religions, such as Dionysism. Similarly, the idea that gods could descend from the heavens with a message or mission was also well-established. To this, Christianity added the motif of the God's descent as an act of love for humans, his martyrdom or sacrifice for humans while on earth, and his subsequent rebirth and return to heaven in spiritual form. These themes of descent and ascent are offset in the ritual of baptism. The proselyte ascending to heaven meets God on God's descent to earth.

Neoplatonist philosophers and Gnostics elaborated the idea of divine descent. In their treatises, God descends to matter and puts on material form to create the world and thus have an object for his love. The soul's ascent enacts in reverse the stages of God's descent, releasing spirit from matter. The metaphor of undressing is often used in neoplatonic accounts to describe this process. As God puts on material form to descend, mortals must strip off their material form to enter heaven.

A second important development has to do with the role of mediating spirits. In the *Symposium*, Diotima establishes the special nature of Eros as a *daimōn*, or spirit, at the beginning of her dialogue with Socrates. Since Eros is desire for the beautiful and good, she argues, he must lack these qualities, and therefore he cannot be a god. At the same time, Eros is not so entirely lacking in these qualities that he is ignorant of them—he knows enough to seek the beautiful and the good, and this divine spark elevates him above most mortals. Eros, Diotima observes, is thus akin to the philosopher, who seeks but does not yet know truth.

Now, the value of a mediating spirit is related to the fact that in ancient Greek belief the gods normally had no contact with humans.

This was impossible, as they were immaterial, humans material. As Diotima explains, "A god does not have direct contact with a human being; on the contrary every interchange and conversation between gods and human beings is through a *daimōn*" (203a). Eros can transverse the planes of earth and heaven and establish communication between them. Thus, he is linked with divination and priestcraft "and all soothsaying and sorcery." In this regard, he represents the underlying unity of the cosmos, offsetting the dualism of older cosmologies in which heaven and earth are distinct and opposite domains.

Eros' double nature mirrors that of humans. Where humans are mortals with a divine spark within them, Eros is a spirit with human shortcomings. Osborne points out how Socrates is in many respects the model for Diotima's description of Eros. A philosopher, Socrates exemplifies the relentless desire for the good and the beautiful that leads from the material to the immaterial, the sensible to the insensible. In Christianity, Jesus fulfills the role of Eros/Socrates. However, there is an important difference in how this role is conceptualized. Spirits, as Diotima points out, are by definition not gods. But Jesus, in Christian belief, is a god, one who has descended to earth, and not, therefore, a spirit.

A third development has to do with the role of choice. For both Plato and Jesus, passionate love is a form of spiritual possession. In Plato, this is largely involuntary. For Jesus, however, uniting with God (or the spirit of God represented by himself) is an ethical choice. God does not unite with humans unless they prepare themselves and seek such a union. Further, for Plato, the ethical dimensions of spiritual eros are largely limited to the care and nurturing that occurs between lovers and the social contributions that are the offspring of their love. There is no counterpart in Plato to Jesus' command to express agape toward everyone, not only God and one's family and friends, but even one's enemies.

Plato's spiritual eros — the feeling of care and nurturance for another arising from sexual desire and union — becomes in Jesus' teachings, agape, feelings of care and nurturance to all others, even one's enemies. From an historical perspective, however, agape is not a break from but a development of spiritual eros. As shocking as it may seem to today's conservative Christians, Christian ideals of love are rooted in a philosophical tradition inspired by homosexual desire. Of course, Plato and Jesus cited examples of devotion between parents and children and between married couples. But when it came to describing the ethical and spiritual dimensions of love, same-sex relationships were their foremost example.

In sum, we find in both Plato and Jesus the same connection between same-sex love and heavenly ascent, the same surprising marriage of mysticism and social reform. In both, the love of comrades is associated with experiences of spiritual possession, rapture, and apotheosis — humans becoming divine. At the same time, same-sex love benefits society. It is creative, giving birth to spiritual and social contributions. It offers a model for social relations of equality and reciprocity. To love one's enemies was to love those who belonged to different groups and had different social statuses. Indeed, for Jesus, unconditional love dissolves social differences.

Thus, the example of love between members of the same sex inspired an ethical and spiritual program whose ultimate aim is the suspension of all hierarchies and status differences. This agenda is most explicit in the teachings of Jesus, who seems to have envisioned something like an army of comrades ushering in a New Age. But even Plato, who focused on individual and interpersonal dimensions of same-sex love, described alternative relationships that challenged the social conventions of his time.

CHAPTER SEVEN
God from Man

Some time in the century before Jesus was born, a Greek author named Theognetus produced a grand synthesis of ancient mythology known as the *Sacred Speeches in 24 Rhapsodies*, or simply the *Rhapsodic Theogony*. Although the original text has not survived, scholars have reconstructed Theognatus' epic by compiling quotations of it from various neoplatonic writings.

The *Rhapsodic Theogony* begins with the birth of a figure unique in Greek mythology—a double-sexed being called Phanes (among other names) from whom all other creation springs:

> Of this Chronos, the ageless one, whose counsels never perish,
> was born Aither and a great yawning gulf on this side and
> on that: and there was no limit to it, no bottom nor foundation.
> (All things were in confusion) throughout the misty darkness.
> Then great Chronos fashioned in the divine Aither a silvery egg.
> And it moved without slackening in a vast circle.
> And at the birth of Phanes the misty gulf below and the
> windless Aither were rent.
> First-born, Phaethon, son of lofty Aither.
> Whom they call Phanes…because he first appeared in
> the Aither.
> With four eyes looking this way and that.
> With golden wings moving this way and that.
> Uttering the voice of a bull and of a glaring lion.
> Female and Father the mighty god Erikepaios.
> Cherishing in his heart swift and sightless Eros.
> The key of Mind.
> A great daemon ever treading on their tracks.
> An awful daemon, Metis, bearing the honoured seed of the
> gods, whom the blessed on tall Olympos were wont
> to call Phanes, the Firstborn.
> The Firstborn none saw with his eyes, unless it were holy
> Night alone. But all the others marvelled when there
> burst upon their gaze the unlooked-for light in the
> Aither; so gleamed the body of immortal Phanes.

Protogonos, Phaethon, Erikepaios, Metis, Phanes—yet other texts identify him as Dionysos and Eros, and describe "him" as possessing both male and female sex organs. Following his cosmic hatching, Phanes resides in a cave and mates with himself, giving birth to a series of gods.

He (the pronoun used despite his hermaphroditism) later mates with his own daughter, Night, who gives birth to Heaven (Uranos) and Earth (Ge). Phanes creates the sun and the moon and establishes a place for both gods and humans to live. Then he is swallowed by the upstart god, Zeus. Assimilating Phanes, Zeus acquires his creative powers and his kingship. "He held the body of all things in the hollow of his own belly; and he mingled with his own limbs the power and strength of the god [i.e., Protogonos]. Therefore together with him all things in Zeus were created anew."

This imagery is echoed in Paul's description of the son of God in the Letter to the Colossians: "He is the image of the invisible God, the first-born of all creation; for in him all things in heaven and on earth were created, things visible and invisible, whether thrones or dominions or rulers or powers [i.e., other spirits] — all things have been created through him and for him. He himself is before all things, and in him all things hold together" (1:15-17).

THE BLESSINGS OF MADNESS

The *Rhapsodic Theogony* belongs to the sacred literature of Orphism, a mystery religion with a long history in the ancient world. Orphism was flourishing in Plato's time, and it was still influential when the Roman Empire officially adopted Christianity centuries later. Yet much about Orphism remains uncertain, including its origins, its practices, and the scope of its appeal.

The Orphics were followers of the legendary figure Orpheus, who reputedly had the power to enrapture birds, animals, even rivers and trees with his singing. On the expedition of the Argonauts, he outsings the Sirens, saving the adventurers from their deadly seduction. In another account, he travels to the underworld seeking the release of his deceased wife. Pausanius describes Orpheus as a culture-bearer who introduced "divine mysteries, rites to purify wicked actions, cures for diseases, defences against the curses of heaven" (9.30.3). In yet another story, he survives death when a band of Thracian women, enraged by his influence over their husbands, cut off his head. The head continues to sing.

Over the centuries, the Greeks attributed numerous writings, teachings, and rites to Orpheus. Whether there was an organized religion of Orphism, however, remains the subject of debate. In his classic study, *Orpheus and Greek Religion*, W. K. B. Guthrie argued that the Orphics were a small band of devotees, not a popular movement, whose basic message appealed primarily to philosophers. Orphism's ideal was union with the divine as a means to immortality. The Orphic life aimed "at the exaltation and purification of our Dionysiac nature in order that we may in the end shake off the last trammels of our earthly selves and become actually, what we are now potentially, gods instead of mortals." The Orphics believed this could be achieved through certain rites and procedures, which could deliver the soul from punishment, and through right living.

Belief in an afterlife was a prominent feature of Orphism. The Orphic poems inscribed on gold and buried with the deceased describe the soul's journey to heaven in terms similar to the mystical writings we have already seen. According to one plate found in south Italy and dated to the fourth or third century B.C.E.:

> But so soon as the spirit hath left the light of the sun,
> Go to the right as far as one should go, being right
>   wary in all things.
> Hail, thou who has suffered the suffering. This thou
>   hadst never suffered before.
> Thou art become god from man.
> A kid thou art fallen into milk.
> Hail, hail to thee journeying the right hand road
> By holy meadows and groves of Persephone.

The most striking passage here is the reference to man becoming god. In the oldest myths of the ancient Near East and Greece, neither humans nor their souls entered heaven, let alone were deified. The belief that one could become a god, or godlike, was one of the ways that Orphics departed from conventional Greek religion. They also declared allegiance to a fixed and written creed, and they believed that their daily conduct had an effect on their life after death. Rather than passively honoring the gods through offerings—the typical mode of pagan peity—the Orphics introduced rituals for self-perfection. Their belief that souls were judged in the afterlife reflected a doctrine of the immortality and transmigration of the soul. All this made Orphism less like pagan cults and more like Christianity.

Orphism had a disproportionate impact in relation to the number of its followers. Over the course of ancient history, many philosophers and authors cited Orphic texts and beliefs. But none was more influenced by Orphism than Plato. "Plato paraphrases Orpheus everywhere," as one ancient author observed. Consequently, Plato's writings, in Guthrie's words, "alone were sufficient to ensure that, even had all other channels been closed, the doctrines of the Orphics would have been well known, and have made an irresistible appeal, to the later religious thought of Europe."

Whereas Plato refers many times to "the wise" or "the initiators" or "the old and sacred writings," Orpheus is one of the few authorities he cites by name. In the *Cratylus*, he writes:

> Now some say that the *sōma* [body] is the *sēma* [a word
> meaning both "sign" and "tomb"] of the soul, as if it were
> buried in its present existence; and also because through it
> the soul makes signs of whatever it has to express, for in this
> way also they claim that it is rightly named from *sēma*. In my
> opinion it is the followers of Orpheus who are chiefly
> responsible for giving it the name, holding that the soul is
> undergoing punishment for some reason or other, and has
> this husk around it, like a prison, to keep it from running
> away. (400c)

This, of course, is the same idea in the *Phaedrus*: the soul is
imprisoned in the body and yearns to escape it. This separation of body
and soul, physical senses and mind, earthly existence and the heavenly
realm of pure Ideas is one of the most characteristic features of Plato's
thought. Taken up by Christianity, this dualism has had a long history
in Western culture. For Plato, however, unlike Christians, "flesh" and
"spirit" were not irreconcilably opposed; they could be brought into
harmony with the aid of *daimones* and through certain practices.

Plato's *Phaedo*, *Gorgias*, and *Republic* all draw on Orphic origin
myths. The birth of Aphrodite Uranos from her father's severed genitals
as related in the *Symposium* also appears in Orphic theogonies, and the
account of the soul as a wing in the *Phaedrus* draws on doctrines of both
Orphism and Pythagoreanism. The influence of Orphism is also
apparent in Socrates' comment in the *Phaedo* that philosophers seek to
visit the "other world" in search of wisdom, much as others seek
deceased male lovers (*paidikon*), wives, or sons—Orpheus, of course,
descended to Hades seeking his wife, Eurydice (68a). Indeed, as a
philosopher who championed critical inquiry, Plato's frequent resort to
mythology is surprising. But as Guthrie points out, Plato used myths as
an alternative mode of thought whenever he wanted to account for
something that did not lend itself to dialectical inquiry. Such was the
case with the extraterrestrial existence of the soul—one of the subjects of
the *Phaedrus*. As Guthrie concludes, "Plato thought of the Orphic myths
as the complementary mythological expression of profound
philosophical truths." (His use of myths, in this regard, is similar to
Jesus' use of parables.)

Plato's writings illustrate the connections between beliefs about
the immortality of the soul, judgment in the afterlife, and the structure
of the cosmos. In the *Phaedo*, Socrates propounds a tripartite model of
the universe, in which the earth is suspended in the center of the
heavens, while beneath are hollows encircled by subterranean rivers.

When individuals die, a *daimōn*, or spirit, conducts their souls to a place of judgment. Those souls who have not "lived well and piously" are condemned to reside in the various depths of the underworld (108e-113e). As we saw in chapter 2, belief that the soul was immortal and that it made a perilous journey after death was widespread in the ancient Mediterranean. This belief, in turn, was linked to two other ideas: that souls could be reincarnated and that descent to the fiery underworld purified them from their entanglement with matter, returning them to a state of pure spirit.

Eventually, all these ideas were associated with the motif of heavenly ascent—for purified souls escape the confines of the underworld. Their final resting place is the heavens above earth. Descent is a prelude to ascent. Socrates implies as much in the *Phaedo*:

> But those who are found to have excelled in holy living are freed from these regions within the earth and are released as from prisons; they mount upward into their pure abode and dwell upon the earth. And of these, all who have duly purified themselves by philosophy live henceforth altogether without bodies, and pass to still more beautiful abodes which it is not easy to describe, nor have we now time enough. (114b-c)

The followers of Pythagoras took this one step further. Purification, perfection, rebirth could all be attained in one's present life by undergoing mystery rites in which descent, death, and regeneration were enacted. The Orphics sought to attain a similar goal through rites that served to deliver the soul from divine punishment. They also resorted to the use of charms and spells quite similar to those found in the magical papyri. The Pythagoreans as well drew on magical practices. Indeed, Peter Kingsley suggests that early Pythagoreans like Empedocles were, for all purposes, practicing magicians.

Plato, too, subscribed to the ideal of perfection in one's present life, but he rejected this side of both Orphism and Pythagoreanism. In the *Republic*, he wrote:

> They produce a bushel of books of Musaeus and Orpheus, the offspring of the Moon and of the Muses, as they affirm, and these books they use in their ritual, and make not only ordinary men but states believe that there really are remissions of sins and purifications for deeds of injustice, by means of sacrifice and pleasant sport for the living, and that there are also special rites for the defunct, which they call functions [*teletai*, "mystery rites"], to deliver us from evils in

that other world, while terrible things await those who have neglected to sacrifice. (364e-365a)

Much as later generations of Christians distanced themselves from magical practices, Plato purged his borrowings from Orphism and Pythagoreanism of these elements (but see "Plato the Magician"). Even so, he used the language of mystery rites to describe the states of consciousness attained by the philosopher, albeit through sober living and dialectical inquiry. In the *Symposium*, for example, the description of how eros leads to the apprehension of true Being has references to the mysteries held at Eleusis. In the *Phaedrus*, Socrates praises *mania*, including that produced by the very *teletē* Plato disapproves of in the *Republic*. "In reality," he says, "the greatest of blessings come to us through madness, when it is sent as a gift of the gods" (244A). Attaining beneficial or divine madness was the goal of Orphic rites, too. For Plato, however, *mania* was only a starting point in the philosopher's quest.

Plato is our principal source on the *teletē* as practiced in classical Athens; in particular, the rites of the Corybantes. The Corybantes were the Phrygian versions of the Cretan Kouretes, figures with a prominent role in Orphic theogonies. Sons of the goddess Rhea, the Kouretes guard the infants Zeus and Dionysus by dancing wildly outside the caves in which they are hidden, clashing their swords and shields to drown out their cries. Strabo refers to the Corybantes as *daimones* and "ministers of the gods" (10.3.7). In the rites held in Plato's time, individuals were believed to be possessed by these spirits.

Ivan Linforth has reconstructed the Corybantic rites drawing on various sources:

> First there were preliminary sacrifices to propitiate the god— what god, we do not know—and to ascertain whether he was favorable to the undertaking or not. Then, at some point in the procedure, came the "chairing," in which the candidate was seated in a chair [the *thronōsis*, or enthronement] and the ministrants [whom Plato indicates may have been women] danced around him and raised a great din. The effect of this was to rouse his excitement and stir his emotions, so that he gradually lost consciousness of all but the whirling rhythm of the dance. This was followed by what was called the telete proper, in which, we may suppose, the candidate threw himself into the dance with the rest and yielded to the intoxication of the rhythm. In the end, when all was over, the participants emerged from the tumult to a state of calm and tranquility, and their minds were at peace.

As Plato notes, individuals joined these rites hoping to find relief from psychological distress in the form of excessive fear and anxiety. Some hoped as well to erase a blight on their lives due to the failing of an ancestor or because of the anger of the gods. In Plato's words, they suffered "frights" which were due "to a poor condition of the soul" (*Laws*, 790e). Psychologists today might describe these symptoms as "panic attacks" and "obsessive guilt." The rites were believed to cleanse the mind of these emotions. The means of achieving this, as Linforth notes, were homeopathic. That is, the cure involved a dose of the poison—good *mania* to drive out the bad.

The Corybantic rites are referred to at least six times in Plato's writings, leading Linforth to conclude:

> When Socrates and Phaedrus read a speech of Lysias together and their enjoyment of its beauty is compared to participation in the rites, when the inspiration of poets is compared to Corybantic enthusiasm, when the effect of Socrates' words in discourse with his companions is said to be similar to the effect of the rites, when Socrates says that the solemn voices of the laws sound in his ears as imaginary pipes sound in the ears of Corybantic devotees—formal comparisons such as these argue more than tacit toleration of the rites: they imply a recognition of something admirable in them.

FROM TWO-IN-ONE TO ONE-IN-TWO

Plato's concept of the soul, his belief in the perfectibility of one's present life, his understanding of spiritual possession, and his use of myths and origin stories all reveal the influence of Orphism. But what about spiritual ascent? Orpheus *descends* to hell. He does not seek a vision of god or heaven, but the release of his wife from Hades. Where did Plato get the idea of the soul ascending to "the heaven which is above the heavens"?

In fact, imagery of heavenly ascent does occur in Orphic literature. In the *Rhapsodic Theogony*, Phanes, the firstborn, originally lives in a cave (that is, the underworld). The sixth Orphic hymn, however, describes him as "Phanes, called the glory of the sky/On waving pinions through the world you fly." In another fragment, he "sits on the outer ridge of heaven and from his mystic station illuminates the vastness of this temporal world." An ascent seems implied in these references, and with it a cosmology of multiple heavens.

Phanes also represents a theme often associated with same-sex love—the archetype of androgyny. In this regard, he is more like the compound mythical beings of Near Eastern mythologies than the gods of the Greek pantheon found in Hesiod's *Theogony*, whose gender is never in doubt. Ancient Greeks found the concept of androgyny disturbing. Their social approval of male homosexuality was contingent on neither partner being perceived as feminine.

Despite his alien features, Phanes was often identified with the god Eros, whom Hesiod describes as the "most beautiful among the immortal gods" (120). Hesiod's Eros fulfills similar functions as Phanes in Orphic myths. He is the creative principle, the source of life—qualities that ancient Greeks (curiously) attributed to male sexuality. In Aristophanes' comedy, *The Birds*, the birth of Eros is described with imagery borrowed from Orphic mythology: He emerges from a "wind-sown" egg and is referred to as "Eros the lovely, with gold-gleaming wings on his back, the image of wind-spun swiftness" (693ff.). The influence of the Orphic Phanes also can be seen in the account of Eros in the *Symposium* and that of the winged soul ascending to the highest heaven in the *Phaedrus*.

As we saw in the case of early Christianity, androgyny serves to symbolize psychic wholeness and completion. Phanes is not only double-sexed, he is animal, human, and god all at once. With his four eyes, the voice of a bull and a lion, and golden wings, he recalls the *hayyoth* in Ezekiel's vision who had four wings, and human, lion, ox, and eagle faces. He lives in a cave (symbolic of the womb, the Earth Mother, and the unconscious or intuitive mind), but he also ascends to the highest heaven to shed light on the world (symbolizing the achievement of consciousness). He is a *daimōn*, like Eros, a mediating spirit who holds together otherwise divergent elements of the perceptible world (see fig. 9).

Despite all these parallels to Orphism, it is important to note how Plato transformed its teachings. Plato's ideal philosopher does not unite with a god by undergoing a raucous ceremony in which he loses consciousness and dances like a demon. Divine union for Plato is the outcome of the search for beauty—a form of *mania*, yes, but one whose effects are subjective. It does not involve a loss of consciousness in which a god or spirit takes over the mind of the individual, but the coexistence of the individual's consciousness with that of the god—along the lines of the healing reunion of halves described by Aristophanes.

This is what it means to become a god—to acquire the consciousness of a god. In spirit possession, the individual's consciousness is suspended or replaced by that of the spirit. The philosopher, however, reaches heaven through reflection and self-analysis, seeking to realize his eros in its most essential form, as the desire to possess—that is, to hold in consciousness, to be united with—pure Beauty and Good. I would argue that Jesus understood union with

God in a similar way—as the coexistence of individual and divine consciousness. The mass possessions referred to in Acts and Paul's letters, in contrast, entailed a loss of consciousness; others had to be present to hear and interpret what those who were possessed said because they had no awareness of it themselves.

As an androgyne, Phanes does not synthesize male and female as much as he juxtaposes them. He has male *and* female organs. "He" symbolizes not resolution or synthesis, but dynamic tension. In contrast, Plato's symbol of wholeness is male-male union. Its archetypal image as described by Aristophanes is the (re)union of two halves—twins—not opposites. I refer to this as the archetype of the Divine Twins. Occasionally, however, Plato invokes androgynous imagery by employing metaphors based on women's sexuality to characterize the creativity of same-sex love. In the *Theaetetus*, for example, Socrates describes himself as a midwife who delivers others' ideas, while in the *Phaedrus* he refers to spoken discourse as being written on the souls of those who hear it and becoming the speaker's sons. In the course of his career, Phanes, too, bridges the archetypes of the Androgyne and the Divine Twins. Initially he reproduces as a hermaphrodite, copulating with himself. Later he mates heterosexually, albeit with his daughter, Night. Finally, he is swallowed by Zeus in a same-sex encounter, impregnating him with the seed of "all things." Zeus then gives birth to the world anew.

THE ORIGINS OF ORPHISM

Where did Orphic ideas and practices originate? As M. L. West suggests in his study, *The Orphic Poems*, one source may be the mythology of the Near East, in which a primeval ocean, Time as a creator god, the cosmic egg, and reincarnation are key elements. Another likely source is Eurasian shamanism. Orphism combined a doctrine of reincarnation in successive bodies (both animal and human) with a shamanistic theory of spirit helpers, while Orphic accounts of the soul's journey after death parallel, as we will see, shamans' accounts of spirit travel. Indeed, the powers attributed to Orpheus—the ability to control animals and nature, perform healings and initiatory rites, and survive dismemberment—are all typical of shamans.

Such patterns were widespread among the peoples occupying the northern borderlands of the Greek world, in particular the Thracians, whose homeland extended from modern Bulgaria into Turkey. The Greeks, who began to encounter them in the seventh and sixth centuries B.C.E., considered them fractious and backward tribes. Long-haired and tattooed, the Thracians disdained farming, living in open villages rather than cities. According to the ancient historian

Fig. 9. The Orphic god Phanes emerging from the world egg at the center of the cosmos. Encircled by the zodiac and the four winds, s/he bridges heaven and earth, bird and beast, male and female. After an early second-century C.E. relief from Modena, Italy.

Herodotus, "He is held in highest honor who lives by war and robbery" (5.6.2). Thracian religion included animal worship and magical rites. A key deity, Herodotus reports, was a *daimōn* called Salmoxis. Every five years, the Thracians employed a rather gruesome procedure for sending a "messenger" to Salmoxis bearing their prayers. A man, selected by lot, was thrown upon a phalanx of spears. If he died, it was considered a good omen (4.94.2-3). The Thracians also believed in immortality—in Herodotus' words, "that they do not die, but that one who perishes goes to the deity Salmoxis" (4.94.1). Consistent with this belief, they built elaborate burial mounds for their dead and filled them with valuable goods for use in the afterlife.

Herodotus goes on to relate a separate account of Salmoxis that portrays him as an historical figure. Presumably a slave in the household of the philosopher Pythagoras, he obtained his freedom and returned to Thrace, where he instituted various reforms in Thracian religion. This included a doctrine of immortality. To substantiate his teachings, he built an underground chamber and disappeared into it, reappearing four years later to the amazement of his fellow Thracians (4.95.1-5). As Mircea Eliade notes, this was a typical shamanic feat. Other reports of Thracian traditions are suggestive of spirit travel and heavenly ascent. A Thracian king named Kosingas, for example, is said to have threatened to ascend to the goddess Hera by means of a ladder to complain to her of his subjects' misconduct (Polyaenus, *Stratagemata* 7.22).

Other ancient authors identify Orpheus as a Thracian king and credit the Thracians with originating Orphic rites. Thracian rites were also compared to those of the Corybantes (Strabo 10.3.15). In Anatolia, where Thracians settled following the conquest of Troy in 1180 B.C.E., a synthesis of local traditions and Thracian religion gave rise to the cult of Sabazius, a god identified with Dionysus and, like Dionysus, worshiped in ecstatic rites. In neighboring Phrygia, similar rites were performed by the gender-bending *galli* on behalf of the god Attis (see "The *Galli* and Their Kind"). Like Salmoxis, Dionysus was characterized by periodic disappearances (symbolic of death) followed by his revival and return. (The Orphic Phanes was also identified with Dionysus; both shared another common trait of shamans, that of androgyny.) All these figures—Salmoxis, Dionysus, Orpheus, and even Pythagoras— reportedly made descents to the underworld.

In sum, both ancient and modern authorities agree in tracing the shamanic elements of Orphism and Dionysism back to Thrace, and in recognizing the connections of Pythagoreanism to these cults as well. Thracian culture, in turn, typifies those of societies throughout central Asia, such that, as Kingsley concludes, "There can be no separating the Thracian Orpheus from Central-Asiatic shamanic tradition."

One other Eurasian people whose shamanic religion may have influenced the Greeks were the Scythians. Like the Thracians, they spoke an Indo-European language. Their original home, however, is believed to have been in the region of the Altai Mountains in Siberia — their art, for example, is quite similar to that of other Siberian peoples. In the early first millennium B.C.E., they began migrating into the Near East, and by the late seventh century they had entered the steppes north of the Black Sea. Like the Thracians, the Scythians had a reputation of being fierce warriors and master horsemen who cut off the heads of their enemies and drank their blood. Herodotus describes them as "not living by tilling the soil but by raising cattle and carrying their dwellings on wagons" (4.46.3). They, too, buried their elite in elaborate tombs filled with rich goods.

Scythian religion included the worship of the elements, animal sacrifices, and a cult of the dead. Especially elaborate ceremonies were held when the king died, at the end of which participants purified themselves with vapor-baths, throwing cannabis seeds onto hot rocks and inhaling the smoke until they were intoxicated. (The Thracians also may have used hemp to produce trances.) Herodotus says that Scythians had many *manteuontai*, soothsayers or diviners. Among these was a special class known as *enarees*, who, Herodotus reports, were *androgynoi*, "men-women" (4.67.2). The *enarees* employed a special technique of divination that had been taught to them by none other than Aphrodite Uranos, the patron of Plato's higher form of same-sex love. This association with the goddess originated at the time of the Scythian invasion of Palestine in the early seventh century B.C.E., when, Herodotus relates, Scythian warriors robbed her temple in Syria — "the oldest of all the temples of the goddess" (1.105.3). The goddess, in return, punished them with the "female disease," which their descendents have suffered from ever since (1.105.4).

The *enarees* are also mentioned in a text attributed to the Greek physician Hippocrates. After explaining at length why the majority of Scythians are infertile (the men's bodies are moist and cold, and they ride horseback too much; the women are moist and fat), the author adds:

> Moreover, the great majority among the Scythians become impotent, do women's work, live like women and converse accordingly. Such men they call Anaries. Now the natives put the blame on to Heaven, and respect and worship these creatures, each fearing for himself. (*Airs, Waters, Places* 22)

All this sounds quite similar to North American berdaches, or two-spirits — individuals who combined male and female social roles with traits unique to their status in an alternative gender identity, as we will see in chapter 10. Like the *enarees*, berdaches were often religious specialists. Unfortunately, this is the extent of ancient references to them. Some memory of these Scythian traditions seems to have survived, however, among the Ossete people, linguistic descendents of the Scythians in modern Ukraine and Georgia. Their folklore features gender-reversal and male birth, and recent archaeological finds in the region of the Scythians and their neighbors the Samartians confirm the existence of men in alternative gender roles and women warriors — perhaps the prototypes for the mythical Amazons.

Sorting out the connections between Orpheus, Dionysus, Salmoxis, Sabazius, Attis, and the Kouretes, Corybantes, *galli*, and other cult groups is a daunting task, if possible at all. Strabo, writing at the beginning of the Christian era, concluded:

> Whereas some represent the Corybantes, the Cabeiri, the Idaean Dactyli, and the Telchines as identical with the Curetes, others represent them as all kinsmen of one another and differentiate only certain small matters in which they differ in respect to one another; but, roughly speaking and in general, they represent them, one and all, as a kind of inspired people and as subject to Bacchic frenzy, and, in the guise of ministers, as inspiring terror at the celebration of the sacred rites by means of war-dances, accompanied by uproar and noise and cymbals and drums and arms, and also by flute and outcry and consequently these rites are in a way regarded as having a common relationship. (10.3.7)

Two thousand years later, scholars have little to add to this picture. We are dealing here with religious patterns found throughout the ancient world. Underlying the local variations, however, was a shared goal and procedures for attaining it — namely, the production of *mania*, possession by a spirit. As Strabo's comments show, the typical response of pagans when confronted by cultural differences was to seek similarities, to compare and equate. This contrasts markedly with the Judeo-Christian outlook, whose tendency is to reify differences. All we can say now is that "mysteries" — mystery religions, along with their mythologies and rites — are part of the cultural heritage produced by the encounter of Greek, Near Asian, and Eurasian cultures, of West and East. This heritage inspired Orphism and other religious and cultural innovations down to Christianity, with its synthesis of Greek philosophy, Jewish mysticism, and pagan magic (see "Christianity and Paganism: Conflict and Synthesis"). The themes we have been tracing — heavenly ascent and union with the divine, and their connection with androgyny and same-sex love—are integral to this heritage.

We have begun to discern the "queer" underpinnings of Western mysticism and spirituality. But we have yet to exhaust the trail of clues that leads to their ultimate origins.

CHAPTER EIGHT
Soft Man Being

The charge that scholars live in ivory towers is not always easy to deny. For the tenured academic, anyway, a lifetime of guaranteed employment, free to pursue personal interests no matter how specialized or obscure, surrounded by the bright faces of the young, would seem to be one of little risk and many pleasures. But the story told here could not have been told without the contributions of scholars whose work entailed genuine risk; for whom, indeed, the very acts of research and writing were acts of defiance.

Morton Smith, who discovered the Secret Gospel and spent more than a decade preparing his study of it, had no illusions about the reception his findings would receive. "Any attempt to answer such questions, i.e., to explain what ancient authors deliberately concealed, must be conjectural, and many scholars reject on principle all conjectures except their own. Consequently I expected that mine about these problems would be generally rejected, the more so because they introduced notions unfashionable (Jesus practiced baptism) or shocking (and magic!). I was not disappointed." Critics denounced Smith's work as "venal popularization," "a morbid concatenation of fancies," and "science fiction." Yet, to Smith's credit, he explored all the implications of Clement's letter, including those suggested by the phrase "naked man with naked man."

It is important to acknowledge contributions like Smith's because in so many other cases investigators confronted with evidence of same-sex behavior have felt compelled to denounce, dismiss, or ignore it. In my research on gender diversity among Native Americans, I have found only one instance in which a traditional third gender or berdache individual was actually interviewed — and not by an anthropologist, but a retired army general. Even Omer Stewart, a prominent American anthropologist who was himself gay, did not venture to approach the Zuni berdache pointed out to him in 1941, but settled instead for scribbling down gossip. The idea that same-sex behavior and relationships have a marginal role in human history has been a self-fulfilling prophecy of academic scholars.

ONCE IN ETERNITY

One anthropologist who did preserve valuable evidence of queer spirituality is Vladimir G. Bogoraz. Born in 1865 in a Jewish family in Tsarist Russia, Bogoraz faced a future of severely limited opportunity. To evade anti-Semitism, he joined the Russian Orthodox church. But as a student in St. Petersburg in the 1880s, he was drawn into the anti-tsarist movement. He joined Narodnaya Volya (Peoples' Will), a revolutionary party that embraced *narodnichestvo*, or populism, and idealized common people and folk culture. For his political activity, Bogoraz was arrested twice—imprisoned for three years the first time, then exiled for ten more to the region of the Kolyma River in far northeastern Siberia.

Exile, by isolating the individual from meaningful social and intellectual interaction, deprives its subject of one of the basic conditions of humanity. In such a situation, as Solzhinentsyin showed, finding a use of one's mind and abilities, no matter how nominal or symbolic, is a profound statement of defiance. Initially, Bogoraz, still in his twenties, began writing poems and stories. Then he met another exile, Vladimir Jochelson, ten years his senior, who turned his attention to the native peoples living in the forbidding regions around them. Under the influence of *narodnichestvo*, both men were committed to the idea that the culture of folk and tribal people included values and forms of social organization which represented alternatives to modern society. Thus, radicals become anthropologists and anthropologists sometimes radicals.

Bogoraz's cultural and linguistic studies of native Siberians were eventually recognized, and in 1895, although still in exile, he was appointed to the Sibiriakov expedition of the Russian Geographic Society. In 1900, his sentence completed, he joined the famous Jesup North Pacific Expedition. Organized by the pioneer anthropologist Franz Boas and funded by an egocentric American capitalist, the Jesup expedition was a grand attempt to study the peoples and cultures on both sides of the North Pacific, which, it was hoped, would shed light on how North America was originally populated. Between 1897 and 1902, ethnologists fanned out across the northern Pacific rim, on foot, by boat, and in dogsleds, recording languages, folklore, and customs, and collecting artifacts, which were shipped back to the American Museum of Natural History in New York City.

Bogoraz and his wife arrived at the Mariinsky Post on the Pacific coast of Siberia, barely one hundred miles south of the arctic circle, in July 1900. The couple joined the Reindeer Chukchi, who had moved their herds to the coast to escape the plague of insects that infest the Siberian interior during its brief summer. Conditions were "unfavorable," Bogoraz reported to Boas—a measles epidemic had killed nearly thirty percent of the local population. After a few months with the Chukchi, Bogoraz made a twelve-month tour through the territory of the Asiatic Eskimo, Koryak, Tungus, and Kamchadal. The Chukchi, however, remained his central interest.

Meanwhile, Russia was in turmoil. When Bogoraz returned to St.

Petersburg he was swept up in the fervor of the 1905 Revolution. "You will understand," he wrote to anthropologist Franz Boas, "that an epoch like this happens only once in many centuries for every state and nation and we feel ourselves torn away with the current events against our will." Boas, ever the man of science, responded: "If events like the present happen only once in a century, an investigation by Mr. Bogoras of the Chuckchee happens only once in eternity, and I think you owe it to science to give us the results of your studies." But his words fell on deaf ears. Bogoraz was arrested again that fall. When friends posted bail, he fled to Finland, then New York, where he finally completed his reports before returning to Russia permanently. A supporter of the 1917 Revolution, he enjoyed a long and distinguished career as a professor and curator at the University of Leningrad.

Bogoraz's contributions to the Jesup Expedition resulted in seven monographs. With his wife, he collected extensive ethnographic and linguistic data, transcribed 150 native language texts, gathered 5,000 artifacts (including skeletal material, plaster casts of faces, and archaeological remains), recorded somatological measurements for 860 individuals, and made 95 phonographic records. Few anthropologists have ever collected such a quantity of data.

THE CHUKCHI

By the 1700s, the Russians had brought most of Siberia under their control. Tribe after tribe were subdued by the Cossacks and made to pay tribute to the tsar. But when the Cossacks ventured east of the Kolyma River—into that northeast finger of Asia that points toward North America—they encountered a people of unusual belligerence. Normally, they wandered about the tundra in small family-based bands, without any formal social organization. But faced with a common enemy, they united under the leadership of experienced warriors and entered battle with awesome ferocity. If captured, they committed suicide.

These were the Chukchi.

In 1747, when the Chukchi slaughtered a Cossack leader and his party, the Russians gave up their efforts to subdue them. Eventually, they burned their fort and withdrew from the region altogether. It was not until the mid-nineteenth century that they were finally able to lure the Chukchi into paying tribute, and only then in return for gifts that often exceeded the value of the tribute. At the time of the Jesup Expedition, Russia still considered Chukchi territory "not thoroughly subdued." Bogoraz, for his part, concluded that irascibility was the Chukchi's most conspicuous trait. As one man told him, "I am a tundra wanderer! My anger rises suddenly; it comes and goes of its own will."

If a harsh existence can be blamed for short tempers, the Chukchi had ample cause for irritability. They lived in a treeless tundra with an average annual temperature below twenty degrees Fahrenheit. With no wood to build fences, keeping semiwild reindeer herds together was a full-time task. In summer, when the herds wandered to escape swarms of reindeer flies, those in camp survived on berries, roots, and leaves mixed with stale reindeer blood; the herders, to avoid having to slaughter their animals, sucked milk from the cows and gnawed on chips of antler. When a reindeer was killed it was a festive and religious occasion. Bogoraz wrote:

> The Chukchi housewife knows better than the women of the neighboring tribes how to obtain from a carcass the most nutritious parts. The flesh and blood, the rims of the horns and hoofs, the gristle of the ears and nostrils are all consumed, raw or cooked. The half-digested moss taken from the paunch is cooked with fat and roots as porridge; the bones are boiled to extract the marrow, and the remainder is used for feeding the dogs.

At the beginning of the twentieth century, nonagricultural societies that depended on some combination of hunting, herding, fishing, or gathering still could be found in most regions of the world. The Chukchi that Bogoraz observed, in fact, had only recently become reindeer herders. They still relied on gathering, hunting, and fishing to a large extent. Although existence can be tenuous for farmers no less than nomads, the former can indulge the illusion that they exercise control over their food supply. Nomads, in contrast, know that they are dependent on nature and natural forces, and have only their individual efforts — and luck — to feed themselves.

A common goal of religion in many societies is to access unseen forces believed to have influence over nature and human affairs. But where farmers seek the cooperation of these forces, nomads seek direct intervention, in the form of luck and, above all, information — where to find food and water, whether to fight a battle or make peace, what design to use in art, what identity to adopt. This was the original information age. The source of information, however, was the spirit world, and the means of accessing it psychological rather than technical. In this belief system, all living beings and many features of nature are believed to be animated by an indwelling consciousness, or spirit. For people who lack the technical aids available today, attributing consciousness to the natural world makes sense as a way of explaining patterns of nature and human events. The characteristic qualities and movements of the sun and moon, for example, are understood as personality traits, much as human behavior is understood as a function of characteristic dispositions. These animating spirits can exist independently of bodies and objects, however, as immaterial patterns of energy. In this respect, the humans, animals, and objects they dwell in are merely masks or costumes, not their true, ineffable forms.

In such societies, individuals who have the ability to interact with spirits are highly valued. Typical signs of such contact include speaking in voices; appearing to hear or see what others do not; unusual feats of skill, strength, or endurance; and strange or idiosyncratic behavior in general. Such skills are not something that can be learned. They are a talent, a gift which, like all special talents, is understood to be the result of supernatural intervention. Sometimes, however, this contact is of such an intense and overwhelming nature that what is bestowed is not any specific boon but supernatural power itself—or, rather, the capacity to transmit such power. Much as the Corybantic rites expelled bad *mania* with good *mania*, tribal religious experts can control spiritual forces because they have been subjected to them—and survived.

This religious pattern is known as shamanism. Shamanism is not based on sacred texts, an institutionalized priesthood, fixed places of worship, or scripted rituals and ceremonies. It is centered on the individual figure of the shaman. Although shamanism may seem alien to us today, in practice it is the most empirical of all religions. No faith is required. Shamans are judged by their powers and their success in using them. Any theories or ideological claims they make have weight only to the extent that their practice is effective. (Marcel Mauss once made much the same point regarding magic: "Magic is linked to science in the same way as it is linked to technology. It is not only a practical art, it is also a storehouse of ideas. It attaches great importance to knowledge—one of its mainsprings. In fact as far as magic is concerned, knowledge is power.")

Of the powers attributed to shamans, the most common is healing. Shamans are able to diagnose illness—by identifying malevolent spirits or objects that have been "shot" into their patients—and to heal—by removing these objects and driving malevolent forces out. They can also retrieve lost souls by undertaking a spirit journey on behalf of their patients. Other roles of shamans include divination; leading funerary rites; serving as psychopomps, or conductors, for the souls of the dead; functioning as hunting magicians; and (more rarely) serving as sacrificial priests and leading tribal ceremonies.

As Bogoraz found, the Chukchi epitomized shamanism to a remarkable degree. Nearly one in every three Chukchi claimed to be a shaman, and every family owned a shaman's drum. On ceremonial occasions, these were brought out and all the family members took turns beating it and going through the motions of the shaman's trance. True séances, however, were conducted by professional shamans. It was to these that Chukchi turned when in crisis.

Chukchi shamanism was based on beliefs concerning the structure of the universe reminiscent of those in the ancient Near East and Mediterranean. As Bogoraz wrote, "According to the cosmogonical beliefs of the Chukchee, there are several worlds situated one above another, in such a manner that the ground of one forms the sky of the one below. The number of these worlds is stated as five, seven, or nine. They are arranged symmetrically above and below the earth, each of the lower worlds having a corresponding one above it." In this hierarchy, the sky is occupied by a distant creator figure, who is referred to variously as "Upper Being," "Dawn," "Zenith," "Noon," and "Owner-of-the-star-with-the-stuck-snake," a reference to the fixed polar star. "This Being," Bogoraz reports, "gives protection and assistance to men, who, oppressed by their foes in their earthly life, come to him." The underworld—and the far borders of the Chukchi territory—are home of the *ke'let*, evil spirits who steal humans' souls and eat them. As one shaman told Bogoraz, "We are surrounded by hostile spirits who walk about us invisibly with gaping mouths, and…we distribute gifts to such spirits on all sides."

Chukchi shamans communicated with the spirit world by entering a trance or altered state of consciousness. The exact nature of this state is the subject of ongoing study by anthropologists and psychologists. In fact, trances can take different forms. One pattern is that of the spirit journey, or shaman's flight, in which the shaman has an experience of out-of-body travel and encounters with spirit beings. The Chukchi believed that by this means shamans could travel on all the planes of the cosmos, passing through holes that connect them. Traveling to the heights of heaven, they viewed the universe from the perspective of the sky god himself. Traveling to the underworld, they retrieved souls that had been lost or stolen.

Travel to the spirit world is made possible by the aid of one or more intermediaries, helper or guardian spirits. Individuals acquire spirit helpers, who typically appear in animal form, as part of their induction into the shamanic profession. This usually occurs in response to a life crisis, such as a serious injury or illness, or a vision or dream. In the course of surviving and recovering from this crisis, the individual acquires a spirit helper. Among the Chukchi, the helper might take the form of a wolf or walrus who appears in the wilds at a moment of danger and rescues the individual.

Such an experience serves as both an initiation into shamanism and as training in shamanic powers. As one shaman told Bogoraz, when he was a youth, a voice commanded him, "Go into the wilderness: there you will find a tiny drum. Try it and prove its qualities!" When he obeyed the voice and beat the drum, he found that he was able to see the whole world, to mount to the sky, and even set up his tent in the clouds—he had ascended to heaven.

Bogoraz observed several ceremonies conducted by Chukchi shamans. They were held at night, in a dark tent. They began with the shaman stripping to the waist, smoking his pipe, and then beginning to beat his drum and sing. Every shaman had his or her own songs. The melodies were simple, without words. After a while participants heard the voices of the spirits coming from every direction around them, even from beneath the ground and far away. These were different kinds of spirit than the soul-stealing *ke'let*. They personified animals and natural forces, with names like Wild-Reindeer-Spirit, She-Walrus-Spirit, Walking One (that is, the bear), or they were inanimate objects, such as the Long One, the spirit of the needle.

Eventually, one of these spirits entered the shaman's body. The shaman would begin moving his head rapidly and crying out in falsetto. This was the voice of the spirit itself, who typically spoke in a kind of gibberish, which had to be translated by an assistant (as in Paul's churches). When the spirits were present in the shaman's tent, strange things occurred: objects levitated, the tent shook, it rained stones and bits of wood. Through the shaman, the spirits of the dead conversed with the audience, offering advice on any number of matters. Sometimes the shaman fell to the ground unconscious, at which point his soul was believed to have left his body to seek advice from the spirits. Chukchi shamans also visited the spirits in their sleep, awaking with the patient's lost soul in their hands in the form of a fly or a bee. They then returned it to the patient's body by opening his or her skull. Shamans also healed by blowing their own spirit into their patients or by replacing a lost soul with one of the spirits that they controlled.

Performances like these have often been misunderstood by Western observers, who have dwelled on the fact that some of these effects are "tricks"—objects sucked out of patients' bodies are actually secreted on the shaman's person, voices are produced by ventriloquism, and so forth. (Bogoraz, however, admitted to witnessing many demonstrations of shamanic power that he could not easily explain.) Unsympathetic observers, especially colonial officials and missionaries, denounced shamans as frauds who misled and deceived their people. But shamans' demonstrations of power are really no different than the "trick" by which bread is turned into the body of Christ, and wine into blood in the Christian mass. In fact, Bogoraz found that many Chukchi were quite aware that shamans used sleight of hand, but this in itself was considered an inspired skill, and, in any case, the Chukchi viewed such demonstrations much as Christians view their mass—its spirituality resided not in the gestures and formulas themselves, but in the ineffable mysteries they represented.

Perhaps the most remarkable aspect of Chukchi culture uncovered by Bogoraz was what he referred to as a "branch" of shamanism of a "special character." Some Chukchi, in the course of becoming shamans, experienced a change of gender—"in part, or even completely." Unlike other anthropologists, Bogoraz avidly collected data on this subject. He not only interviewed shamans who had been transformed, he stayed with one in his tent, making observations of his daily life. As a result, his monograph provides a unique glimpse into the queer underpinnings of Eurasian shamanism.

Unfortunately, Bogoraz's account is at points unclear. He describes a category of "transformed shamans," apparently a minority, but he also discusses "degrees" and "stages" of gender transformation affecting a much larger number of individuals. In fact, as we will see, different phenomena are involved in these "stages," and one stage does not necessarily follow another.

The first form of transformation Bogoraz describes involves males who braid their hair in a female style. "This usage is widespread among the Chukchee," he reports, "and is adopted not only by shamans at the command of the 'spirits,' but also by sick persons at the bidding of shamans. In the latter case the aim is to change the appearance of the patient so as to make him unrecognizable by the 'spirits.'" Whether this practice is adopted permanently or on a temporary basis is not clear. In any case, it suggests that the Chukchi considered the symbols of gender to be transferable. That is, female symbols representing female powers could be used by men as well as women. This is because, as we will see, gender was not regarded as fixed or immutable. Indeed, when it came to gender assignments among the Chukchi, social and supernatural factors often outweighed anatomical sex. Gender, to use the current jargon, was "constructed." As such, it could be reconstructed.

The second "stage" described by Bogoraz includes individuals who are instructed by spirits during a spiritual or health crisis (which were considered largely the same) to adopt the clothing of the opposite sex. Such individuals did not, however, otherwise alter their lifestyles. If they were married men and had children, they continued in that role. Bogoraz described one such cross-dresser and noted that his appearance could create "no misunderstanding about the sex to which he really belonged."

Whereas Bogoraz's first two "stages" do not result in a change of basic lifestyle or gender identity, the third "stage" entails a "complete" transformation. Those who undergo it enter a new category altogether—distinct from that of men or women. The Chukchi referred to transformed males as "soft men beings," while women who experienced gender transformation were referred with a term that meant "similar to a man."

119

As Bogoraz learned, these transformations occurred at the command of the spirits when the individual was at the critical age of early youth in which shamanism typically manifested itself:

> A young man who is undergoing it leaves off all pursuits and manners of his sex, and takes up those of a woman. He throws away the rifle and the lance, the lasso of the reindeer herdsman, and the harpoon of the seal-hunter, and takes to the needle and the skin-scraper. He learns the use of these quickly, because the "spirits" are helping him all the time. Even his pronunciation changes from the male to the female mode. At the same time his body alters, if not in its outward appearance, at least in its faculties and forces. He loses masculine strength, fleetness of foot in the race, endurance in wrestling, and acquires instead the helplessness of a woman. Even his physical character changes. The transformed person loses his brute courage and fighting spirit, and becomes shy of strangers, even fond of small-talk and of nursing small children. Generally speaking, he becomes a woman with the appearance of a man.

According to Bogoraz, many youths "dreaded" such a call. This has often been cited as evidence of a negative view of gender transformation among the Chukchi. Bogoraz's comment, however, needs to be placed in context. From a Western, heterosexual point of view, the prospect that a dream or vision could dictate an unwanted transformation of one's gender and sexuality no doubt is dreadful (but certainly no less dreadful than having to pretend to be heterosexual when one is not or having to accept an arranged marriage to an undesirable partner). At the same time, as Bogoraz admits elsewhere, young people had reason to dread any shamanic calling, whether it entailed gender transformation or not. Shamans trafficked with malevolent spirits; it could be nasty business. Even spirit helpers were dangerous—failure to carry out their idiosyncratic commands could result in instant death.

In any case, Bogoraz's case histories of soft men do not support the assertion that they dreaded their calling. Indeed, the life of the soft man was not without its rewards:

> The "soft man" begins to feel like a woman. He seeks to win the good graces of men, and succeeds easily with the aid of "spirits." Thus he has all the young men he could wish for striving to obtain his favor. From these he chooses his lover, and after a time takes a husband. The marriage is performed

with the usual rites, and I must say that it forms a quite solid union, which often lasts till the death of one of the parties. The couple lives much in the same ways as do other people. The man tends his herd and goes hunting and fishing, while the "wife" takes care of the house, performing all domestic pursuits and work. They cohabit in a perverse way, *modo Socratis* [the Socratic mode, or anal intercourse], in which the transformed wife always plays the passive rôle. In this, again, some of the "soft men" are said to lose altogether the man's desire and in the end to even acquire the organs of a woman; while others are said to have mistresses of their own in secret and to produce children by them.

Here, there is no mention of dread and no evidence that the soft man was under compulsion to engage in sexual practices that he did not desire. Indeed, Bogoraz's account suggests quite the opposite: soft men were free to form relationships with women as well as men, although most apparently related to other males. The role of "soft man" accommodated rather than determined sexual orientation.

In Western terms, these relationships would be considered homosexual. The Chukchi view was more complex, since the soft man occupied a different gender status from that of both men and women. Whether this status amounted to a third gender role or simply a variation on being male (much as contemporary gay men are classified as a subset of men) can be debated. Chukchi terminology suggests that, despite the ways in which they behaved like women, "soft men" were still classified as male. According to Bogoraz, transformed men always kept their male names.

Chukchi attitudes toward soft men were revealing. According to Bogoraz, "The state of a transformed man is so peculiar that it attracts much gossip and jests on the part of the neighbors. Such jests are of course interchanged only in whispers, because the people are extremely afraid of the transformed, much more so than of ordinary shamans." In other words, gender transformation made shamans more powerful—it was a *source* of power. Bogoraz recorded a Chukchi story that illustrates this belief:

> In a tale widely circulated among the Chukchee, a "soft man," clad in a woman's dress, takes part, with other members of the family, in corralling the reindeer-herd. The wife of his brother taunts him, saying, "This one with the women's breeches does not seem to give much help." The "soft man" takes offence, and leaves the family camp. He goes away to the border-land of the Koryak, who assault him

in his travelling-tent. He, however, snatches his fire-board implement, and with its small bow of antler, shoots the wooden drill at his adversaries. Immediately it turns into a fiery shaft and destroys all of them one by one. He then takes their herds, and, coming back to his home, shows his newly acquired wealth to his relatives, saying, "See now what that of woman's breeches was able to procure for you."

The transformed shaman's sexuality was also a source of power — and the means by which he bonded himself to his helping spirits:

Each "soft man" is supposed to have a special protector among the "spirits," who, for the most part, is said to play the part of a supernatural husband, ke´IE-husband, of the transformed one. This husband is supposed to be the real head of the family and to communicate his orders by means of his transformed wife. The human husband, of course, has to execute these orders faithfully under fear of prompt punishment. The husband often takes the name of his wife as an addition to his own name; for instance, "Ya´tirgin, husband of Tilu´wgi." Otherwise, the same is done by the children with the name of their father.

Male shamans who are not transformed have *ke´le* wives, who similarly participate in the daily life of the house. As we will see, marriage to — and sex with — spirits is one of the most common methods by which shamans throughout Eurasia accessed the spirit world.

Bogoraz adds:

"Soft men," of course, are supposed to excel in all branches of shamanism, including the ventriloquistic art, notwithstanding the fact that they are supposed to be women. Because of their supernatural protectors, they are dreaded even by untransformed shamans, who avoid having any contests with them, especially with the younger ones, because they are exceedingly "bashful," and readily stand back before the pretensions of other people; but afterward the supernatural husband [of the soft man] retaliates for the slight.

Bogoraz's account of the soft man Tilu´wgi is worth quoting at length (see fig. 10). Here we see Victorian anthropology at its most odious — inquisitorial and voyeuristic — despite Bogoraz's attempt to mask his relentless will to know behind an ironic and entertaining tone:

Fig. 10. The Chukchi soft man Tilu´wgi, 1895. After Waldemar Bogoras, The Chukchee, Memoirs of the American Museum of Natural History XI, part II, *Fig. XXXIII, Fig. 1, (p. 453).*

I met him at a small trade-gathering among the camps of Reindeer people on the Wolverene River. He, together with a party of traders, came from the Chukchee Peninsula. He was of Maritime origin [a branch of the Chukchi]; but his family had some reindeer, and spent most of their time tending the herd. Tilu´wgi was young, and looked about thirty-five years of age. He was tall and well developed. His large rough hands especially exhibited no trace of womanhood.

I stayed for two days in his tent, and slept in his small inner room, which was hardly large enough to accommodate four sleepers. Thus I had a chance to observe quite closely the details of his physique, which, of course, were all masculine. He refused obstinately, however, to permit himself to be fully inspected. His husband, Ya´tirgin, tempted by the offered price, tried to persuade him, but, after some useless attempts, was at last silenced by one scowling look from his peculiar "wife." He felt sorry, however, that I had been baffled in gratifying my curiosity, and therefore offered me, to use his own words, his eyes in place of my own.

He described the physique of Tilu´wgi as wholly masculine, and well developed besides. He confessed that he was sorry for it, but he hoped that in time, with the aid of his ke´let, Tilu´wgi would be able to equal the real "soft men" of old, and to change the organs of his sex altogether, which would be much more convenient than the present state. Notwithstanding all this, and even the brownish down which covered his upper lip, Tilu´wgi's face, encircled with braids of thick hair arranged after the manner of Chukchee women, looked very different from masculine faces. It was something like a female tragic mask fitted to a body of a giantess of a race different from our own. All the ways of this strange creature were decidedly feminine. He was so "bashful" that whenever I asked a question of somewhat indiscreet character, you could see, under the layer of its usual dirt, a blush spread over his face, and he would cover his eyes with his sleeve, like a young beauty of sixteen. I heard him gossip with the female neighbors in a most feminine way, and even saw him hug small children with evident envy for the joys of motherhood; but this even the ke´lE-husband could not place within the limits of transformation.

The human husband of Tilu´wgi was an undersized fellow, shorter than his "wife" by at least half a head. He was nevertheless healthy and strong, a good wrestler and runner, and altogether a normal, well-balanced person. He was a cousin of Tilu´wgi, as generally the transformed shamans prefer to choose a husband from among their nearest relatives.

The division of labor between the two followed, of course, the usual rules. In the evening, Ya´tirgin would sit idly within the inner room while Tilu´wgi busied himself outside with the hearth and the supper. Ya´tirgin received the best pieces of meat, and the transformed "wife," according to custom, had to be content with scraps and bones. In the more serious affairs of life, the voice of the "wife" was, however, dominant.

I heard also from their neighbors a curious story, that one time, when Ya´tirgin was angry at something and wanted to chastise his giant wife, the latter suddenly gave him so powerful a kick that it sent him head foremost from their common sleeping-room. This proves that the femininity of Tilu´wgi was more apparent than real.

The transformation in Tilu´wgi began in his very early youth, after a protracted illness from which he freed himself by the song and the drum. He gave a shamanistic séance in my presence, which had no peculiar features, except that the ke´IE-husband often appeared and talked to the public, extolling the shaman. In the very beginning, Tilu´wgi called him and asked him to mend the drum, which, as he pretended, had not the proper ring. We heard the ke´IE-husband blow with great force over the cover of the drum, after which its sound at once improved.

Bogoraz briefly describes several other soft men. E´chuk was about forty, "tall and strong, of rather indecent behavior and strongly peppered talk." He boasted that he had given birth to two sons from his own body with the help of his protector spirit. Kee´ulin was an old man of sixty. He had had a female wife, who had born him several children, and a male lover, with whom he had lived for more than twenty years. Both had died, however. Dressed as a woman, his face was covered with gray stubble. "He was quite poor, and even the shamanistic power had gone from him to a considerable degree. He was said, however, to have a new lover, — another old man who lived in the same house with him." Two other soft men were young and lived with their parents. "One was a nimble young fellow and a very able herdsman; but the people accused him of perverting all his young companions, who beset him with their courtship, to the great detriment and offence of the lawful beauties of the camp."

Finally, Bogoraz reports two cases of transformed women:

[She] was a widow of middle age, who had three half-grown children of her own. She received at first an "inspiration" of a more usual kind, but later the "spirits" wanted to change her to a man. Then she cut her hair, donned the dress of a male, adopted the pronunciation of men, and even learned in a very short time to handle the spear and to shoot with a rifle. At last she wanted to marry, and easily found a quite young girl who consented to become her wife.

The transformed one provided herself with a gastro-cnemius [tendon] from the leg of a reindeer, fastened to a broad leather belt, and used it in the way of masculine private parts. I have said before that the gastrocnemius of a reindeer is used by Chukchee women for the well-known unnatural vice. After some time the transformed husband, desiring to have children by her young wife, entered into a bond of mutual marriage with a young neighbor, and in three years two sons were really born in her family. According to the Chuckchee interpretation of mutual marriage, they were considered her own lawful children. Thus this person could have had in her youth children of her own body, and in later life other children from a wedded wife of hers. Another case was that of a young girl who likewise assumed man's clothing, carried a spear, and even wanted to take part in a wrestling-contest between young men. While tending the herd, she tried to persuade one of the young herdswomen to take her for a husband. On closer acquaintance, she tried to introduce the same implement, made of a reindeer gastrocnemius tied to a belt, but then was rejected by the would-be bride. This happened only a few years ago; the transformed woman is said to have found another bride, with whom she lives now in her country on the head-waters of the Chaun River.

Bogoraz concludes his discussion of soft men with a survey of similar roles across the northern Pacific rim, among the Koryak, Kamchadal (Itel'men), Asiatic Eskimo (Iupik), and Kodiak of Alaska. More recently, Marjorie Balzer has added the Northeastern Yukaghir, the Nivkh (Gilyak), and the Nanai (Gold) to the list of Siberian groups with gender-transformed shamans, while other researchers have noted vestiges of gender transformation in Central Asia among Turkmens, Uzbeks, Abkhazians, and others. Already in Bogoraz's time, these groups were under pressure to suppress such roles. He describes a

Russian administrator who considered soft men to have "a great and baleful influence" among the Asiatic Eskimo, so he actively discouraged them. When the last soft man at Indian Point died in 1900 from measles, Bogoraz reports, "Other inhabitants did not undertake to follow his practices, remembering, perhaps, the reproofs of Mr. Gonatti" (but see "Repression and Revival").

Given all that Bogoraz reports on gender transformation among the Chukchi—from the symbolic cross-dressing of the first "stage" to the alternative gender identities of soft men and women "similar to a man"—it seems misleading to refer to these practices as a "branch" of Chukchi shamanism. A more accurate characterization would be that gender difference, a certain degree of "queering," to use current jargon, is essential to shamanism, not only among the Chukchi, but almost everywhere that shamanic patterns are found. The widespread employment of cross-dressing and cross-gender symbols by "untransformed" shamans, in other words, are attempts to imitate the more complete, awe-inspiring gender transformation of soft men and thereby acquire some of the supernatural power of gender mediation and homosexuality.

The casual use of cross-gender symbols and garments by shamans—Bogoraz's first two "stages"—is, in fact, more widely documented than the presence of roles like that of soft men. So perhaps in another sense it is correct to view queer shamanism as a "branch" of a broader pattern or to say that shamanism, like many other social and cultural patterns in the nonwestern world, was fully capable of accommodating a sexual minority. What is key, however, is appreciating the relationship of queer shamanism to shamanism in general. Far from a deviation, gender-bending shamans who form same-sex relationships represent the fullest realization of shamanic beliefs and practices. Indeed, they exemplify the shape-shifting, boundary-crossing, identity-changing powers of the shaman, which are the very qualities of the spirit world itself.

We began with agape—the unconditional love of God for humans that Jesus imparts to humanity. In tracing this idea back in history, we have ended up in an unlikely place and with an unexpected conclusion. It is not the family that gives rise to this love. After all, it is a love that by definition exceeds what kinship and marriage require. Rather, the origins of selfless love lie within the ancient heritage of shamanism and the practice of uniting with spirits by means of sexual desire and, through this union, aiding others. The model for agape is not the duty-bound love of relatives, but voluntary love between equals. As Jesus says in Luke and Matthew, "Whoever comes to me and does not hate father and mother, wife and children, brothers and sisters, yes, and even life itself, cannot be my disciple" (Luke 14:26; Matt. 10:37).

CHAPTER NINE
The Shaman's Queer Power

As remote as they may be, the Chukchi typify beliefs and religious practices widely shared across a region of Eurasia that borders on the Mediterranean world. As Mircea Eliade wrote in *Shamanism: Archaic Techniques of Ecstasy*, "Throughout the immense area comprising Central and North Asia, the magico-religious life of society centers on the shaman." These societies, as Eliade noted, share several features:

> The Arctic, Siberian, and Central Asian peoples are made up chiefly of hunters-fishers or herdsmen-breeders. A degree of nomadism is typical of them all. And despite their ethnic and linguistic differences, in general their religions coincide. Chuckchee, Tungus, Samoyed, or Turko-Tartars, to mention only some of the most important groups, know and revere a celestial Great God, an all-powerful Creator but on the way to becoming a *deus otiosus*. Sometimes the Great God's name even means "Sky" or "Heaven"; such, for example, is the Num of the Samoyed, the Buga of the Tungus, or the Tengri of the Mongols.... Even when the concrete name of the "sky" is lacking, we find some one of its most characteristic attributes—"high," "lofty," "luminous," and so on. Thus, among the Ostyak of the Irtysh the name of the celestial god is derived from sänke, the primitive meaning of which is "luminous, shining, light." The Yakut call him "Lord Father Chief of the World," the Tatars of the Altai "White Light" (Ak Ayas), the Koryak "The One on High," "The Master of the High," and so on. The Turko-Tatars, among whom the celestial Great God preserves his religious currency more than among their neighbors to the north and northeast, also call him "Chief," "Master," "Lord," and often "Father."
>
> This celestial god, who dwells in the highest sky, has several "sons" or "messengers" who are subordinate to him and who occupy lower heavens. Their names and number vary from tribe to tribe; seven or nine "sons" or "daughters" are commonly mentioned, and the shaman maintains special relations with some of them. These sons, messengers, or servants of the celestial god are charged with watching over and helping human beings.

All this is surprisingly reminiscent of the cosmological scheme of the ancient Mediterranean. In some Siberio-Asiatic traditions the heavens are believed to be connected by stairs or a ladder as they are in Hellenistic and Near Eastern cosmologies. But is Siberian shamanism the source of the ideas and practices we have been tracing? Or are Siberian and Mediterraenan cosmologies independent developments and their similarities coincidental?

We can only speculate now, but if Eurasian shamanism influenced Greek religion it did so indirectly, through intervening groups, such as the Turko-Tatars of the Central Asian steppes, and Indo-Europeans, such as the Thracians and Scythians. As Eliade argues, Indo-European religions share several features with Siberio-Asian shamanism:

> In both there is the same importance of the great God of the Sky or of the Atmosphere, the same absence of goddesses (so characteristic of the Indo-Mediterranean area), the same function attributed to the "sons" or "messengers" (Ashvins, Dioscuri, etc.), the same exaltation of fire. On the sociological and economic planes the similarities between the protohistorical Indo-Europeans and the ancient Turko-Tatars are even more strikingly clear: both societies were patriarchal in structure, with the head of the family enjoying great prestige, and on the whole their economy was that of the hunters and herdsmen-breeders.... Given the economic, social, and religious parallels between the ancient Indo-Europeans and the ancient Turko-Tatars (or, better, Proto-Turks), we must determine to what extent the various historical Indo-European peoples still preserve shamanic survivals comparable to Turko-Tatar shamanism.

All these traditions of heavenly ascent have one common denominator—belief in a supreme god who occupies a supreme heaven. Other gods, as we have seen, are not necessarily eliminated in this system, but rather are demoted to subordinate spirits and assigned to lower heavens. Thus, while Orphic myths promote Zeus to the status of supreme god, they also attribute an important role to mediating figures like Phanes-Eros, who can traverse the realms between heaven and earth. And, as we have seen, both Jewish and Christian tradition, despite their ostensible monotheism, admit of a multiplicity of lesser supernatural beings—"spirits," "demons," "dybbuks," "angels," "saints," and so forth.

In fact, shamanic themes and practices can be found in so many religions as to be practically universal. This led Eliade to reserve the term "shamanism" for only those religions in which a specific set of traits is present: "special relations with 'spirits,' ecstatic capacities permitting of magical flight, ascents to the sky, descents to the underworld, mastery over fire, etc." Above all, Eliade considers out-of-the-body travel synonymous with shamanism: "A first definition of this complex phenomenon, and perhaps the least hazardous, will be: shamanism = *technique of ecstasy*.... The shaman specializes in a trance during which his soul is believed to leave his body and ascend to the sky or descend to the underworld."

As Eliade shows, throughout northern Eurasia individuals became shamans as a result of a crisis—a life-threatening illness or injury, a dream, a vision, or, in its most extreme form, a seizure. Among the Chukchi, the hallucinatory experiences this entailed might include an ascent to the sky and a dialogue with celestial gods; a descent to the underworld and dialogue with the spirits and souls of dead shamans; an attack by gods or spirits resulting in dismemberment followed by a restoration to life; or revelations of esoteric knowledge. Once again we can see the pattern of the initiation rite—suffering or torment resulting in symbolic death followed by rebirth. Eliade notes:

> Any "sickness-vocation" fills the role of an initiation; for the sufferings that it brings on correspond to initiatory tortures, the psychic isolation of 'the elected' is the counterpart of the isolation and ritual solitude of initiation ceremonies, and the imminence of death felt by the sick man (pain, unconsciousness, etc.) recalls the symbolic death represented in almost all initiation ceremonies.

This ritual structure (death, transformation, rebirth) explains why underworld descent and spiritual ascent are so often linked—the former corresponds to the phase of suffering and death, the latter to rebirth and resurrection.

Eliade distinguishes shamanic spirit travel from possession. Shamans who travel out of their bodies communicate with the dead and with spirits without becoming their instrument. In the case of possession, the individual's consciousness and personality are temporarily supplanted by that of the spirit. Similarly, while their ecstatic experiences are involuntary at first, shamans eventually learn to call up spirits more or less at will. Eliade argues that the shaman's vocalization of spirit and animal voices, which resembles possession, is, in fact, "a *taking possession of his helping spirits by a shaman*. It is the shaman who *turns himself* into an animal.... Or, again, we might speak of a *new identity* for the shaman, who becomes an animal-spirit, and 'speaks,' sings, or flies like the animals and birds."

This distinction is useful for understanding the most important power of shamans—their ability to heal. If it were simply a matter of spirits speaking through them, it would be hard to explain how shamans are able to affect the health of their patients. But shamans are not passive instruments of spiritual forces. They actively identify themselves with spirit beings and are able to induce similar identifications on the part of their patients. By mobilizing these powerful dynamics, shamans impact the psychological and physical health of others.

Shamanic rites throughout Eurasia follow the pattern Bogoraz observed among the Chukchi. The shaman begins by invoking helping spirits. This is accompanied by singing and drumming. With the aid of these spirits, the shaman identifies the cause of the illness—usually a particular evil spirit or objects that have been put into the patient's body. These are expelled or extracted by the shaman, who may also make a spirit journey on behalf of the patient.

In the process, the shaman creates a mythical and symbolic representation of the patient's illness, portraying it emotionally and subjectively, much as the patient experiences it—as an internal combat between parts of the body with an accompanying loss of physical control, disruption of body image, and desocialization. What gives shamanic rites their potency are the means the shaman employs to interject the patient (and his or her body) into this myth. The shaman goes to great lengths to create analogies between symbols and myths, and the patient's body. They may portray themselves as moving into the patient's body and, with elaborate metaphors, naming the affected parts and describing their pains. Then, at a crucial moment, the distinction between symbol and reality is erased. The shaman produces a foreign object from the patient, or, even more dramatically, transfers evil spirits from the patient into his or her own body, struggling with them and sometimes suffering even more than the patient. In Yakut (Sakha) healing ceremonies, the shaman (in Eliade's words) "lays ahold of the trouble, carries it to the middle of the room and, never stopping his imprecations, chases it away, spits it from his mouth, kicks it, drives it with his hands and breath."

In his analysis of a South American Indian curing ceremony, anthropologist Claude Lévi-Strauss shows how the shaman makes the patient conscious of his or her physiological experience by portraying their suffering. The cure, Lévi-Strauss concludes, lies in making the emotional situation of patients explicit and making acceptable to them pains that their bodies refuse to tolerate. The shaman reintegrates the experience of illness back into a meaningful whole. Lévi-Strauss compares this to psychotherapy: both shamans and psychotherapists seek to establish communication between conscious and unconscious mind, although in psychotherapy the patient provides his or her own myth, while in shamanic healing this is provided by the shaman.

In the ritual Lévi-Strauss analyzes, the shaman breaks down the mind-body separation, thereby inducing "the release of the physiological process, that is, the reorganization, in a favorable direction, of the process to which the sick woman is subjected." Simply put, the shaman uses myths and symbols to trigger organic reactions normally beyond conscious control. In Lévi-Strauss's words, symbols have an "inductive property"; their underlying structure is similar to the structure that shamans hope to establish at the organic level—one of balance and health.

Psychologist C. G. Jung also recognized the power of myths and symbols to heal. The symbolic structure most analogous to a physical and psychic state of well-being, he suggested, was the mandala—an image in which disparate elements are organized in symmetrical patterns around a central point. As his patients moved toward an integration of their unconscious and conscious selves, Jung observed that they spontaneously created or dreamed mandala images:

> The severe pattern imposed by a circular image of this kind compensates the disorder and confusion of the psychic state—namely, through the construction of a central point to which everything is related, or by a concentric arrangement of the disordered multiplicity and of contradictory and irreconcilable elements. This is evidently an *attempt at self-healing* on the part of Nature, which does not spring from conscious reflection but from an instinctive impulse. [emphasis in original]

Jung theorized that symbols serve not only to represent and express experiences of psychic and physical illness, they can convert psychic energy from one form to another. Another symbol associated with wholeness and unity, which often represents the "Self," Jung's term for the totality of conscious and unconscious mind, is the figure of the Androgyne, an archetype we have encountered already in the history of heavenly ascents.

Shamans' ability to forsake their own identities and assume the consciousness, personality, and physical condition of others—including other beings and other genders—is an extension of the primal shamanic motif of death and rebirth. In abandoning their own identities, shamans die. In assuming other identities they are reborn. In psychological terms we would say that the ego boundaries of shamans are weakly defined and their body images fluid, a consequence of the physical traumas and transformations they endure.

Identification with others is essential to empathy—the ability to sympathetically feel the experience of another—which is recognized as one of the most important skills of therapists. Helping professionals express empathy by carefully attending to what their clients say, paraphrasing their statements, and validating their emotions. What greater expression of empathy could there be than the act of the shaman who takes another's illness into his or her own body and then suffers as the patient suffers?

This capacity for identification is crucial to another skill—that of acting. Indeed, when we consider the shaman's use of stories, symbols, music, demonstrations of powers, and impersonation of spirits using masks and other means, it is easy to imagine theater originating in shamanic rites. In Korea, where female shamans (*mudang*) are still common alongside occasional male shamans (*paksu mudang*) who are typically gay, all the traditional arts, from music to dance and theater, are believed to have been derived from the ancient ceremonies of shamans. In the same way, Greek theater developed out of rituals that depicted the death and rebirth of Dionysus. The Greeks believed that by producing catharsis, drama had therapeutic powers. Today, therapists and counselors seek to tap these powers through a branch of the helping professions known as drama therapy.

These powers are familiar to us now; they are the same that Plato attributed to the rites of the Corybantes: the suspension of anxieties and fear, the release of repressed emotion, the acting out of inner dramas— catharsis. In the ancient world, such rites were a means of purifying and perfecting one's self in anticipation of union with the divine and ascent to heaven, the Orphic-Platonic ideal.

In the ancient heritage of shamanism—its myths, images, and rites— teachers like Plato and Jesus perceived a special form of love, one that drew on powerful psychological processes of identification and empathy, and bonded humans in equal and reciprocal relationships with each other and with the divine, a way of loving with the potential to transform society.

What else can we call the shaman's willingness to forsake his or her own identity to assume another's, to die and be reborn in the course of relieving another's pain, except a selfless act of love? What better example could be found of the ideal Jesus held up when he told his disciples, "No one has greater love than this, to lay down one's life for one's friends"? (See "Was Jesus a Shaman?")

Shamans, of course, are not philosophers. Although they might apply their powers to aid others and perfect themselves, they could just as easily use them for personal gain and even to harm others (in which case shamanism becomes "witchcraft"). Ancient magicians, too, sought to control spirits, sometimes to achieve ascents to heaven, but just as often to win a lover, find a lost object, or secure luck in gambling. The teachings of Plato and Jesus, however, focus on union—between friends of the same sex, between the human in me and the divinity in the other I love, between mortals and mediating spirits who lead the way to heaven. Spiritual union, not spirit possession or control of spirits, is the means of perfecting oneself and experiencing heaven on earth.

Sexuality has remained in the wings of this story so far—sublimated in Plato's theory of love and hinted at by phrases like *gumnos gumnō* and Paul's metaphorical use of marital relations to describe union with Christ. But now we can begin to see the connection of sex to the themes of spiritual union and heavenly ascent.

Eliade discounted the practice of shamans marrying and having sexual relations with spirits, labeling it a "deviation." Others, however, have concluded that sexuality plays a central role in shamanism. Lev (Leo) Shternberg, who was a member of the Jesup Expedition along with Bogoraz, found that throughout Siberia shamans were "prompted to shamanistic service by a special spirit who offered them love and with whom they cohabit in sleep." Shternberg recorded a revealing account of a shaman's relationship with his spirit wife. The shaman is from the Gold (Nanai) Tribe, a Southern Tungus people along the Amur River (the present-day boundary of China and Russia):

> Once I was asleep on my sick-bed, when a spirit approached me. It was a very beautiful woman. Her figure was very slight, she was no more than half an arshin (71 cm) tall. Her face and attire were quite as those of one of our Gold women. Her hair fell down to her shoulders in short black tresses. Other shamans say they have had the vision of a woman with one-half of her face black, and the other half red. She said: "I am the *ayami* of your ancestors, the Shamans. I taught them shamaning. Now I am going to teach you. The old shamans have died off, and there is no one to heal people. You are to become a shaman."
>
> Next she said: "I love you, I have no husband now, you will be my husband and I shall be a wife unto you. I shall give you assistant spirits. You are to heal with their aid, and I shall teach and help you myself. Food will come to us from the people."
>
> I felt dismayed and tried to resist. Then she said: "If you will not obey me, so much the worse for you. I shall kill you."
>
> She has been coming to me ever since, and I sleep with her as with my own wife, but we have no children. She lives quite by herself without any relatives in a hut, on a mountain, but she often changes her abode. Sometimes she comes under the aspect of an old woman, and sometimes under that of a wolf,

so she is terrible to look at. Sometimes she comes as a winged tiger. I mount it and she takes me to show me different countries. I have seen mountains, where only old men and women live, and villages, where you see nothing but young people, men and women: they look like Golds and speak Goldish, sometimes those people are turned into tigers. Now my *ayami* does not come to me as frequently as before. Formerly, when teaching me, she used to come every night. She has given me three assistants—the *jarga* (the panther), the *doonto* (the bear) and the *amba* (the tiger). They come to me in my dreams, and appear whenever I summon them while shamaning....

There can be no shaman without an *ayami*. What assistant spirit will come to him without one? The *ayami* is the shaman's teacher, he is like a god of his. A man's *ayami* is always a woman, and a woman's—a man, because they are like husband and wife. Some shamans sleep also with all their assistant spirits, as with a woman. There was one great shaman woman who lived without a husband. She had many spirit-servants, and she slept with them all. They say there is one shaman whose *ayami* comes to him as a man. I have not seen such shamans myself. But the *ayamis* are also of great variety....

With the striking image of the Gold shaman being borne by his spirit-wife in the form of a winged tiger on a journey through the sky we are once again in the presence of the motifs of spiritual union and heavenly ascent.

Although the shaman in this account says that men's *ayamis* are always female, he nonetheless mentions a male shaman whose spirit spouse was male. In fact, in the complex psychodynamics of shamanism, every shaman's gender is transformed at some point. While the marriage of a male shaman to a female spirit conforms to heterosexual protocols, when the shaman is possessed by his spirit, he becomes female, speaking with a female voice. Equally so, the soft man, when hosting his male spirit-husband, becomes—once more—male. The shaman's powers of identification unfix gender assignments. The shaman becomes what he or she desires.

And this is the centerpiece of Plato's philosophy of love. In the spiritual development described by Diotima, the desire to possess the other (common eros) is transformed into the desire to become the other (heavenly or spiritual eros). This gives rise to the capacity to love another as if oneself. As Socrates tells Phaedrus, lovers, perceiving their own god in the beloved, "are inspired by him [the beloved] and derive their customs and practices from him, insofar as it is possible for a human being to be like a god" (*Phaedrus* 253a).

The "god" that the lover attributes to his beloved is the archetypal figure governing his own personality. By loving the beloved, the lover realizes himself, even as he leads his beloved toward the realization of his own inner divinity. All this presumes the dynamics of a same-sex relationship, the mutual and unfettered identification possible between individuals who see themselves as the same rather than opposites. Friends, in Socrates' words, "belong" to one another, because they share "some disposition, demeanour, or cast of soul" (*Lysis* 221e).

In the case of heterosexual relationships, becoming the other necessarily entails a measure of gender-crossing. In societies like the Chukchi this is not problematic. Male shamans possessed by female spirits can become temporary women or enter the alternative status of the soft man. Most societies of Central Asia and those of the ancient world, however, were patriarchal, and in the ideology of male superiority, men who become women and sexual relations that compete with heterosexual marriage are viewed dimly. It is not surprising, therefore, that roles like that of the Chukchi soft man are rare outside Siberia—the Scythian *enarees* being an exception. In the Greek world, there were no institutionalized roles for "not-men," and those gods and myths that featured androgyny were generally considered non-Greek in origin—like Dionysus, who was said to have come from Thrace. In patriarchal societies, male heterosexual desire can only be desire-to-possess, never desire-to-become a woman. Homosexual desire is disallowed for the same reason—it turns men into women. In the phallic-centered sexuality of patriarchy, one partner must be dominant and the other subordinate, a role that is always viewed as female, whether fulfilled by a woman or a boy or a man.

An exception to this rule is the institutionalized homosexuality of Classical Greece. What made these affairs acceptable was the requirement that the younger partner not submit (or at least not eagerly) to penetrative sex and that he give up his subordinate role once he became an adult. As long as these protocols were observed, both partners were men. Consequently, desire-to-possess could become (or be combined with) desire-to-become without resulting in a change of gender status. And both partners could benefit from the shamanic powers of identification and empathy unleashed.

Same-sex love occupies a special place in the patriarchal imaginary of Western cultures—as compulsory heterosexuality's "other," the unexplored territory of mutuality and mutual self-realization. Same-sex love became patriarchy's repressed dream. Only now, after two millennia of religiously-inspired homophobia and repression, has it become possible for individuals from the broad mass of humanity to enter the untrammeled paths of this dream, to discover for themselves what it enfolds.

Before our appreciation of the history of queer shamanism is complete, however, we have two more threads to trace. One leads from Siberia across the Bering Straight to the so-called New World; the other leads back to the Near East where this story began.

CHAPTER TEN
The Changing One

One day in the early 1880s a young Navajo Indian was riding his horse along the edge of a desert canyon in the arid mountains of eastern Arizona. Suddenly, the bank gave way, and the boy found himself rolling down the canyon wall, the horse's hooves striking him repeatedly. When he came to rest, his body was racked with pain. His collarbone had been shattered and two or three ribs broken. He couldn't move his legs. Likely, he had a fractured pelvis.

Given the resources of tribal medicine, these were life-threatening injuries. The fact that the youth survived was considered evidence that he had supernatural protection. Even so, he underwent two healing ceremonies before he was able to walk again. These were complex rituals incorporating lengthy prayers and chants, masked dances, herbal remedies, and the creation of mandala-like images from colored sand and other materials representing scenes from Navajo mythology. At the climax of the ceremony, the patient was led onto the sandpainting, and material from it was rubbed on his body, literally identifying him with the gods and interjecting him into their myth.

In the course of undergoing these ceremonies, the injured youth memorized both the prayers and the sandpainting designs. He now had the right to perform them himself. By this twist of fate, he became a medicine man.

The boy's name was Klah. As an adult, he was addressed as Hastíín Klah, using the Navajo term for "sir." By the time of his death in 1937, he was one of the most accomplished medicine men of his tribe and one of the most well-known Native Americans in the United States (see fig. 11).

In fact, there was nothing unusual about the way that Klah became a medicine man. Serious illness or injury followed by supernatural intervention and healing was, among the Navajo as among the Chukchi, the typical way that individuals entered that profession. But there was something else about Klah that ensured an exceptional career. During the course of his recovery, his family determined that he was a *nádleehí*, a member of a distinctive class of individuals believed to have special spiritual propensities. *Nádleehí* literally means "one who is constantly changing." The "change" is between genders, but not in the sense of crossing from one gender to another, but of a continual fluctuation between male and female, and between androgyny (*both* male and female) and third gender (*neither* male nor female).

Such individuals, referred to as "berdaches" by anthropologists and as "two-spirits" by many contemporary Native Americans, have

139

been documented throughout North and South America. Two-spirits occupied a distinct status that combined the work and social roles of men and women with traits unique to their identity. Many Navajo *nádleehí* cross-dressed, although Klah did not. Two-spirits typically formed sexual relationships with members of the same (anatomical) sex, although not other two-spirits. In most tribes, they were not only well-accepted, they were believed to have special powers.

Given Klah's *nádleehí* attributes and his skill in learning complex ceremonies, his extended family decided to devote its resources to his continued training. For three decades, Klah studied under various medicine men, eventually mastering eight ceremonies—more than any medicine man of his generation or, for that matter, since. At the age of forty-nine, he declared his apprenticeship complete and held a week-long ceremony and festival attended by some two thousand Navajos and members of neighboring tribes.

Klah's accomplishments were not limited to religion. He was equally talented as an artist. Taking advantage of his *nádleehí* status, he single-handedly transformed one of the most important arts of his tribe—weaving. Weaving was women's work, but as a "changing one," Klah was trained in this skill as well as the skills of a medicine man. He mastered the techniques of weaving brightly-colored blankets with intricate geometric designs. Then, in the early 1920s, he began to weave designs based on sandpaintings. In the years that followed, he produced dozens of these large-scale tapestries, most of which were purchased by wealthy collectors and museums. His intent was to help preserve the religious knowledge he had spent a lifetime accumulating.

Klah formed close friendships with Anglo-American traders, scholars, artists, and art collectors. Among these was the wealthy Bostonian spinster, Mary Cabot Wheelwright. With Klah's support, she founded a museum in Santa Fe devoted to preserving Navajo religion and art—today called the Wheelwright Museum of the American Indian. Klah died a few months before the museum's opening in 1937, but many of his tapestries and ceremonial accoutrements, along with extensive recordings of myths told by him and drawings of his sandpaintings, formed the centerpiece of the museum's collections. Wheelwright recalled her friend in these words:

> I grew to respect and love him for his real goodness, generosity—and holiness, for there is no other word for it. He never had married, having spent twenty-five years studying not only the ceremonies he gave, but all the medicine lore of the tribe. He helped at least eight of his nieces and nephews with money and goods.... When I knew him he never kept anything for himself. It was hard to see him almost in rags at

Fig. 11. Hastíín Klah (1867-1937), Navajo medicine man, weaver, and two-spirit.

his ceremonies, but what was given him he seldom kept, passing it on to someone who needed it....

Our civilization and miracles he took simply without much wonder, as his mind was occupied with his religion and helping his people. It was wonderful to travel with him, as he knew the ceremonial names and legends of all the mountains, rivers and places, and the uses and associations of plants and stones. Everything was the outward form of the spirit world that was very real to him.

THE SHAMANIC ORIGINS OF NATIVE AMERICAN RELIGION

Until recently, conventional wisdom held that the native peoples of the Americas were Asiatic in origin, arriving by way of the Bering land bridge some 12,000 to 15,000 years ago. Recent archaeological findings, however, have reopened the debate about how and when the so-called New World was populated. At a site in Chile, human remains have been found that are at least 12,500 years old, indicating that the migration from Asia began much earlier than previously believed—some experts now think as long as 40,000 years ago. Complicating the picture further is tantalizing evidence that at least some peoples reached the New World from Polynesia, Asia, and even prehistoric Europe.

However long humans have lived in the Americas, it has been long enough for their cultures to evolve in diverse ways. Over four hundred languages were spoken in North America alone, belonging to more than a dozen independent language families. This and other evidence indicates that the Americas were populated in waves at widely dispersed points in time. Even so, it remains a significant fact that the New World was occupied primarily in a north to south direction, by peoples originally accustomed to life in an arctic setting.

Arctic cultures share several features. Most are based on hunting and most (if not all) have a shamanistic religion. It is not surprising, therefore, that many native religions in both North and South America have shamanistic elements. Even complex, collective religions with priesthoods and temples, such as those of the Aztecs, Mayans, and Incans had pronounced shamanic features. In this regard, in terms of religious history, the dichotomy of Old World and New is arbitrary and misleading. Hastíin Klah drew on a body of beliefs and practices rooted in northern Asian shamanism, the same patterns we found underlying ancient Mediterranean and Near Eastern traditions of heavenly ascent.

Given these connections, it is not surprising to find parallels in North America to each of the "stages" of gender transformation Bogoraz found among the Chukchi. Shamans in tribes such as the Tolowa of northern California wore women's basket hats with otherwise male clothing—Bogoraz's first stage—while cases of adult men cross-dressing as a result of a dream or vision while remaining heterosexual—Bogoraz's second stage—have been recorded in several tribes. But even more common were two-spirit roles, like that of the Navajo *nádleehí*, corresponding to Chukchi soft men and women "similar to a man." Such roles have been documented in over 150 North American tribes and among Central and South American groups as well.

Of course, there are tribal differences between these roles. Among the Navajo, *nádleehí* enjoyed exceptional opportunities for social and economic success. A mythical *nádleehí* plays an important role in the tribe's origin myth, and a prominent Navajo god was *nádleehí*. As among the Chukchi, only a minority of medicine men fulfilled this alternative gender role, but far from being a "branch" of Navajo religion, *nádleehí* personified the transformative powers all medicine men were believed to have.

The case of the Navajo is interesting because their ancestors, speakers of Athabaskan languages, may have been the last Asian immigrants to reach North America (along with the Inuit). Athabaskan physical features, for example, are more like those of modern northern Asians than other Native Americans. This being the case, historic Navajo culture is that much closer to its arctic origins.

Athabaskans initially settled in a wide arc across the subarctic region of Alaska and Canada. Then, about one thousand years ago, groups began to move south. Some reached the Great Plains and adopted a Plains Indian lifestyle. Others reached the coast of northern California (such as the Tolowa) and settled in permanent villages. And some entered the American Southwest, perhaps only a century or two before the arrival of the Spanish conquistador, Hernando Cortés, becoming the historic Navajo and Apache tribes.

Southwestern Athabaskans underwent rapid cultural change as a result of their contact with the indigenous village-dwelling Anasazi. They added farming to their subsistence strategies and borrowed a variety of religious practices, including sandpainting, the use of masks and dances, and an extensive body of carefully preserved myths. Even so, the basic patterns of Eurasian shamanism can still be discerned in Navajo religion. In myths, for example, a protagonist typically encounters spirit beings, is stricken or killed by them, and then restored. At the same time, there are differences between Navajo religion and the patterns we saw among the Chukchi. Contact with spirits is not always involuntary. In some myths, the hero consciously, even brazenly seeks such contact. He is, in short, a mystic—in the words of the Mithras Liturgy, an "inquirer." Further, the knowledge he acquires is not merely magical, but practical. The hero learns techniques of farming, house building, and making tools. Then he returns to the community and shares this knowledge. In these accounts, he is less a shaman in the Chukchi style and more of a culture hero, like Orpheus or Dionysus.

The development of Navajo religion is evident in the evolution of the *nádleehí* deity Begochídíín. In *Navajo Hunter Traditions*, Karl Luckert argues that Begochídíín was among the original gods of the Athabaskans when they arrived in the Southwest. They were at that time nomadic hunters-and-gatherers, and Begochídíín was the patron of hunters with power over game animals. His character was that of a pansexual trickster. He snuck up on individuals at embarrassing moments and grabbed their genitals or got between couples when they were making love.

Luckert believes that a change in Begochídíín's character occurred when the Navajos shifted from hunting and gathering to horticulture and, with the arrival of the Spaniards, sheepherding. Begochídíín came to be credited not only with the creation of game animals but domestic animals as well, and with providing the first seeds. He was considered the inventor of pottery and the first *nádleehí*.

In Klah's time, Begochídíín was a complex figure. According to one account, he was born from a flower impregnated by a ray of sunlight; in another, from a sunbeam and a sun ray. He is, like Phanes, a radiant being. Because he is the youngest offspring of the Sun, he was spoiled and given dominion over many things. He is the source of a medicine made from flowers, and he has power over wind and insects. Having been born from sunlight, he is usually invisible, but he can appear at any time and take many forms.

In Klah's version of the Navajo origin myth, the earth goddess, Changing Woman, travels to her home in the Pacific Ocean where she is greeted by Begochídíín, walking across the water. According to Klah, "His hair was shining and little rays of light shone and sparkled from him." Elsewhere, Klah describes him as fair-skinned, with red or yellow hair and blue eyes, and dressed as a woman. Other accounts describe him as an old man, or as a boy who turns into a man, or as alternating between old and young—much as the term *nádleehí*, "the one who is changing," suggests. In tribal societies, gender and age are basic social distinctions, and Begochídíín transcends both.

In another myth told by Klah, Begochídíín appears as a malevolent and protean being, first a boy, then a worm, then a man from whose mouth pours hordes of insects that sting the people until they are unconscious. Only when he is given an appropriate ceremonial offering does he draw the insects back into his mouth. According to Klah, "Then they saw that the man was Begochiddy, and were greatly amazed.... Begochiddy told the people that he would go with them and watch over them, and the people were glad and went on their way, when suddenly

Begochiddy disappeared from their midst and they did not see him go, so they knew that he had gone up into the sky." He had ascended to heaven.

Donald Sandner, a Jungian analyst who studied Navajo medicine men, considers Begochídíín "a reconciling symbol which brings together good and bad, high and low, pure and impure, male and female, and as such he is one of the most daring intuitive concepts of American Indian religion—an ingenious attempt to express the basically paradoxical nature of man in the image of a god." As Jung observed, tricksters like Begochídíín typically combine traits of animals, humans, and gods. For that reason, they often serve as symbols of the Self, the total psyche in both its conscious and unconscious dimensions.

As we have seen, androgyny was as a symbol of wholeness and spiritual healing for early Christians. Jesus is credited with preaching the transcendence of gender, and in Christian literature and art he is often portrayed in an androgynous manner. However, as Jung argues, the orthodox image of Christ is not an ideal symbol of the Self, because Christian belief splits off any negative aspects of God and projects them onto figures of evil—Satan, the anti-Christ, demons, and spirits. In Navajo tradition, Begochídíín's malignant side is neither ignored nor suppressed, and this makes him a more apt representation of the Self— he is god, human and animal; good and evil; male and female; a Navajo who is fair-skinned. Begochídíín the trickster became a transcendental savior.

As Navajo religion evolved, so did Navajo social roles. The tribal shaman who healed the sick, predicted the future, and helped hunters find game became a medicine man, a ceremonialist, and a priest whose ability to heal was based on his mastery of rituals and myths. Klah, with his knowledge of so many ceremonies, with their myriad prayers, chants, myths, and sandpaintings, epitomized this evolution. And sadly he culminated it as well. No Navajo medicine man since Klah has been qualified to conduct so many ceremonies; indeed, knowledge of several died with him.

The evolution of shamans into priests occurred in the Old World as well. The followers of the gods Cybele and Attis, called *galli*, functioned as temple priests and, in Anatolia (modern Turkey), served as priest-kings of theocratic city-states, such as Pessinus. Their rituals and performances, however, incorporated shamanic techniques, including gender transgression, ecstatic dancing, supernatural feats, such as blood-letting with knives and swords, and the attainment of trance states in which they foretold the future.

To find the oldest instance of this development we need to return to the Near East and the home of the world's first literate, urban civilization, that of the Sumerians. Beginning in the mid-third millennium B.C.E., cuneiform texts document a class of priests known as *gala*, who were specialists in singing lamentations. This role originally may have been filled by women—the hymns sung by *gala* were in a dialect known as *eme-sal*, which is normally used to render the speech of female gods. *Gala* also appear to have been homosexual. According to a humorous Sumerian proverb, "When the *gala* wiped off his ass [he said], 'I must not arouse that which belongs to my mistress [i.e., the goddess Inanna].'" (In fact, the word *gala* was written using the cuneiform signs "penis+anus.")

Like professional mourners in other cultures (including present societies in the Near East), *gala* sang lamentations to memorialize the dead, express the grief of survivors, and seek the intercession of the gods for the benefit of the community. Their hymns were believed to calm the heart of the deity by praising and pleading with it. Indeed, lamentation became the model for all human interaction with the gods in Sumerian religion.

Gala appear in Akkadian texts (the language of the Assyrian and Babylonian successors of the Sumerians) as *kalû*. The role of *kalû* was, if anything, greater than that of their Sumerian predecessors. A related class of Sumerian priests were known as *kur-gar-ra*. They appear in Akkadian texts as *kurgarrû*, usually in conjunction with priests called *assinnu*. All these figures—*kalû*, *kurgarrû*, and *assinnu*—were typically identified as servants of Ishtar, Inanna's Akkadian counterpart. As a Babylonian myth relates, the god Enki created *gala* to sing "heart-soothing laments" for Inanna. These priests also shared variant gender and sexual attributes. In the case of the *kurgarrû* and *assinnu*, Ishtar is said to have changed their "masculinity" into "femininity." Akkadian omen texts instruct men to have intercourse with *assinnu* to obtain luck (much as Sioux warriors in North America had sex with *winkte*, or two-spirits, for luck in battle).

While *gala* sang lamentations to "ease the mind" of the deity, the rites performed by *kurgarrû* and *assinnu* seem to have been intended to actually provoke the fury of the god (or perhaps portray it) and then resolve it. Descriptions of these rites sound remarkably similar to those of the Corybantes and *galli* (see "The *Galli* and their Kind"). The *kurgarrû* performed a war dance to the music of flutes, drums, and cymbals, apparently in a trance state. They brandished swords, knives, and clubs and may have engaged in blood-letting. They also portrayed the goddess by wearing masks and cross-dressing. *Kurgarrû* and *assinnu* were prominent in "crisis rites" as well. These were held during the New Year festival and on the occasion of lunar eclipses, when *kurgarrû* "dissolved the evil." (Something similar is suggested in a text that describes the *assinnu* as "grabbing" sickness and taking it away.) At this stage of development, the rites of the *kurgarrû* and *assinnu* begin to resemble theater.

Underlying these complex rituals were ancient techniques of lamentation. As the myth known as the "Descent of Inanna" illustrates, these techniques involved the same powers of identification and empathy at work in the rites of shamans. In this myth, Inanna travels to the land of the dead to attend the funeral of the husband of her sister, Ereshkigal, Queen of the Underworld. This infuriates Ereshkigal, who kills Inanna and turns her into a waterskin, which she hangs from a peg on a wall. Meanwhile, the disappearance of Inanna from the surface of the earth causes all life to come to a halt. Animals no longer mate; men and women no longer have intercourse. To rescue Inanna, Enki creates twin figures, a *kurgarrû* and a *kalatur* (from Sumerian *galatur*, probably "little *gala*"). Both are described as creatures who are "neither male nor female" — they are spirit beings and, as such, lack fixed gender.

Following Enki's instructions, the *kurgarrû* and a *kalatur* cross the boundary between the world of the living and the dead by slipping through the cracks of the gates to the underworld like flies. They encounter the goddess Ereshkigal in state of extreme distress, moaning like a woman about to give birth, her breasts uncovered, her hair swirling about her head. They proceed to restore her peace of mind in what may be the oldest recorded example of psychotherapy.

> Ereshkigal was moaning:
> "Oh! Oh! My inside!"
> They moaned:
> "Oh! Oh! Your inside!"
> She moaned:
> "Ohhhh! Oh! My outside!"
> They moaned:
> "Ohhhh! Oh! Your outside!"
> She groaned:
> "Oh! Oh! My belly!"
> They groaned:
> "Oh! Oh! your belly!"
> She groaned:
> "Oh! Ohhhh! My back!!"
> They groaned:
> "Oh! Ohhhh! Your back!!"
> She sighed:
> "Ah! Ah! My heart"
> They sighed:
> "Ah! Ah! Your heart!"
> She sighed:

"Ah! Ahhhh! My liver!"
They sighed:
"Ah! Ahhhh! Your liver!"

Finally calmed, Ereshkigal stops wailing and looks at the two sexless beings. "Who are you?" she asks, "Moaning—groaning—sighing with me? If you are gods, I will bless you. If you are mortals, I will give you a gift." The gift they desire is Inanna, whose lifeless body hangs from a peg on the wall. Thus, they trick Ereshkigal into releasing her nemesis. Sprinkling the "food of life" and the "water of life" on Inanna, the *kurgarrû* and *kalatur* restore her to life.

These figures have qualities of both the Two-Spirit or Androgyne archetype and the archetype of Divine Twins. The lack of differentiation between them, their sameness, is the basis of their empathic powers—just as they reflect each other, they reflect the emotions of Ereshkigal back to her. By acknowledging and validating these emotions they restore her peace of mind.

Having begun with Jesus' teachings on love and traced their history backwards to their original forms we have come to some surprising conclusions. Western ideals of love are rooted in ancient beliefs and practices, many of which seem alien to us today—in spells in which magicians entreat spirits, "For you are I, and I, you"; in shamans' ability to identify with spirit beings and become one themselves. This heritage of queer shamanism is woven through the entirety of Western religious history. From the shaman who foresakes his or her identity to assume that of spirits and of their patients, and who, by uniting with spirits (sometimes sexually), is able to travel to the underworld and to heaven; to Plato's lovers, who reflect each other's archetypes and by uniting attain the perfection that makes spiritual ascent possible; to Jesus, who teaches his followers to love others without regard for differences and, by uniting with him, enter heaven. But this story is not complete without a final chapter.

CHAPTER ELEVEN
Lover and Perfect Equal

The storm of controversy that greeted Morton Smith's *Clement of Alexandria and a Secret Gospel of Mark* when it was published in 1973 was followed by a strange silence. Although the authenticity of Clement's letter along with some, if not all, of Smith's arguments about it have been quietly accepted by many scholars, few have been willing to defend Smith in print, and there have been almost no follow-up studies. As Shawn Eyer comments, "When seen in light of the massive literature which has been produced by the other major manuscript finds of our century, the Dead Sea Scrolls, Nag Hammadi codices, the comparative dearth of good studies on this piece [the Secret Gospel] in particular cannot be explained in any other way than as a stubborn refusal to deal with information which might challenge deeply-held personal convictions."

In the early 1980s, Smith's book was remaindered—publishers' lingo for declaring a book out of print and selling off remaining copies to discount booksellers. That was when longtime gay activist Don Kilhefner gave a copy to Harry Hay, who, in turn, presented it to me and my lover, Bradley Rose, when we arrived at his home in Los Angeles in the spring of 1982. "I think there's something in here we should be concerned with," he said mysteriously—"us" meaning gay men.

Hay himself was a figure of some historical import, having founded the first grassroots gay organization in the United States in 1950. In subsequent years, he was active in a variety of political causes, while pursuing extensive research on gay roles in history and across cultures. In the 1970s, he wrote a series of provocative essays that helped spark a movement among gay men to explore their spirituality. Harry had an uncanny knack for capturing the imagination of others.

And "captivated" perfectly describes the effect Smith's book had on Brad and me. We were fascinated by everything about it—how Smith had found Clement's letter secreted away in a desert monastery, his painstaking analysis of its authenticity, and above all the possibility of a gospel that brings us closer to the historic Jesus than the ones we have now. Smith's study was also the most scholarly book Brad or I had encountered. It cites ancient sources in five languages and presents untranslated material in various alphabets. It incorporates comments from other authorities, as well as Smith's own conclusions at different points in time. It was arcane, complex—and thoroughly engaging.

Harry, Brad, and I poured over Smith's monograph—my copy has notes in all three hands. Following Smith's argument required locating, and sometimes translating, obscure ancient sources. One of Harry's friends started to give us lessons in ancient Greek. Soon we had exhausted the resources of the Los Angeles Public Library.

At the time, my attention was drawn primarily to the secret baptism and its homoerotic overtones. I wanted to know what sort of procedure "naked man with naked man" was and how it could have triggered an altered state of consciousness. What I failed to appreciate at the time was the connection of this ritual to ideas about love with a hallowed history. Jesus was not a "homosexual baptizer" (as John Crossan characterizes Smith's interpretation of the Secret Gospel) — his own sexuality remains a mystery — but he was someone for whom love between men could embody some of the highest ideals of humanity.

The idea that same-sex love has its own emotional dynamics was not new to me. I had come out in 1975, in a gay studies class offered at, of all places, the University of Montana. Our textbooks were the fervid manifestos and treatises, the coming-out stories and front-line accounts of the gay liberation movement. In these works, gay love was discussed often.

Gay liberation had burst forth following the 1969 Stonewall riots in New York City. Many of its activists had already been involved in the tumultuous politics of that decade. They brought with them ideals from both feminism and the antiwar movement. These movements, in their critique of American society, converged on a key point: male aggression was the source of many social problems. Pacifists challenged the American glorification of violence and the socialization of men as warriors. Feminists sought to change gender roles so that women could engage in pursuits that had been restricted to men and men could engage in activities, such as housework and childcare, and develop skills such as nurturing and cooperation that were considered feminine.

Many of the young men who joined the early gay liberation movement saw themselves as fulfilling both pacifist and feminist ideals. They opposed the war in Vietnam not only because it was morally wrong, but because it was their inclination to love other men, not kill them. They epitomized the popular slogan "Make Love Not War." But as Harold Norse declared in his 1973 poem, "I'm Not a Man," gay men's nonviolence was part of a general rejection of the patriarchal male role:

I'm not a man. I cry when I'm unhappy.
I'm not a man. I do not feel superior to women.
I'm not a man. I don't wear a jock strap.
I'm not a man. I write poetry.
I'm not a man. I meditate on peace and love.
I'm not a man. I don't want to destroy you.

Just as gay men were seen as challenging conventional masculinity, lesbians were seen as escaping the confines of femininity. Gay liberationists turned the conventional judgment of homosexuals on its head. Rather than rejecting stereotypes of lesbians and gay men, liberationists embraced gender difference as a challenge to patriarchal sex roles. If society overcame its hostility toward homosexuality, they argued, then everyone—male and female; heterosexual, homosexual, and bisexual—could escape these rigid roles and define their own sexual and gender identities. As Dennis Altman wrote in his introduction to *The Gay Liberation Book*:

> Once men are no longer so frightened of homosexuality— and it is this fear of being branded a "fag" or a "sissie" that underlies many of the more unpleasant instances of male violence and aggression—men will be able to relate more genuinely and more lovingly, not only to each other but also to women. We may even reach a time when the sight of two men making love is not considered obscene, but when two men fighting is.

This is claiming a good deal more than most of today's "queer" activists are willing to assert. Three decades after Stonewall, the standard argument of the lesbian/gay/bisexual movement is merely that same-sex love is morally neutral and should be neither criminalized nor persecuted. For gay liberationists, however, gay love was an alternative social practice that could change society as a whole. As the 1971 manifesto of the London Gay Liberation Front declared, "Gay men don't need to oppress women in order to fulfill their own psychosexual needs, and gay women don't have to relate sexually to the male oppressor, so that at this moment in time, the freest and most equal relationships are most likely to be between homosexuals."

In the course of the 1970s, gay historians found precedents for these ideas in the writings of nearly forgotten nineteenth-century reformers such as Karl Heinrich Ulrichs, John Addington Symonds, and Edward Carpenter. Others began reevaluating well-known gay figures, such as Walt Whitman. Gay liberationists, they discovered, were not the first to suggest that same-sex love could contribute something valuable to society.

"ABSORBING ALL TO MYSELF"

There is a school of thought that would explain the ideas of Plato and Jesus strictly in terms of the contexts in which they lived and what others had already said and written. I would argue, however, that their

151

ideas at least partly reflect their experiences of same-sex love. This is why, despite the different times and cultures in which they lived, both came to similar insights, and why those insights have been rediscovered by others since. This is not because there is something "essential" about those who love the same sex. What *is* essential, however, is the fact that in most societies heterosexuality is both privileged and regulated by social convention. Same-sex relations, in contrast, are often less structured, because they do not involve family alliances and the production of heirs, and because they are stigmatized. Consequently, they unfold in less conventional ways, even as they vary from culture to culture. Same-sex love offers different opportunities—sexually, emotionally, and socially.

The individual who most of all deserves credit for rediscovering the mystical dimension of same-sex love in modern times is Walt Whitman. Much as Plato is considered the father of philosophy, Whitman is called the father of American poetry. In fact, Whitman's ideas about same-sex love resonate with those of both Plato and Jesus. Like them, he passionately loved others of his own sex, and like them his thinking was deeply influenced by these experiences.

When I first read Whitman in a college English class, I was amazed by its unabashed homoeroticism. As he declares at the beginning of the "Calamus" section of *Leaves of Grass*:

> I proceed for all who are or have been young men,
> To tell the secret of my nights and days,
> To celebrate the need of comrades.

And yet, until the 1970s, literary critics rarely commented on Whitman's homosexuality. If it was noted, it was said that there was no evidence that Whitman actually had sex with men and that, in any case, his concept of comradely love was spiritual, not physical. As Robert K. Martin observed in his 1979 book, *The Homosexual Tradition in American Poetry*, "The record of lies, half truths, and distortions is so shameful as to amount to a deliberate attempt to alter reality to suit a particular view of normality. If Whitman is to be a great poet, he must be straight." Thanks to Martin's work and that of others, however, it is no longer possible to deny that Whitman was homosexual or that his poetry was inspired by his homoerotic experiences.

As Martin shows, these experiences were the source of Whitman's belief that all things in the universe were cosmically connected. In his poems, this cosmic vision is attained in the dream-like moments following sexual release. In "Song of Myself," for example, he describes a thinly veiled act of fellatio:

I mind how once we lay such a transparent summer morning,
How you settled your head athwart my hips and gently turned
    over upon me,
And parted the shirt from my bosom-bone, and plunged
    your tongue to my bare-stript heart,
and reach'd till you felt my beard, and reach'd till you held
    my feet.

A revelatory state of consciousness immediately ensues:

Swiftly arose and spread around me the peace and knowledge
    that pass all the argument of the earth;
And I know that the hand of God is the promise of my own,
And I know that the spirit of God is the brother of my own,
And that all the men ever born are also my brothers, and
    the women my sisters and lovers...

As the poet's consciousness continues to expand, it enfolds nature as well as humanity—"Absorbing all to myself and for this song." This desire for inclusiveness underlies Whitman's poetic style—in particular, his frequent listing and cataloging. For Whitman, as Martin observes, "The drive of one individual toward another is the first step toward a perception, in visionary terms, of one's union with the world. The move is always from the particular to the general, from love of one person to love of all."

Whitman's poem, "The Sleepers," relates a dream vision with all the characteristics of a shamanic spirit journey. The poet's consciousness leaves his body. Like the shaman who ascends to heaven, he views the world from the perspective of the sky god. Passing through the night, he witnesses the full spectrum of humanity, from its greatest to its lowest. Here and there, he pauses to rest beside the sleeping figures or, like the spirits that shamans encounter, to have sex with them ("I roll myself upon you as upon a bed"). The poet's desire leads him not only to unite with others sexually, but to identify with them as well: "I dream in my dream all the dreams of the other dreamers, / And I become the other dreamers." This unitary consciousness erases the distinction between subject and object, the very basis of the modern, Western worldview. The result is an alternative view of reality in which the intuitive and empathic capacities typical of shamanism are given free play.

The love Whitman expresses, like Plato's heavenly love and Christian agape, is not possessive or acquisitive. In Whitman's poems, the lover does not seek some quality from the beloved that he lacks to complete his own psyche. Rather, in "The Sleepers" and other poems, the lover merges with the beloved—the "two become one," in

Aristophanes' words. In this psychic synthesis, both partners are transformed, their old personalities die, and new ones are born.

We saw how the ability to identify with others, human and supernatural, was the source of the shaman's powers. Whitman's all-encompassing consciousness is based on a similar capacity. This is what made it possible for him to project a vision based on his homosexual experiences that speaks to men and women regardless of their sexuality. Loving men, he could identify with men who loved women. Having received tenderness from men and having given it himself, he did not find it threatening to identify with women or imagine their sexual desires and pleasures.

Whitman discovered something else about his capacity to identify with others. It could have a healing effect. He came to this realization during the Civil War, when he lived in Washington, D.C. and visited sick and wounded soldiers in the numerous hospitals set up throughout the city. As he later wrote, "I have met very few persons who realize the importance of humoring the yearnings for love and friendship of these American young men, prostrated by sickness and wounds. To many of the wounded and sick, especially the youngsters, there is something in personal love, caresses, and the magnetic flood of sympathy and friendship, that does, in its way, more good than all the medicine in the world." In fact, Whitman believed his own "magnetism" could be literally transferred to others with a healing effect. In any case, the young soldiers, who lay sick and injured in unsanitary, overcrowded hospitals that were little more than death wards, responded to Whitman's care with childlike sweetness and affection.

These Civil War experiences were the source of Whitman's belief that all men had the capacity to express loving tenderness toward each other. At first, he did not have a name for this way of loving. In the 1855 version of "Song of Myself," he wrote that he could not tell "the pinings I have…the pulse of my nights and days." But in 1860, in the "Calamus" section of *Leaves of Grass*, he gave this "pulse" a name: "O adhesiveness! O pulse of my life!" Whitman borrowed the term "adhesiveness" from the popular pseudoscience of phrenology (the reading of bumps on the head). He gave it a completely new meaning, however, when he applied it to same-sex love and contrasted it to "amative," or heterosexual, love.

Whitman believed that adhesive love had a particular role to play in democratic society. As he declares in "Calamus":

Come, I will make the continent indissoluble,
I will make the most splendid race the sun ever shone upon,
I will make divine magnetic lands,
    With the love of comrades,
    With the life-long love of comrades.

Having witnessed the carnage of the Civil War, Whitman's concern was how a democratic society could overcome the centrifugal forces of geography, race, and ethnicity. In a society of equals, civic order and unity cannot be imposed from above by a hierarchical social order. Whitman, however, had seen how same-sex desire crossed lines of class and race, and how it could arise instantaneously, sometimes by eye contact alone. The fewer social differences between individuals, Whitman concluded, the more freely love could flow. And so he believed that if men's capacity for adhesive love was given free expression it could provide the glue to unite a diverse population. The result would be a society held together by love, instead of authority. As he wrote in his essay, "Democratic Vistas," "It is to the development, identification, and general prevalence of that fervid comradeship, (the adhesive love, at least rivaling the amative love hitherto possessing imaginative literature, if not going beyond it) that I look for the counterbalance and offset of our materialist and vulgar American democracy, and for the spiritualization thereof."

It is important to note that Whitman lived in a time when the word "homosexual" had not yet been invented. His readers did not automatically assume that passionate expressions of love between men signaled homosexuality. For Whitman, erotic love was merely a special case of passion between men. By the end of the nineteenth century, however, the new science of psychology had defined those who had same-sex relations as a distinct type of diseased and abnormal person. Society and individuals alike began to scrutinize all relationships between members of the same sex for signs of sexual motives.

Whitman was a visionary. Instead of practical plans for sexual liberation, he offered dream-visions, spiritual union, an all-inclusive consciousness. But his writings influenced individuals who did have practical plans for liberating homosexuals. One was the Englishman John Addington Symonds, who carried on a twenty-year correspondence with Whitman and wrote one of the first modern defenses of homosexuality. Another was Edward Carpenter, who described the impact of Whitman's writings as "working a revolution within me." Carpenter later compiled extensive cross-cultural and historical evidence to argue that homosexuality was neither abnormal nor pathological.

Vision and politics came together in the career of Harry Hay as well. Hay drew on years of experience as a political organizer in left and labor organizations when he helped found the early gay organization, the Mattachine Foundation, in 1950. He had also devoted years of research and reflection in order to come to an understanding of homosexuals as a minority group and not just a disparate collection of "sick heterosexuals." Hay credits his accidental discovery of a book by Edward Carpenter in his youth with giving him his first positive view of homosexuality. Like Carpenter, Hay became a lifelong socialist, drawn to spirituality and mysticism.

In 1971, as the early gay liberation movement was reaching its peak, Hay moved to northern New Mexico and spent the rest of the decade living among the Tewa Indians. While the gay movement around the country was becoming less radical and more accomodationist, Hay continued working within the vein of gay liberation ideas—speculating on gay sexuality and gay love in relation to critiques of capitalism and patriarchal gender roles. While he considered himself a Marxist thinker, his involvement in the 1960s counterculture and his years of contact with Native Americans fostered an appreciation for visions and ritual. These interests converged when he argued that gay people, like women and members of ethnic and racial minorities, had a particular consciousness or worldview.

In 1976, Hay wrote an essay arguing that egalitarian, same-sex relationships encouraged a mode of thinking he termed "subject-subject." This insight occurred to him one night when he was remembering his childhood dream of finding another boy like himself:

> Oh, I knew that all the other kids around me were thinking of girls as *sex objects*, to be manipulated—to be lied to in order to get them to "give in"—and to be otherwise treated with contempt (when the boys were together without them). And, strangely, the girls seemed to think of the boys as objects, too.... [But] in that long-ago fantasy, he whom I would reach out in love to was indeed projected as being another me—*and the one thing we would not be doing* was making objects of each other. Just as in my dream (which I would go on having for years), he'd be standing just before dawn on a golden velvet hillside...he'd hold out his hand for me to catch hold of, and then we would run away to the top of the hill to see the sunrise, and we would never have to come back again because we would now have each other. We would share everything, and we'd always understand each other completely and forever!

In pinpointing the root cause of social problems—from sexism and racism to the destruction of the environment—in the underlying worldview of Western society, Hay was not alone. During the same period, feminists were pointing out how, in the Western worldview, only men who fulfilled patriarchal roles were considered full human beings, subjects with inalienable rights, while others who were not male or not Western were less than fully human and classified, along with the natural world itself, as objects, not subjects. Hay termed this Western mode of thought "subject-object" consciousness. In subject-object consciousness, not only are the thoughts, feelings, and experiences of those defined as "other" discounted, they are often not even recognized as existing.

In subject-subject consciousness, however, the other who is equal and the same is seen as a subject just as one sees oneself. Since one knows oneself, one instantly knows the other who is the same. No effort is necessary to establish empathy—it is always-already present. When this outlook is extended to all humans and to the natural world, the result is a truly different view of reality. For Hay, subject-subject consciousness is equivalent to a visionary or altered state of mind, much like the all-inclusive consciousness Whitman describes.

In this regard, Hay went beyond most gay liberationists. He viewed same-sex love as not only having distinct social traits; he recognized it as having a spiritual dimension as well. Unlike Whitman, however, who only talks about types of love, not people, Hay believed same-sex love is characteristic of a distinct group in society. Both views are still being debated. It could be argued, for example, that if adhesive love really is a capacity all men have, then the cause of gay liberation is relevant to all men. On the other hand, who will lead the way in developing this capacity? And in challenging society's homophobia, who will go first? For Hay, individuals who actively express and seek out same-sex love are different from those for whom adhesive love is a latent capacity.

Whitman, Carpenter, and Hay were not alone among those pioneers of gay liberation who were deeply influenced by their encounter with the queer heritage of Western spirituality. The social circumstances of modern homosexuals and gender-different people is such that a personal quest for meaning is inevitable. Not surprisingly, issues of spirituality and religion have arisen throughout the short history of the "LGBT" movement. This will continue to be the case as long as society refuses to see us as part of history and acknowledge our contributions to the social fabric. Whitman, Carpenter, and Hay each represent different approaches to this quest. Whereas Whitman sought the meaning of his difference through self-examination and personal experience, discovering adhesive love by singing the "song of myself," Hay and Carpenter turned to the study of other cultures and other times to find the spiritual dimension of same-sex love. These paths— experience and memory—are not exclusive, however. Ultimately, all three men based their thinking on personal experiences of love and mysticism.

Jesus and the Shamanic Tradition of Same-Sex Love

In 1979, I attended a retreat where Hay passionately presented his ideas concerning subject-subject consciousness and called on us as gay men to foster it. At that event I discovered I was not alone in yearning to incorporate a spiritual outlook into my life. For many of us, a spiritual inclination began in childhood with a fantasy life that included talking to trees and animals, and inventing rituals. As we shared these experiences at the 1979 retreat, we realized that gay spirituality begins with reclaiming the child-like awareness we had before the crippling and stifling influence of homopobia penetrated our lives. Whitman had a similar intuition and frequently celebrated boyhood. In "There Was a Child Went Forth," he describes the child's awareness in terms that resonate with Hay's concept of subject-subject:

> There was a child went forth every day,
> And the first object he look'd upon, that object he became,
> And that object became part of him.

But in 1979 adhesive love and subject-subject consciousness were ideals, not realities. In those years, it was difficult to see anything redeeming in the way that gay men were pursuing love. The activist, experimental era of gay liberation was over. A grassroots movement of volunteer and self-help organizations was being replaced by agencies staffed with professionals. Gay marches had become gay parades, and gay social life was shifting from public and community-organized events to commercial venues.

Discussions of gay love gave way to a narrower focus on sexuality. Self-identified sex radicals claimed that simply having gay sex challenged the social system, while moderates claimed that sex was the only thing that distinguished lesbians, gay men, and bisexuals from heterosexuals, and since it was a private act, it was an invisible difference. In either case, sex had become the lynchpin of gay identity. To be gay or bisexual was to have sex. At the same time, many gays, lesbians, and bisexuals were rejecting the idea advanced by earlier liberationists that they might be gender-different. The assimilationist mantra took its place: "We're no different from heterosexuals except for what we do in bed."

In the 1970s, to live up to their image as sexual athletes, gay men began using drugs and alcohol at rates far in excess of the general population. Our sexual experiences became increasingly intense, but they occurred in contexts that attributed them with no particular significance. Gay men began referring to sex as "play"—it became a form of recreation, to be consumed much as entertainment or travel or fashion. Far from posing a challenge to the social order, it turned out that a sexual minority community whose identity was derived from what it consumed was perfectly compatible with postindustrial capitalism.

All this occurred as an organized antigay opposition was emerging. In 1977, Anita Bryant's campaign in Dade County, Florida overturned legislation to protect gays from discrimination. Soon gay civil-rights protections were being repealed throughout the country. Heterosexual Americans were not ready to see gay lifestyles or relationships as equal to theirs in any way, nor were they willing to entertain the possibility that gays were different in ways that might be beneficial. Indeed, gays themselves increasingly rejected such speculations as elitist, throwbacks to a discredited model of homosexuality as inborn and essential. Lesbian and gay intellectuals, under the influence of Michel Foucault and the theory of social constructionism, not only decried the idea of queer differences; the very desire to explore the meaning of one's sexual identity was dismissed out-of-hand.

In 1982, at the same time I was reading *Clement of Alexandria*, I decided to write an essay expressing my dismay at the role of sexual objectification in the gay men's community. Instead of healing the wounds inflicted on us by a homophobic society, we were perpetuating low self-esteem. And the consequences of this, I argued, could be seen in a growing range of health problems appearing among gay men — from alcoholism to sexually transmitted diseases to recent reports of a new and mysterious illness that was taking gay men's lives.

My essay, titled "Desperate Living" (after a popular John Waters' film), was published about the same time that I put down Smith's book. Our extended stay with Harry and his partner John in Los Angeles was over. Brad and I were still young, in our twenties, and life flowed in strong currents. We found ourselves back in San Francisco, immersed in new jobs and new projects.

Fifteen years passed before I took up Smith's book again. It was 1997, and I had been invited to speak at Gay Spirit Visions, an annual conference held outside Atlanta, Georgia. The theme was mentoring. As I thought about this topic, it occurred to me that gay men needed not only mentors — teachers, guides, role models — but also some form of initiatory experience to mark their passage from the closet to community and from gay childhood to gay adulthood.

Then I remembered the mystical rite of initiation uncovered by Morton Smith. As I began rereading his book, I saw connections that had escaped me before. I realized how Jesus' secret baptism drew on ideas and images with a long history, and how it was that same-sex love could be part of — indeed, give rise to — visionary experiences. I realized as well that the insights I was having now were the result of what I had experienced in the fifteen years since I last picked up Smith's book.

Jesus and the Shamanic Tradition of Same-Sex Love

Those were the years when the AIDS epidemic swept through our lives like wildfire, whisking away acquaintances, friends, and lovers — and, eventually, my own life partner.

THE GREATEST LOVE

The epidemic unfolded as a series of horrifying realizations. In 1982, only two hundred gay men had been diagnosed with what came to be known as Acquired Immune Deficiency Syndrome (AIDS). Even that number was alarming, but we were still hopeful. Perhaps the outbreak was limited, and the disease was not transmissible. After all, those who were getting sick seemed to be gay men leading fast lives — and if it were a matter of fast living, well, we could change that. Then it became clear that an infectious agent was involved. So we hoped that it was not easily transmitted. But it was. Then we hoped that the virus had been discovered before many of us had been infected. But HIV's long incubation period and government inaction had ensured that hundreds of thousands of gay men were already infected. So then, desperately, we hoped that infection did not always result in illness, and that illness did not always lead to death.

Ultimately, all these hopes were dashed.

By the mid-1980s, all we could hope for was that oneself and one's friends were somehow not among those infected. But nearly fifty percent of gay men in San Francisco were already HIV-positive. In the end, no one in my generation, which include those who had launched gay liberation and created many of the institutions that lesbian, gay, bisexual, and transgendered people take for granted today, escaped the gruesome touch of HIV.

So it was that Brad came home from the neighborhood health clinic one day and announced that he was HIV-positive. ("Well, my attitude is positive, too," he joked.) At that time, patients lived an average of eighteen months from the time of their initial diagnosis. Brad lived nine years — a blessing, but a mixed one, for they were years stalked by crises and fear of crises. He died in June 1996 — too late to benefit from the new treatments introduced later that year, which have so dramatically altered the face of the epidemic (at least in the northern hemisphere).

At the height of the epidemic, a diagnosis of AIDS was considered a death sentence. As such, it was an immediate catastrophe. Many, like Brad, had no health insurance, and so the very first challenge was to find some means of getting around insurance policies that denied coverage to people with preexisting conditions. Or one could dispose of all savings and property, as Brad eventually did, to qualify for Medicare. Then one had to find a doctor familiar with treating HIV who would accept a new patient. To get adequate care, one had to learn about

160

complicated and experimental treatments and wrestle with doctors, hospitals, and HMOs to obtain them. These health-care providers were often unfamiliar with and unsympathetic toward gay men; their bureaucratic requirements Kafkaesque. All this had to be dealt with, even as one lay wasting in a hospital bed.

As members of a stigmatized population, gay men are rejected not only by the larger community but often by their own families as well. Very little of the care provided to the AIDS patients I knew came from family members. And the care they needed was extensive, both in the hospital and when they returned home, often prematurely discharged under the regimens of HMO cost-cutting. This happened twice to Brad, who had to be readmitted after emergency room visits in the middle of the night. And the admitting process! What worse agony than to be desperately ill, vomiting, wracked with fever from some unknown infection—but no matter, one still had to wait in line, fill out endless, repetitive forms, explain one's symptoms again and again. The hours I spent sitting with friends in emergency and admitting rooms as they waited in agony for care remain, for me, the most disturbing memories of the epidemic.

Brad and so many others suffered this and more. And our role, those who were not sick (or not yet sick), was to witness it helplessly, as the ones we loved agonized toward death. Until finally, exasperated with unresponsive doctors and fearful of overworked nurses, we often moved into the hospital with our loved ones, and spent the nights in the chair next to their beds, offering cool water and bits of food, changing linens, pressing the call button one more time.

"I don't want to be a burden," Dennis, my hometown friend, said, crying softly as he perched on the edge of his bed during his first hospital stay. But terminal patients *are* burdensome; it can't be helped. In the end, they require twenty-four-hour care. In extreme pain, fearful, suffering from dementia, they are not always cooperative or pleasant, either. And young men in their prime do not die easily. AIDS patients lingered for weeks, even months. Time and again I saw the spirit yield before the body, and fear of the hospital and its treatments conquer fear of death. For Brad and me, that moment came after a sleepless night in the sixth week of his last hospitalization, when he tearfully said, "Let's go home."

But as the crisis deepened, something happened that I would not have predicted earlier. That abstraction called the "gay community" actually began to function as such, as a collective of people who identified with and cared for each other. As one gay man after another was diagnosed, friends came forward to help. Others volunteered and helped strangers. The gay community bridged the chasm between an inadequate health-care system and the breakdown of the American

161

family (not the breakdown conservatives blame on gays, but the real breakdown represented by distant families too fearful of AIDS and too riven with homophobia to offer support to their own kin).

As gay men became ill, friends took over their care. They organized themselves into what they called support groups and circles. They held meetings and divided up responsibilities. They assigned themselves shifts and took turns providing care, around-the-clock if needed. They cooked and cleaned, they shopped and took their friends to countless medical appointments. They became advocates for their treatment, monitoring and coordinating the care provided by doctors, nurses, hospitals, and other agencies. They did research, they filled out forms, they made phone calls. They found lawyers to prepare wills, agencies to deliver food, and nurses to provide in-home care. When the family arrived on the scene—often unprepared to deal with their sons' homosexuality, let alone their imminent deaths—they took them in hand, answered their questions about their sons' lifestyle and about AIDS, and helped them process their loss. Above all, they showed the families of the victims something they may have doubted: that their homosexual sons were loved.

And they did more. They made it possible for the dying to chose the time and manner of their death. They created peaceful and beautiful environments for their passing. And when death had finished its work, they invented original and moving ways to honor their friends' lives, from private ceremonies to public expressions of grief such as the AIDS Quilt. Friends did all this, even as they fretfully monitored their own HIV status.

In two decades of the epidemic, I have witnessed many different responses to the crisis and many human dramas. Not everyone rose to the occasion. Sometimes those who had been closest vanished from the lives of those stricken. And sometimes those who had been distant moved to the center. When my friend Dennis developed dementia and was unable to care for himself, a high-school friend he had not seen for some years took an unpaid leave of absence from his job in Seattle to fly to San Francisco and spend two weeks providing Dennis with day-to-day care while he marshaled the services Dennis needed.

In the end, the most awful point of the epidemic for me was not when I waited for Brad to take one more breath and he didn't. With his friends and family gathered around, all I could say was, "Thank God it's over." A much worse moment came two weeks later, after the simple memorial we held for him in Golden Gate Park. As the last friend was leaving, I suddenly realized how truly alone I was. It was as if the war had ended, the battlefield had been cleared, but I was still sitting in my foxhole with my buddy's brains splattered all over me, wondering why him instead of me. I don't know how I would have survived that night if our friend, Sam, had not offered to stay with me. We weren't especially close, but that night, and the next day when he took me into the sunshine for San Francisco's annual Gay Pride Day celebration, he was the best friend in the world.

A few days later, I received a phone call from Brad's nursing service. I was eligible to join a ten-week support group for gay men who had lost their partners to AIDS. Ten sessions hardly seemed enough to repair a decade of losses, but I was willing to try anything that might help me feel better.

It was a profound experience. I was not alone. Of course, I knew intellectually that others shared my experience. But to sit in a room of seven men and hear their stories—my story, my pain—conveyed something much more than a comforting platitude. I wasn't the only gay man who made the commitment to stand by his lover through his illness—and found that commitment stretch out over years. I was humbled by the sacrifices these men had made. Each had spent months caring for their bedridden lovers, even as they struggled to meet job and other responsibilities. Several had dealt with much more frightening situations than I had—worse illnesses, worse doctors and hospitals, hostile relatives, longer death watches. And yet, when one man said that he would have been willing to provide that care forever, if only his lover could have lived, everyone in the group echoed his sentiment. We had all been devastated by the loss of something the larger world hardly recognizes—the love one man can feel for another.

Relatives and families are expected to aid each other in crisis. Acts of love are urged upon them by social and legal conventions. What should we call it, then, when unrelated people make voluntary commitments to each other that society neither recognizes nor accepts, and fulfill those commitments through unimaginable trials? What should we call the sacrifices of friends who helped friends in the AIDS epidemic? Isn't this what Jesus meant by the highest love—laying down one's life for one's friends? Friendship, as Andrew Sullivan has observed, may be the greatest legacy of the plague years.

Of course, nongay friends and family members were also among those who helped. I remember how another of Dennis' high-school friends, Helen, suddenly arrived at the open ward where he spent his last two weeks. She brought her eleven-year-old daughter, Celeste, who joined us standing in a circle holding hands with Dennis as he took his last tortured breath. When Celeste returned to Montana, she took it upon herself to educate her class about AIDS and what it means to lose a friend.

My observation, however, is that the support groups that nongay friends and relatives joined arose out of the realities of gay men's lives and values. After all, what brought the members of these circles together was a gay man who loved them. Further, these gay men loved others, whether in sexual or nonsexual relationships, as equals, as multidimensional individuals like themselves, same-to-same, subject-to-subject. When nongay friends and relatives joined these circles of caretakers, they learned how to love this way, too.

Here is where the arbitrary definition of lesbians and gay men in terms of sexuality, a holdover of the psychiatric/medical model of homosexuality, does everyone a disservice. It blinds gay people to traits, values, and experiences they may share that are not sexual in nature, and it blinds society to the contributions sexual minorities can make because of their difference. Gay men's friendships are often just as distinctive as their sexual relationships. Passionate and intense, physically intimate without being sexual, and emotionally complex, they are typically based on shared interests and emotional openness — and are often both turbulent and tenacious as a result. Gay men spend hours on the phone with their friends talking about their ideas and feelings. They sleep over at each other's houses; they travel together; they might live together as roommates but entertain and socialize like a couple. Or they might have started as a couple and ended up as friends. A study by Kath Weston found that the ex-lovers of gay men and lesbians are much more likely to remain close friends than is typical for divorced heterosexuals.

The psychologist C. J. Jung also noted this capacity:

> Since a "mother-complex" [in Jungian theory, the "cause" of male homosexuality] is a concept borrowed from psychopathology, it is always associated with the idea of injury and illness. But if we take the concept out of its narrow psychopathological setting and give it a wider connotation, we can see that it has positive effects as well. Thus a man with a mother-complex may have a finely differentiated Eros instead of, or in addition to, homosexuality.... This gives him a great capacity for friendship, which often creates ties of astonishing tenderness between men and may even rescue friendship between the sexes from the limbo of the impossible. He may have good taste and an aesthetic sense which are fostered by the presence of a feminine streak. Then he may be supremely gifted as a teacher because of his almost feminine insight and tact. He is likely to have a feeling for history, and to be conservative in the best sense and cherish the values of the past. Often he is endowed with a wealth of religious feelings, which help to bring the *ecclesia spiritualis* into reality; and a

spiritual receptivity which makes him responsive to revelation.

In the midst of the unfolding horror of AIDS, gay men demonstrated the capacity for passionate love that Socrates and Aristophanes describe in the *Symposium*. They laid down their lives for each other as Jesus challenged his disciples to do. They created new families in the process, and this has had an impact on society at large, as Whitman once dreamed adhesive love might have. I have seen gay love heal, if not the body, then the spirit of those tormented by disease and those devastated by grief. The social and spiritual potentials of same-sex love ennobled in writings from Plato to Whitman are a living heritage.

This story of queer shamanism and same-sex love culminates here—for now—with a disaster of historic proportions and the response of one community. The epidemic saw not just lone individuals like Walt Whitman on a shamanic journey through the hospital corridors of the Civil War, not just a small band of disciples inspired by a charismatic leader, but countless gay men and their friends, fulfilling the highest ideals of love by caring for each other when society as a whole would not. The challenge to this community now is to remember this painful history in order to claim its emotional, moral, and spiritual legacy.

It was the epidemic that enabled me to see the real significance of the Secret Gospel of Mark. Love between equals and sames—agape, subject-subject love—is heaven on earth.

The philosophy of love that emerges from Whitman's poetry is not only critical of hierarchical social relations, it pinpoints their origins in patriarchal masculinity. Whitman believed, in Robert Martin's words, that "love between men implicitly challenges traditional Western ideas of male superiority and of male hardness and female softness.... To call oneself the 'tenderest lover' is to accept one's femininity or, more accurately, to challenge all social prescriptions of behavior according to gender. Whitman's ideal is nonactive, nonproductive; his joy is in companionship, in being, not doing."

In Classical Greece, the patriarchal nature of sexuality meant that those who were sexually penetrated (whether women, men, or boys) were inferior and subordinate to those who did the penetrating. For this reason, Plato had to separate sex from love to imagine reciprocal and egalitarian same-sex relationships—and so began Western civilization's misguided dichotomy of flesh and spirit, body and mind. Whitman, however, could imagine two men being sexually receptive and affectionate with each other without either being inferior or subordinate. In "Democratic Vistas," he describes adhesiveness as "manly friendship, fond and loving, pure and sweet, strong and life-long," and claims that such love will make the American character "unprecedently emotional, muscular, heroic, and refined."

Whitman was well ahead of his time. Until the 1960s, most homosexual men saw themselves in gendered terms. They were "female men," "intermediate types," a kind of androgyne, and the partners they were seeking were "real men," technically not homosexual because they were "masculine." For a variety of reasons, this self-image changed dramatically in the 1960s and 1970s. Gay men began to define themselves as Whitman did: They were men, different from other men because they were nonpatriarchal, not because they wished to be women. Equally significant, they defined their ideal partner as other men like themselves. The masculine/feminine roles of an earlier generation were rejected. This created the basis for subject-subject relationships in Harry Hay's terms, for Whitman's adhesive love—love between sames and, by virtue of their sameness, equals.

As I argued in chapter 6, the images and motifs associated with same-sex love are typically those of twins and twinning. Aristophanes uses this imagery in the *Symposium* when he describes how the two halves of originally doubled beings seek to reunite. Whitman evokes this imagery as well, when he declares in "Calamus": "Lover and perfect equal!" and in his essay, "Democratic Vistas," he writes, "I say democracy infers such loving comradeship, as its most inevitable twin or counterpart, without which it will be incomplete, in vain, and incapable of perpetuating itself (240)."

In contrast, the archetype underlying queer shamanism and roles like that of the Chukchi soft man is the Androgyne, a figure who mediates, juxtaposes, or blends in some way male and female. Androgyne imagery and themes continue to play an important role in the imaginary life of gay men today. Indeed, Whitman himself, in his ability to identify with the sexuality of women, can be viewed as androgynous, but Whitman's androgyny was based on a capacity for empathy that he experienced in relationships with others who were the same sex as he, his psychic twins.

Of course, archetypes, as Jung theorized, are symbolic representations of psychic energies, and as such can convert from one form to another—twinning leads to androgyny, androgyny to same-sex love. Historically speaking, one could say that the archetype of Divine Twins arises from a synthesis of shamanic androgyny and Mediterranean traditions of age-based homosexuality. Both archetypal patterns foster a suspension of social hierarchies and differences—the Androgyne by merging gender differences, the Twins by transcending them through their sameness. When this happens, when under the influence of either of these archetypes, individuals shed social and gender differences, they approach the state of the spirit world itself—a cosmic dance of pure, formless energy.

THE DESCENT OF HEAVEN

In Whitman's poem, "The Sleepers," the narrator attains a vision of essential beauty after witnessing the diversity of humanity. "I swear they are all beautiful," he declares, "Every one that sleeps is beautiful, every thing in the dim light is beautiful." In the next stanza, he goes on to echo Plato's theory of the soul, but with an important difference. For Whitman, the soul was not imprisoned in the body, and its characteristic movement was not escape from material form and ascent to heaven. Rather, Whitman describes the soul as descending from heaven at the moment of conception and delighting in its attainment of physical form:

> The myth of heaven indicates the soul,
> The soul is always beautiful, it appears more or it appears less,
>   it comes or it lags behind,
> It comes from its embower'd garden and looks pleasantly on itself
>   and encloses the world,
> Perfect and clean the genitals previously jetting, and perfect and
>   clean the womb cohering,

The head well-grown proportion'd and plumb, and the bowels
and joints proportion'd and plumb.
The soul is always beautiful,
The universe is duly in order, every thing is in its place...

For Plato, self-perfection could be achieved through philosophy and divine madness, and desire could be purged of possessiveness and transformed into spiritual love. Early Christians also believed in self-perfection, but by renouncing the body and sexuality altogether. Whitman, in contrast, believed that self-perfection lay in removing the guilt and shame surrounding the body, so that fulfilling sexual desires becomes redeeming rather than demeaning. In "The Sleepers," the soul, the essence of beauty, delights in acquiring material form and no longer yearns to escape it. We do not need to ascend to enter heaven. Heaven will come to us. Or rather, we can find it within ourselves.

With Whitman, this psychomythic pattern comes full circle—from the early myths of the ancient Near East in which heaven and earth are incongruous, to the dream of ascending to heaven pursued by mystics, to the descent and humanizing of God in Christianity, to, finally, the fulfillment of humanity's potential for divinity in this life, on this earth, a possibility revealed in the light cast by the exemplar of same-sex love.

A final word is in order. Although this story began in the mode of historical narrative, it has become increasingly personal as it has continued, which is to say more and more centered in my own experiences, those of a gay man of a certain generation, living in a specific place, having a particular experience of a calamity that has affected many others, often in other ways. Nonetheless, I maintain that my story speaks to all gay men and all those different in terms of sexuality and gender. And I unapologetically suggest that heterosexuals can learn from it, and from the experiences of gay men in general. I do so in all humility, not because I believe homosexuality is more special than heterosexuality, but simply because that, in being different, it offers other possibilities. Learning about these possibilities represents an opportunity for everyone to become more whole, more aware, more able to find a bit of heaven on earth.

As I argued in the Preface, the intense love and mutual identification that can arise between sames and equals is a function of the sociological features of such relationships, not any essential traits that only certain people have. Plato, Jesus, and Whitman all believed that the particular kind of love they advocated could be learned by everyone, that if same-sex lovers sometimes exemplified it they had no monopoly on it. What this means is that as society becomes more egalitarian and personal relationships become more equal, then spiritual eros — agape, adhesive love, subject-subject consciousness — can be more widely expressed and experienced. For love, in the words of the Gospel of Philip, "never calls something its own.... It never says, 'This is yours' or 'This is mine,' but 'All these are yours.'"

Today one of the most powerful forces for social equality is the international women's movement. To the extent that women achieve equality with men and the differences between the sexes are no longer tied to differences in status and power, the dynamics of heterosexual relationships will be similar to those of same-sex relationships. If same-sex love is heaven on earth, this does not mean that everyone must be gay to enter heaven, nor that we must ascend to reach heaven. Rather, everyone might benefit from embracing the possibilities represented by same-sex love — equality, reciprocity, mutuality, identification.

Opposite-sex love has its own history and its own spiritual dimension. Jung's transpersonal psychology is substantially based on the idea that heterosexual union provides the model for psychic wholeness, which entails the integration of a repressed opposite-sex component in each of our psyches. Jung found that for men especially the encounter with their anima, or feminine psyche, could be a profoundly spiritual experience. One need only turn to Robert Graves' paean to the archetypal feminine in *The White Goddess* or Joseph Campbell's insights into sacred marriage in *The Hero with a Thousand Faces* to find examples of heterosexual men keenly attuned to the spiritual potentials of opposite-sex love.

Jung, however, and many other heterosexual thinkers, believed that the psychic dynamics of his theory of sexual intimacy were not, in fact, "heterosexual" but "human," common to all, even those whose "sacred marriage" was with the same sex. But the dynamics of union between sames and equals are distinct from those of heterosexuals — neither better nor worse, but different. Where the union with an opposite results in a more complete, self-realized individuality, the union of sames produces a completely new individual altogether. Psychologist Mitch Walker has described these dynamics as Magickal Twinning. "The action of Magickal Twinning," he writes, "is a kind of duplication where the spirit-essence of one object is infused into another, making spirit twins, yet where the two duplicates are bound together through their common spirit-essence into a third object, an indivisible unity."

Something similar is hinted at in Paul's references to the mystical meaning of baptism. "For if we have been united with him in a death like his, we will certainly be united with him in a resurrection like his. We know that our old self was crucified with him so that the body of sin might be destroyed." The conquest of the flesh was, of course, Paul's particular obsession, but the overall pattern is the same: through spiritual union, one's old self dies and another is born—humans become God, God becomes human—and "we walk in newness of life" (Rom. 6:4-6).

Whereas the archetype underlying opposite-sex love is that of marriage to a god, the archetype of same-sex love is that of union with a god. Through this union, mortals and gods trade places. Joseph Campbell's hero, in contrast, does not become a god as a result of his encounter with the goddess. Rather, he completes his development as a man and returns from his journey still mortal, albeit bearing gifts and talents for his community. But same-sex union with divinity dissolves boundaries of body and ego, erases masculinity and femininity, and effects a death and rebirth—lovers become shamans. This is why same-sex love is so often associated with initiatory archetypes.

In the end, in the lived world, these archetypes—sacred marriage and spiritual union—are never neatly distinct nor the essential traits of any particular person. They are part of a human psychological heritage and to some degree a component of all of our psyches, regardless of whether we primarily love the same or opposite sex or both. In the history of Western religion, where the supreme deity has for so long been male, union with divinity is, for men, necessarily a same-sex experience. That for some this encompasses sexual and romantic union should be no more surprising than traditions of sacred marriage to a goddess found in other, less male-dominated cultures.

And so I end this story expressing hope for a day when the immemorial patterns of same-sex love revealed in our times by the AIDS epidemic will be claimed by people of all genders and sexualities; when love, in all its forms, is valued for its spiritual and—there is no better word—magical as well as its social and sexual dimensions. For it is by loving that we become most like God and catch such glimpses of heaven as we are likely to attain in our mortal lives. Indeed, as I learned from those gone before me, love is all there really is time for.

In Whitman's words, "Love, love, love! That includes all. There is nothing in the world but that—nothing in the world at all. Better than all is love. Love is better than all."

Spell-Checking the Word of God

> *Sacred Scripture* is the speech of God as it is put down in
> writing under the breath of the Holy Spirit. (*Catechism of the
> Catholic Church* §81)

Although the various books comprising the Bible are understood by
Christians to be the word of God, no original manuscript of any biblical
text has survived to the present day, nor indeed any copy that is not
many copies removed from an original. The oldest known gospel
manuscript is represented by a tiny fragment of papyrus from the early
second century with parts of the Gospel of John (the Papyrus Rylands).
Following this is the Papyrus Bodmer II from somewhat later in the
second century, which contains an almost complete copy of John. Also
dated to the second century is the Egerton Papyrus, which appears to be
a noncanonical version of John. The earliest manuscript containing more
than one gospel (Luke and John) dates from the late second or early
third century. The Chester Beatty Biblical Papyri, from the third century,
includes the four gospels and other New Testament texts, but the oldest
complete Greek manuscript of the Bible, the Codex Sinaiticus (or Codex
Aleph), comes from the fourth century.

In any case, the bibles we use today are not translations of any of
these early manuscripts, many of which were not discovered until
modern times, but of later copies from the fourth and fifth centuries,
which are believed to better preserve the original texts. By comparing
these copies, modern scholars are able to identify variations, copying
errors, and extraneous material — referred to as "corruptions" — and
correct these to produce a synthesized version. The most authoritative
Greek Bible is the Greek New Testament published by United Bible
Societies. What it presents as the "original" text is the product of
consensus by an editorial committee based on all the available
variations. Alternate wordings are graded from "A" for "virtually
certain" (that is, authentic) to "D" for "high degree of doubt." In some
cases, the committee considered none of the versions original and
selected the "least unsatisfactory reading."

The Greek New Testament records thousands of variants, which is
not surprising considering over five thousand handwritten Greek
manuscripts have survived. Scholars have been able to reconstruct the
genealogy of most of these texts, identifying which copies they are
copies of, and grouping them into several distinct types based on where
their originals were made. Thus, biblical manuscripts are referred to as
being of an Alexandrian, Caesarean, Antiochan (or Syriac), Western (or

171

Roman), or Byzantine type, with Antioch being where New Testament manuscripts were first, in the words of one scholar, "polished stylistically, edited ecclesiastically, and expanded devotionally." When Constantinople emerged as the center of Greek-speaking Christendom in the fourth century, the Byzantine type began to replace the others. Today, however, scholars believe that the Western type is closest to the original New Testament manuscripts.

The Authorized or King James Version of the Bible (first published in 1611) is based on the Greek New Testament published by Erasmus in 1522. Unfortunately, Erasmus relied on manuscripts now known to be inferior, and as a result he produced, in the words of one scholar, a "debased form of the Greek Testament." Jerome's Latin translation of the Bible, known as the Vulgate, was based on a European Latin text that had been produced in the mid-fourth century based, in turn, on two earlier types of Greek texts. The most reliable surviving copy of Jerome's Vulgate, the official scripture of the Catholic church, was produced at a Benedictine monastery in England in 716. Over the centuries, however, the process of copying the Vulgate introduced so many corruptions that the Catholic Church has twice issued revised versions — in the late sixteenth century and again in the twentieth century.

In sum, the furthest back scholars can trace New Testament manuscripts is to a time when distinct variants existed. The differences between these variants are usually minor, but some are significant. Certain manuscripts of Mark, for example, end abruptly at chapter 16, verse 8, while others include an additional twelve verses. The "word of God" as we know it is not a little the product of scholarly guesswork and faith in the reliability of copyists in an era before digitization and spell-checking.

Even if an original manuscript of a New Testament text were found today, publishing it in its original language would still require choosing between alternate readings where the handwriting, punctuation, spelling or grammar are not clear — ambiguities certain to arise given the way ancient manuscripts were written, in a style known as uncial or majuscule, which uses all capital letters and runs words together without punctuation. This often results in phrases equivalent to "GODISNOWHERE," which could be read "God is now here" or "God is nowhere."

Translation, of course, introduces even more potential for misconstruing or altering original meaning. The words of one language chosen to translate those of another never correspond exactly but invariably carry connotations not present in the original language. Some nuances in one language simply can't be conveyed in others. Greek, for example, cannot convey the conceptual and linguistic nuances of Hebrew, while other languages fail to capture the richness and precision of Greek. Given that Jesus spoke Aramaic, and that his speech survives only in Greek translations, a conceptual and linguistic divide will always separate us from what he really said.

Yet, contradictions, ambiguities, and poor penmanship have not led the moralists to temper their assertions. In the words of a popular bumper sticker, "God spoke it, the Bible says it, I believe it"; or, to quote a TV evangelist, "The Bible says what it means, and it means what it says." Yes—but only if we ignore the problematics of transmission, translation, and interpretation. As Morton Smith once observed, "Blessed are the pure in heart for they shall not see difficulties."

Some Christians, of course, acknowledge the role of interpretation in the reading of scripture, but then claim special access to God which makes their interpretations authoritative. Such is the position of the Catholic church as well as many religious cult leaders. Others, when confronted with discrepancies and ambiguities in biblical texts, retreat to another position: It is not the words of any specific manuscript or book of the Bible that Christians believe in, but the Word of God, a vague sum total of its general meaning. Then, finally, there is the position of liberal theologians, which admits that God's words have been subjected to an historical process, but one that God himself directed (thus, in effect, editing his own words).

Aside from the question of whether the word of God is truly represented by today's bibles, there is the question of which texts truly contain God's words and which do not. Jesus neither wrote gospels nor gave instructions regarding writings his followers should use. Christianity grew and spread for three centuries without agreement on the contents of the New Testament. Among the surviving manuscript fragments from the second and third century, both canonical and noncanonical works are equally represented.

It is fairly certain, for example, that none of the gospels were written by actual disciples of Jesus or by individuals who witnessed his ministry. The Gospel of Mark, the oldest book of the New Testament, is believed to have been written around 75 C.E.; Matthew and Luke in the early nineties. The Gospel of John was written even later, at the beginning of the second century. Textual analysis reveals that Luke and Matthew depend on Mark (but possibly two different versions) and on an earlier text known as "Q" (from the German *quellen*, or source), which has not survived.

In other words, the books comprising the New Testament are neither the original nor the oldest writings of Christianity. Rather, these were probably collections of sayings, teachings, and notable acts, of which Q is an example. Some may have been in Aramaic, the language Jesus spoke, others in Greek. John Crossan has recently pushed the

173

reconstruction of these original writings back even further by identifying material common to Q and the noncanonical Gospel of Thomas, which appears to represent an early tradition independent from the gospels. He calls this shared material the "Common Sayings Tradition" and argues that it circulated in the 30s and 40s C.E. The biographical narratives of Matthew and Luke, with their detailed accounts of Jesus' infancy and his resurrection, were constructed much later, perhaps from oral traditions.

In sum, the writing of the New Testament was not complete until sometime after 100 C.E. Agreement on the scriptural status of these texts and their compilation into an anthology with a fixed order took two more centuries to coalesce.

Among the second generation of Christian authors, the so-called Apostolic Fathers, who were active between 95 and 130 C.E., some knew one or more gospels and collections of Paul's letters, but none of them knew all the gospels, and only Papias (70-160 C.E.) was familiar with the Gospel of Mark. Many drew on oral traditions and texts that have not survived. None of them considered these writings to be "scripture" — that term was reserved for the books of the Hebrew Bible. Some in this period considered Paul's letters the only authority for Christianity; others deemed Paul a heretic and rejected all his writings. This state of affairs continued up to Clement's time in the late second century, with different Christian authorities relying on different gospels and different versions of the same gospels. A synthesis of all four gospels, the *Diatesseron*, became popular in Syria, but in the fifth century it was suppressed and copies systematically destroyed.

The first Christians to treat writings now part of the New Testament as scripture and to define a canon were the Gnostics Basilides of Alexandria and Marcion of Rome in the early second century. In response, orthodox church leaders began creating their own lists of approved writings. The first authority to explicitly declare certain books as scriptural was Irenaeus, who, around 185 C.E., named the four gospels and those alone. It was not until 327 C.E. that Athanasius of Alexandria issued a listing that included all twenty-seven books of the present New Testament, and even this list did not reach its final form until the sixth century.

When the Synod of Hippo bestowed its blessing on Athanasius' list in 393, it was merely acknowledging a consensus, not creating one. But it took centuries for this consensus to develop, and during that period, in various times and places, many writings were suppressed, not only by Christians seeking to impose orthodoxy, but by Romans seeking to suppress Christianity altogether, especially during the Great Persecution of the early fourth century during the reign of the Emperor Diocletian. In the end, God's word, as Burton Mack observes, was the product of "a fiercely fought cultural conquest."

Sex and Spirit in Corinth

Soon after Paul left the Greek city of Corinth where he had spent a year and a half missionizing in the mid-50s, he received a letter from his congregants seeking guidance on several troublesome issues. Competing leaders had emerged, each claiming to have spiritual powers and attracting their own following. Dissension had reached the point that church members were suing each other in court. Paul's response, in the First Letter to the Corinthians, offers a revealing glimpse into the social dynamics of early Christianity. It turns out that many of the issues that perplex Christians today—in particular, sexuality and the status of women—were present at its origins.

At the beginning of his letter, Paul adopts a paternalistic tone, addressing the Corinthians as his brothers and sisters and professing to come to them with "love in a spirit of gentleness," rather than "with a stick" (1 Cor. 4:21). He admonishes them not to quarrel among themselves or "boast about human leaders," for to do so is to remain "of the flesh" and behave "according to human inclinations" (1 Cor. 3:2; 3:21). Then he abruptly switches to the subject of sex. "It is actually reported that there is sexual immorality among you," he writes. Apparently, a church member was having sex with his stepmother. Worse, this was not an isolated incident. Some congregants were even "boasting" about such misdeeds (1 Cor. 5:6).

The Greek word translated here as "sexual immorality" is *porneia*. In Classical Greece, *porneia* and its derivatives referred to commercial sex—*pornē* was a prostitute, *porneion* a brothel, *porneuō* "to prostitute," *pornophilas* "loving prostitutes," and so forth. By Paul's time, the term had acquired a more general meaning, referring to "illicit" or "unlawful" sexual acts in general—"law" in this context being social custom. Traditionally, *porneia* has been translated into English as "fornication" (and *pornos* as "fornicator"), which, in Christian usage, refers broadly to all forms of extramarital sex. In conveying the sense of prohibited acts, however, "fornication" is actually a better translation of *porneia* than "sexual immorality."

Paul's comments on *porneia* indicate that the Corinthian church was winning converts from some socially marginal groups. In chapter 6, verses 9-11, he lists, "fornicators [*pornoi*], idolaters, adulterers, male prostitutes [*malakoi*], sodomites [*arsenokoitai*], thieves, the greedy, drunkards, revilers, robbers—none of these will inherit the kingdom of God. *And this is what some of you used to be.* But you were washed, you were sanctified, you were justified in the name of the Lord Jesus Christ and in the Spirit of our God" (my emphasis; the last verse alludes to baptism).

Here again the English translation leaves something to be desired. The word *malakoi*, derived from *malakos*, or "soft," was widely applied in the ancient world to any man seen as less than upstanding or respectable. Any number of behaviors might cause a man to be labeled *malakos*, ranging from profligacy to masturbation to effeminacy (which did not necessarily imply homosexuality). The philosopher Philo, for example, referred to men who remarried their divorced wives as *malakos* (*Special Laws*, 3.30-31). Likewise, *arsenokoitai* literally translated means "men of the marriage bed" and may refer to male prostitutes, although we cannot be certain because there are so few occurrences of it outside of the two in the New Testament—in 1 Corinthians and 1 Timothy.

Neither of these terms has the same meaning as the modern word "homosexual," which identifies a much broader category of individuals in terms of same-sex preference. In fact, recent studies have shown that there was no social or linguistic category in Greek, Roman, or Semitic cultures that corresponds to the modern notion of homosexual persons. In any case, Paul does not single out "men of the marriage bed" as more or less sinful than fornicators, adulterers, idolators, drunks, or thieves. Nor can his denunciation of male prostitutes be taken as a general condemnation of all same-sex relations, unless we also take his denunciation of adultery as a condemnation of heterosexuality. We cannot even be certain if Paul was condemning *arsenokoitai* for homosexuality or for prostitution.

Clearly, Paul's mission drew not a few outcasts. This should come as no surprise, however, given that Jesus himself trafficked with such people—"very unattractive characters" in the words of one scholar—including victims of disfiguring diseases and mental illness; eunuchs, a category in ancient times that included not only men unable to have sex with women but those lacking the desire to do so; men who, like the one carrying a water jar who leads the apostles to the location of the last supper, do women's work (Mark 14:12); and even prostitutes, if that indeed was the profession of the "woman of the city, who was a sinner," who washes Jesus' feet with her tears and anoints him with oil (Luke 7:37). Of course, Jesus himself transgressed social roles, no more strikingly than in John, when he places himself in the position of a servant and performs the preeminently female task of washing his followers' feet. The movement Jesus launched seems to have had the character of a "rescue mission"—an outreach to the alienated and outcast offering hope and a means of personal transformation, a kind of ancient twelve-step program.

Paul's letter to the Corinthians suggests that some of these reformed sinners were falling off the wagon. Worse, they were justifying their lapses by citing his own teachings, which included the assertion "all things are lawful for me" (1 Cor. 6:12, 10:23). Paul had Jewish dietary and religious laws in mind, but some Corinthians were interpreting this maxim to include not only "unlawful" foods but *porneai*, unlawful acts.

Were these deviations the result of thought-out libertine and Gnostic interpretations of Paul's theology? Paul thinks the Corinthians simply misunderstood his teachings on baptism, secret knowledge, and freedom from the law, and so he reiterates these at the beginning of his letter. The Corinthians are interpreting his doctrines in "human" terms, using their new-found spiritual knowledge for human purposes. But they are still "infants," still of the flesh (literally "fleshly"). They have interpreted spiritual (that is, metaphorical) teachings in worldly (literal) terms (1 Cor. 2:13-3:3).

Paul goes on to address several questions posed by the Corinthians concerning sexual behavior. That sexuality would be a source of contention in early Christian congregations was inevitable considering that the movement attracted both Jewish and gentile converts whose sexual ethics differed in several ways. Thus, some Corinthians were advocating sexual freedom; others, celibacy. There were vexing questions as well regarding divorce, marriage to non-Christians, circumcision, slavery, and eating food that had been offered to idols (which is to say, eating with pagans).

On all these issues, Paul splits the difference. Why belabor matters that were soon to be rendered moot by the return of Christ? So he instructs the Corinthians that if one cannot practice "self-control" as he does, "better to marry than to burn"; that women should not divorce, but if they do, they should not remarry; that the uncircumcised should remain so, while the circumcised should not hide it; that virgins should remain chaste, and those who are married stay so; and that converts who are slaves should accept their lot in life (1 Cor. 7:27).

Yet other problems were related to the forms of worship practiced at Corinth. It seems that in their enthusiasm for *pneumatikos*, or "spiritual things," the Corinthians were getting out of control. It is difficult for us today to appreciate the role of *pneuma*, or "spirit," in early Christianity. Services in Paul time did not follow the kind of orderly proceedings typical of today's churches. Worshipers prayed for the "spirit" to descend upon them, and when it did entire congregations were possessed, spirits speaking and acting through them. Paul lists several kinds of spiritual gifts, or *kharismata*, sought after by his followers. They include: utterance of wisdom (*sophia*), utterance of knowledge (*gnōsis*), faith, gifts of healing, working of miracles, prophecy (which he defines as discernment of spirits—that is, distinguishing "good" from "bad" spirits), speaking in tongues, and interpretation of tongues (1 Cor. 12). Of these, Paul valued most of all speaking in tongues, which he claims to have had "more than all of you" (1 Cor. 14:18). This phenomenon, known as glossolalia, has been widely documented in both Western and non-Western settings. In the context of emotional and dramatic proceedings, individuals lose consciousness and begin uttering streams of a seemingly alien language. Closer analysis reveals these utterances to be mostly gibberish. Related to glossolalia is what Paul calls "prophesizing," trance-state speech in intelligible language but of a cryptic nature, thus requiring interpretation by others. At Corinth, these practices were creating a variety of problems. With the entire congregation babbling in tongues, no one had the slightest idea what anyone was saying. Paul feared that outsiders would consider Christians insane (1 Cor. 14:23). He advises the Corinthians to cultivate "the power to interpret" tongues and prophesy.

Yet another problem had to do with communion meals. Apparently the Corinthians were using these services as occasions to drink and gorge themselves (1 Cor. 11:21). They should eat at home, Paul advises, so that they can await the arrival of all church members and conduct the service in a seemly manner. "So, my friends," he concludes, "be eager to prophesy, and do not forbid speaking in tongues; but all things should be done decently and in order" (1 Cor. 14:39-40).

Before this long discussion of spiritual gifts, however, the very first form of "disorderliness" that Paul addresses has to do with the role of women. Women appear to have been prominent members of the Corinthian church. Paul refers to them as praying and prophesizing, that is, exercising *kharismata* (1 Cor. 11:5). Indeed, some of these women seem to have been claiming social equality with their Christian brothers by appearing in public with their heads uncovered. Since this was a male style, one scholar has characterized the Corinthian women as engaging in transvestism. Again, these problems appear to be a result of Paul's own teachings. As he tells the Corinthians, "Nevertheless, in the Lord woman is not independent of man or man independent of woman" (1 Cor. 11:11), an echo of the formula in Galatians: "There is no longer male and female; for all of you are one in Christ Jesus" (3:28). Such a slogan could certainly be interpreted as authorizing sexual equality.

Paul, however, insists that women remain subordinate to men. Just as God is the head of Christ, he reasons, Christ is the head of every man, and husbands are the heads of their wives. Hence, women should wear veils in church, as a "symbol of authority" and "because of the angels" (1 Cor. 11:10; probably a reference to Genesis, chapter 6, where angels succumb to the charms of mortal women). Paul ends, rather lamely, by appealing to "nature itself": Since nature provides women with long hair, it must be meant to cover their heads! Later, in the same letter, Paul prohibits women from even speaking in church (14:33-35)—which suggests that, in fact, they were—although some scholars believe these verses were inserted by a conservative follower of Paul.

Sometime after writing the First Letter to the Corinthians, Paul returned to that city. Now he found himself confronting not only wayward members of his own church but competing Christian missionaries as well. Consequently, the tone of the Second Letter to the Corinthians is very different from the first, as he mounts a formidable polemic against his competitors.

These missionaries, he writes, proclaim "another Jesus" and "another gospel," and they receive "a different spirit" (2 Cor. 11:4). Paul concedes that they are better speakers than he and that they even have spiritual powers equal to or greater than his. They also have better authority than Paul. They bear letters of recommendation and call themselves "apostles" and "ministers" *from* Christ (2 Cor. 3:2; 11:13; 11:23). They also claim to be "Hebrews" and "descendants of Abraham," that is, Jews from Palestine—perhaps a rival mission from the Jerusalem church. In response, Paul asserts his own Jewish background and claims, "I am not the least inferior to these super-apostles," as he sarcastically calls them, and, as proof, he relates his experience of being "caught up to the third heaven" and receiving "exceptional" revelations—his vision on the road to Damascus (2 Cor. 12:2).

If these super-apostles are the same opponents mentioned in other letters by Paul, then they probably represent the "circumcision party"— Jewish Christians who still observed Jewish laws. At the same time, like Gnostics and Hekhalot mystics, they exalted the powers of angels, which they sought to gain control over, and they made visionary ascents to heaven. If they were indeed ministers "from Christ," they may have known Jesus personally, something Paul could not claim.

Because Paul deals with sexual issues in both Corinthian letters, scholars have assumed that these opponents were also promoting libertine practices. However, the super-apostles are not mentioned in the First Letter to the Corinthians, and Paul's comments there on sexual immorality are addressed to his Corinthian followers, not outsiders. In his Second Letter to the Corinthians, he makes the statement at the beginning, "We have renounced the shameful things that one hides" (2 Cor. 4:2), but nothing indicates that this refers to the super-apostles. Later, *after* he concludes his polemic against the super-apostles, he proposes to visit the Corinthians a third time, but he fears that he will find quarreling, jealousy, anger, and so forth among them—the problems of the First Letter—and that those who had sinned had yet to repent "of the impurity [*akatharsia*], sexual immorality [*porneia*], and licentiousness [*aselgeia*] that they have practiced" (2 Cor. 12:21)—again, the issues of the First Letter.

In sum, the transgressions that Paul deals with in his letters to the Corinthians took two forms: libertinism, on the one hand, reflected in the prominence of women, the practice of sexual freedom, and orgiastic communion meals (*agapai* or "love-feasts"), and, on the other hand, experiments with Gnosticism, including the pursuit of secret knowledge and contact with angels. The libertine development appears to be based on the Corinthians' interpretation of Paul's own teachings. Neither tendency is yet part of a fully articulated, competing belief system, the form Gnosticism would take by the second century, and while there are competing leaders within the Corinthian church, dissension has not led to schism. Christianity in Paul's time encompassed diverse views and people—Jews and gentiles, slaves and their owners, women and men, and those who engaged in same-sex relations as well as those who were heterosexual.

Compared to Paul's mission, the nature of Jesus' ministry is harder to ascertain. Gospel accounts of his teachings on Jewish laws are contradictory. Some scholars believe that references to Jesus "eating and drinking" with sinners and his comments on freedom from the law are Pauline insertions, while the original movement was a form of zealous Judaism. Others argue that libertine and Gnostic tendencies originated with Jesus but were subjected to Judaization by James and others after his death. Yet another possibility is that the "Hebrews" and "Hellenists" mentioned in Acts and Paul's letters were different parties within Jewish Christianity, reflecting a preexisting division between rigorous and lax approaches to Jewish law. The more conservative party, the "Hebrews," appear to be the source of the mystical and Gnostic tendencies in early Christianity.

As an alternative, Morton Smith suggested that Christianity had aspects of both an esoteric sect and a popular movement from its beginning. Thus, conflicting gospel accounts of how Jesus taught are due to the fact that he had two sets of teachings—one secret (as Mark portrays it), for his followers only, and one public (as Matthew would have it). The secret teachings were mystical and libertine, while Jesus' public pronouncements were more cautious. Under James, the Jerusalem church appealed to these public teachings and gained control of the movement. At that point, the libertine tradition went underground.

Libertine groups appear to have been widespread at an early date. Already they are attacked in Matthew, Mark, Luke, Acts, and other New Testament texts. According to the Letter to the Ephesians, "It is shameful even to mention what such people do secretly" (5:12). In 2 Peter and Jude, those who think Christian liberty is an opportunity for carnal indulgence are called false prophets. They will be punished, like the cities of Sodom and Gomorrah. Indeed, the libertinism of some early

Christian sects went so far as to include homosexuality (at least, outsiders believed so).

Whatever the origin of the mystical and Gnostic tendencies in early Christianity, they were well-represented until the end of the second century. Indeed, the orthodox party within Christianity may have been in the minority up until that time. When it did gain ascendancy in the third century, it suppressed its competitors and destroyed their writings, canonizing only those texts that supported its views of church doctrine and history.

The current consensus among New Testament scholars emphasizes the Jewishness of Jesus. While acknowledging that he was a magical healer, exorcist, and miracle worker, scholars now question whether he truly rejected the Law of Moses as some gospel passages suggest and as Paul certainly did. Morton Smith, however, argued that the libertine branch of early Christianity was too well-developed and widespread to have been based on misunderstandings of Paul's teachings. Rather, it originated with Jesus himself and the secret baptism. As for Paul, while his mission to the gentiles placed him at odds with the Jerusalem church, he had been raised as a Pharisaic Jew and studied under a rabbi. As Smith asks, would he have rejected Jewish law so vehemently if it was not an actual teaching of Jesus?

Hetero-androgyny in Early Christianity

Paul's statement in the Letter to the Galatians, "There is no longer Jew or Greek, there is no longer slave or free, there is no longer male and female, for all of you are one in Christ Jesus" (3:28), is probably a paraphrase from the liturgy of baptism as he knew it. One scholar has termed it the "baptismal reunification formula." Because its endorsement of social and sexual equality is more radical than what Paul says elsewhere, William Countryman suggests that it may be pre-Pauline, which is to say from the time of Jesus himself. Paul echoes the formula in First Letter to the Corinthians (12:13) and in Colossians (3:11).

The reunification formula had a long life. Variations of it can be found in several early Christian texts. According to logion 22 in the Gnostic Gospel of Thomas:

> Jesus saw infants being suckled. He said to His disciples,
> "These infants being suckled are like those who enter the Kingdom."
> They said to Him, "Shall we then, as children, enter the Kingdom?"
> Jesus said to them, "When you make the two one, and when you make the inside like the outside and the outside

> like the inside, and the above like the below, and when you make the male and the female one and the same, so that the male not be male nor the female female; and when you fashion eyes in place of an eye, and a hand in place of a hand, and a foot in place of a foot, and a likeness in place of a likeness; then will you enter the Kingdom."

The references to being like children and entering the kingdom of heaven, along with the reunification formula, are all baptismal motifs, as we have seen.

Paul's phrasing ("*is* no longer male and female") describes an end state, the outcome of being united with Christ during baptism. In the Gospel of Thomas, the phrasing ("when you *make* the male and the female one") makes explicit how this was achieved: by unifying male and female. Underlying this idea was the belief held by many early Christians that humanity's original state was androgynous, as symbolized by Adam before Eve was extracted from him. As an exemplar of a perfect and complete state of being, the androgynous Adam, in turn, prefigured Christ, who, as the Gospel of Philip declares, "came to repair the separation which was from the beginning and again unite the two" (70.13-14). This identification of Adam as the predecessor of Christ can be traced back to Paul. The Gospel of Thomas and other Gnostic texts frequently invoke androgynous imagery.

Although the reunification formula could be taken as an endorsement of sexual equality, both the formula and the androgynous imagery it inspired were linked to strong ascetic tendencies within early Christianity. Achieving spiritual androgyny was viewed as a way of surpassing sexual desire—if one was complete, there was no need to desire anything, and to be freed of desire was to escape the bonds of the material world and thereby gain entry to spiritual domains.

This antisexual bias is evident in the version of the formula found in a letter attributed to Clement of Rome from the early second century:

> For the Lord Himself, when asked by someone when His Kingdom would come, said: "When the two shall be one, and the outside as the inside, and the male with the female neither male nor female." Now, the "two are one" when we speak truth to each other, and there is one soul in two bodies without dissimulation. And "the outside as the inside" means this: the inside is the soul and the outside the body. Therefore, just as your body is visible, so let your soul be apparent in your good works. And "the male with the female neither male nor female" means that a brother seeing a sister has no thought of her as female, nor she of him as male. "If

you do this," He says, "the Kingdom of my Father shall come." (2 Clement 12.1-6)

Clement of Alexandria quotes a condensed version of this from the lost Gospel According to the Egyptians:

When Salome asked when what she had inquired about would be known, the Lord said: When you have trampled on the garment of shame and when the two become one and the male with the female (is) neither male nor female. (iii.92.2)

Salome was often cited as an authority by Gnostics. Disrobing and "treading on the garments of shame" was a procedure in baptism rites in Syria, Africa, and Spain in the second century. In these rites, the proselyte stood with outstretched arms (the posture of praying) on a piece of sackcloth, while the priest, dressed in white linen robes, pronounced an abjuration or exorcism of Satan.

Ultimately, Christian ideas about androgyny are heterosexist as well as antisexual. The idea that reuniting "the two" creates a completeness that neutralizes desire assumes that there are only two genders and only one sexuality, the attraction of opposites, male and female. In fact, early Christians (and others in the ancient world) viewed desire as intrinsically female. Consequently, men who felt too much desire, including desire for women, were feminized; they became *malakos*, or "soft." The essence of masculinity, on the other hand, was spiritual, based on men's superior self-control. Achieving androgynous wholeness, therefore, involved different things for men and women. To become more spiritual, Christian men sought to purge themselves of feminizing desire. Some (perhaps many judging from the numerous canon laws against it) resorted to self-castration. Women, on the other hand, became spiritual by becoming male. As the Gospel of Thomas recommends, "For every woman who will make herself male will enter the kingdom of heaven" (114). The First Apocalypse of James echoes this with the statement, "The perishable has gone up to the imperishable and the female element has attained to this male element" (41.15). Apparently, some early Christian women took this advice literally, judging from the legends of female martyrs and saints, such as Hilaria and Porphyria, who dressed and lived as men.

The Letter to the Ephesians illustrates how this heterosexist overlay was added to the baptismal reunification doctrine. The author, probably not Paul but one of his followers, describes how Christ loved the Church, washed it, hallowed it, and placed it beside him in glory, thus enthroning it (5:25ff). Each element of this formula corresponds to a procedure of the Secret Gospel rite—the initiate was anointed, blessed,

183

lifted to heaven, and enthroned. But the reunification formula is missing. Instead, Ephesians uses these baptismal motifs to provide heterosexual marriage advice. Men, the author says, should love their wives like Christ loved the Church, and as they love their own bodies. Since no man hates his own flesh, he who loves his wife therefore loves himself. What this is saying, in effect, is that for a man to treat a wife as an equal, he has to imagine that her flesh is male, like his own. No wonder this is referred to as a "great mystery"! Nonetheless, beneath the heterosexual window dressing the exemplar remains that of love between sames and equals. (Paul's letters are the only place in the New Testament where agape is used in reference to heterosexual relations. Jesus' expressions of love are nearly all directed toward male followers.)

Some early Christians, however, embraced spiritual androgyny without negating sexuality. In the Gospel of Philip quoted earlier, the differentiation of the sexes is considered the source of humanity's ills. The purpose of Christ's coming is to "repair the separation" represented by the division of Adam and Eve. This is achieved through a sacrament referred to as the Bridal Chamber, in which Christ effects a mystical union between individuals undergoing the rite and their angelic counterpart spirits. Having been "unified" in the rite, the individual is immune to malevolent male and female spirits who seek to "unite" with humans of the opposite sex. Just as wanton women and lecherous men refrain from soliciting married men and women, the gospel explains, these spirits avoid those who are already "married" to an angelic spirit. Thus, desire is not eliminated; rather, it is fulfilled through the Bridal Chamber rite. "Fear not the flesh nor love it," the gospel instructs. "If you fear it, it will gain mastery over you. If you love it, it will swallow and paralyze you" (66.4-5). Judging from reports by Hippolytus (*Refutation of All Heresies*, 5.7), Theodotus (21.3), and Irenaeus (*Against Heresies*, 1.21.3) both the Valentians and Naasenes practiced some form of the Bridal Chamber rite.

Paul on Gay Marriage

Union with Jesus, possession by a spirit, ascent to the heavens, liberation from the law—all these elements of Paul's teachings were compatible with libertine Gnosticism. The Carpocratians, for example, interpreted baptism as an experience of resurrection, after which normal social distinctions and social contracts were no longer relevant, much as Paul did. They differed from Paul only in their interpretation of the "freedom" baptism bestowed. For them, as for some of Paul's followers at Corinth, this included sexual freedom, "love-feasts," and perhaps homosexuality. When it came to sex, however, all Paul's instincts went in the opposite direction. "Freedom" meant freedom *from* sexual desire.

Paul's view of heterosexuality was no less dim than his view of homosexuality. As he told the Corinthians, "It is better to marry than to be aflame with passion" (1 Cor. 7:9). Holy matrimony, the litmus test of Christian morality in today's culture wars, was, for Paul, a stopgap for those too weak to forgo sex altogether. It could be argued, therefore, that a genuinely Pauline position on homosexuality would not distinguish it from heterosexual desire, but rather extend to those who "burned" for their own sex the same remedy he holds out to heterosexuals: If one cannot renounced sex altogether, then better gay marriage than gay promiscuity.

Paul's Ascent to the Garden

Paul's claim to have been "caught up to the third heaven" is intriguing not so much because of the assertion that he visited heaven. In that, as we have seen, he had plenty of company. What is interesting is that he refers to three heavens, not seven. In rabbinical literature, the number of heavens is almost always seven, although the *Midrash Tehillim* notes that some authorities count only three. Some versions of the Testament of Levi, from the second century B.C.E., identify three heavens, but this is probably a later revision to what was originally a seven-heaven model, perhaps by a Christian copyist seeking to conform the text to Paul's experience.

2 Enoch (also known as the Slavonic Enoch or the Book of the Secrets of Enoch), written in the late first century C.E., describes ten heavens. The third heaven is the home of the tree of life, "of ineffable goodness and fragrance." Here is where the Lord rests on his ascent to "paradise." According to the text, "Its root is in the garden at the earth's end. And paradise is between corruptibility and incorruptibility" (8.3-5). This description echoes a passage in 1 Enoch, which describes the tree of life standing out among a grove of trees encircling the throne of the Lord atop the highest of seven mountains. The tree is ineffably fragrant. The angel Michael tells Enoch that this is where the Holy Great One will sit when "He shall come down to visit the earth with goodness," and that the fruit of the fragrant tree will be given to the elect for food at the time of the judgment (25.3).

Another echo of Paul's three heavens occurs in the Apocalypse of Moses, which relates legends concerning Adam. Seven heavens are mentioned, but reference is also made to Adam being "borne aloft to his Maker," washed three times, and then lifted up by the archangel Michael "into Paradise unto the third heaven," where "linen clothes" are strewn over him (chapters 38-40).

Paul may have been aware of Mesopotamian models of the cosmos, which typically identified three heavens. Or perhaps he was singling out a motif from the Enoch literature—the third heaven, where the Lord will sit on his throne—because it was compatible with his own eschatology. At the same time, Paul shows familiarity with Hellenistic cosmology. In the First Letter to the Corinthians he writes of "heavenly bodies" and the "glory" of the sun, moon, and stars—the celestial spheres (15:40-41). The synthesis of Hellenistic and Jewish cosmology that we find in Paul and in other early Christian writings became the standard view of the universe in Europe and remained largely unchanged until the intellectual revolution sparked by Copernicus, Galileo, and Newton.

Uprising to Heaven

Behind the baroque accounts of heavenly ascent found in the Hekhalot literature, David J. Halperin sees the yearning of synagogue congregants for a more concrete and tangible God, a yearning that challenged rabbinic authority. The authors of these texts, Halperin suggests, were seeking "to bring a human element into the realm of the divine while at the same time keeping God himself pure and safe from this element." In fact, Halperin points out, the God of the Hekhalot texts is "shamelessly anthropomorphic." He has body parts, he engages in physical contact, he embraces a youth who appears beneath his throne "with a shining face," and he kisses those who enter his presence. As Halperin concludes, "Human nature has infiltrated heaven." This is the real significance of the Hekhalot literature. In these writings, ordinary Jews, through incantations, ritual gestures, and a visionary encounter with divinity, acquired knowledge that was normally the exclusive purview of the rabbis. They achieved the very thing that Isaiah denounced Nebuchadnezzar for boasting: "I will be like the most High."

Why Was Diotima a Woman?

Why does Socrates cite a woman as his authority for his pronouncements on love between men? David M. Halperin (not to be confused with David J. Halperin above) asks this question in an essay in *One Hundred Years of Homosexuality*. The answer, he argues, has to do with the kind of relationship that Plato wanted to idealize. In Classical Greece, creativity and reciprocity were qualities attributed to women and their sexuality. Women were believed to be reciprocal in the sense that they returned the desire, or eros, of the man with their own desire, called *antēros*. Boys, however, were not expected to experience pleasure when they had sex with men. As well, women's sexuality was seen as having a goal—procreation—whereas men's sexuality was oriented only toward particular objects.

Although some scholars have suggested that the low status of women in Greek society was such that readers at the time would have assumed what Diotima says is not to be taken seriously, this underestimates the role of women as oracles and priestesses in Greek religion — and for Socrates, the "way of love" was a religious experience.

This is why, Halperin suggests, Plato used a woman to articulate a philosophy in which male homosexual relationships are described as creative and reciprocal, and the aim of eros as the release of the lovers' creative energies. Such an outlandish claim sounded more credible coming from a woman. In this regard, Socrates used Diotima much like modern New Age advocates cite generic "Native American elders" to lend authority to their innovations.

For Plato, the model for sexual reciprocity was the give-and-take of dialogue. He often used sexual and reproductive imagery to describe the outcome of such exchanges — the birth of ideas. In *Phaedrus*, Socrates speaks of implanting speeches into souls as a kind of fertilization (276e-277a). In Harry Hay's terms, dialogue is subject-subject because it suspends social differences and serves to inspire insight and self-realization rather than impose them.

The Boy Who Became a God

In Greek mythology only one mortal was ever promoted to the ranks of the gods — the Phrygian shepherd Ganymede, borne aloft to Olympus by an impassioned Zeus in the guise of an eagle, where he became the cupbearer to the gods. Diotima evokes the imagery of Ganymede's ascent in the *Symposium*, and it appears in Greek art in depictions of a winged Eros embracing a youth and lifting him heavenward (see fig. 8).

Ancient accounts of Ganymede's ascent to heaven are all quite brief. Here is the story as told by the Roman poet Statius in the late first century:

> From here the Phrygian hunter [Ganymede] was swept away
>   on bronze wings.
> Rising up, Gargara [Mt. Ida] sinks below and Troy recedes,
> his friends stand sadly by, and in vain the noisy hounds tire
>   their voices
> baying at the cloudy sky and chasing after his shadow.
> Thereupon, pouring his flowing wine, he calls in order
> on all the gods of heaven.... (1.548-53)

The story of Ganymede may be a reflection of the male initiation rites held in ancient Crete, as described by Strabo:

They have a peculiar custom with respect to their attachments. They do not influence the objects of their love by persuasion, but have recourse to violent abduction [*harpagēi*]. The lover apprizes the friends of the youth, three or more days beforehand, of this intention to carry off the object of his affection. It is reckoned a most base act to conceal the youth, or not to permit him to walk about as usual, since it would be an acknowledgment that the youth was unworthy of such a lover. But if they are informed that the ravisher is equal or superior in rank, or other circumstances, to the youth, they pursue and oppose the former slightly, merely in conformity with the custom. They then willingly allow him to carry off the youth. If however he is an unworthy person, they take the youth from him. This show of resistance does not end, till the youth is received into the Andreium [the men's house] to which the ravisher belongs.

They do not regard as an object of affection a youth exceedingly handsome, but him who is distinguished for courage and modesty.

The lover makes the youth presents, and takes him away to whatever place he likes. The persons present at the abduction accompany them, and having passed two months in feasting, and in the chase, (for it is not permitted to detain the youth longer), they return to the city. The youth is dismissed with presents, which consist of a military dress, an ox, and a drinking cup; the last are prescribed by law, and besides these many other very costly gifts, so that the friends contribute each their share in order to diminish the expense.

The youth sacrifices the ox to Jupiter, and entertains at a feast those who came down with him from the mountains. He then declares concerning the intercourse with the lover, it took place with his consent or not, since the law allows him, if any violence is used in the abduction, to insist upon redress, and set him free from his engagement with the lover. But for the beautiful and high-born not to have lovers is disgraceful, since this neglect would be attributed to a bad disposition.

The *parastathentes*, for this is the name which they give to those youths who have been carried away, enjoy certain honours. They are permitted to wear the *stolē*, which distinguishes them from other persons, and which has been presented to them by their lovers; and not only at that time, but in mature age, they appear in a distinctive dress, by which each individual is recognised as *kleinos* [praised], for this name is given to the object of their attachment, and that of *philētōr* to the lover. (10.4.21)

The Greek word Strabo uses for the adbuction is the same term used by the poet Theognis in relating the capture of Ganymede by Zeus. It is also the word Paul uses to describe how he was "seized" or "caught up" into the third heaven. Plato, too, uses this language to describe the experience of falling in love.

The separation of the initiates from the larger community is a typical feature of rites of passage. (The practice of living in the mountains and hunting also shows up in the story of Apollo and his lover Hyacinthus.) Following this period of seclusion, the youth receives new clothes, a new name, and a new identity, corresponding to the reincorporation phase of initiation. Recent archaeology lends support to Strabo's account. According to Robert Koehl, a site in the mountains of Crete has yielded remains of animal bones and artifacts that suggest it may have been the location for the feasting Strabo describes. A drinking cup, one of the gifts given to initiates, was also found at the site, painted with a scene depicting just such an exchange of gifts between a man and a youth.

It is a matter of debate whether these practices were native to the Minoan civilization of Crete or were introduced by the Indo-European invaders, the so-called Dorians, who arrived between 1100-1000 B.C.E. Although it seems plausible that the idealized man-youth relationships in Plato's writings evolved from older initiatory practices, there is no direct connection between them. Homosexual relationships in Plato's time, although idealized, were pursued for personal and social, not religious, reasons.

Whatever his origins, the figure of Ganymede has served to symbolize same-sex love throughout the history of Western culture since the Greeks. (The word "catamite" used to identify the younger partner in a homosexual relationship comes from "Ganymede.") His story has been interpreted both erotically and spiritually. Plato gives the myth a spiritual reading in the *Phaedrus*, describing in lyrical language how "the fountain of that stream, which Zeus when he was in love with Ganymede named Desire, overflows upon the lover." But elsewhere Plato claims that the Cretans had invented the myth of Ganymede merely to justify their sexual preferences. Depictions of Ganymede ever since have alternated between the poles of the erotic and the spiritual.

The *Galli* and Their Kind

The identification of the Kouretes in Orphic myths with the Corybantes, patrons of the raucous rites described in Plato's writings, dates back at least to the sixth century B.C.E. Both cult groups were, in turn, equated with figures called Kaberoi. Karl Kerényi has characterized all these groups as "ghostlike phallic demons" in the retinue of the Great Mother goddess. But in Phrygia (central Turkey), where the mother goddess was called Kybele (rendered Cybele by the Romans), the figures who constituted her retinue, and who were often equated with the Kouretes-Corybantes-Kaberoi, were distinctly nonphallic. These were the *galli*. According to some ancient authorities, the mystery rites they led were founded by none other than Orpheus.

During the Hellenistic era, the worship of Kybele/Cybele spread throughout the Greco-Roman world. At some point, she acquired a companion god, Attis, a shepherd from Phrygia like Ganymede. Scholars typically refer to Attis as Cybele's lover or consort, but in fact only one version of his myth portrays him this way. In others, he has only a "chaste passion" for the goddess and is her devoted follower and priest—or he is the object of Cybele's love, which he does not reciprocate. In one version, he attempts to marry a nymph and Cybele, jealous and enraged, drives him mad, leading him to castrate himself. In some accounts he dies; in others he survives. The *galli*, as the priests of Cybele and Attis, presumably followed his example and castrated themselves as well.

The *galli* were the radical gender-benders of the ancient world. As St. Augustine wrote in the early 400s, "Even till yesterday, with dripping hair and painted faces, with flowing limbs and feminine walk, they passed through the streets and alleys of Carthage, exacting from merchants that by which they might shamefully live" (*City of God* 7.26). In Phrygia, they served as temple priests under a leader called "Attis." The Romans encountered *galli* during their military campaigns in Anatolia in 189 B.C.E., serving as intermediaries and ambassadors for their cities, even as they exhibited their characteristic ecstatic behavior (Livy 37.9.9).

Galli began appearing outside of Phrygia as early as the classical period. The Greeks called them *mētragyrtai*, "priests of the Mother." They begged for a living, but also served as missionaries for their goddess. A century before Plato (around 500 B.C.E.) a *mētragyrtēs* appeared in Athens and began initiating women into the mysteries of the Mother of the Gods. The patriarchal Athenian men saw this as a threat and threw the *mētragyrtēs* into a pit, killing him. A plague followed and an oracle bade the city to appease the murdered priest. So the Athenians built a shrine for the Mother of the Gods—the *Metrōon*—although it was actually used as a depository for the city's records.

In 204 B.C.E., the Romans officially adopted the worship of Cybele, building a temple for the Mother of the Gods on the Palatine hill. By the beginning of the Christian era, the worship of Cybele had spread to all levels of Roman society, and the *galli* were a frequent sight in cities and towns throughout the Empire. Traveling in troops, they performed spectacular rites and solicited donations. Apuleius provides a vivid — and undoubtedly exaggerated — account of them in his novel *The Golden Ass*. The narrator has been transformed into an ass and has been purchased by a troop of these priests:

> I saw them apparelled in divers colours, and hideously tricked out, having their faces ruddled with paint, and their eyes tricked out with grease, mitres on their heads, vestments coloured like saffron, surplices of silk and linen; and some wore white tunics painted with purple stripes that pointed every way like spears, girt with belts, and on their feet were yellow shoes; and they attired the goddess in silken robe, and put her upon my back. Then they went forth with their arms naked to their shoulders, bearing with them great swords and mighty axes, shouting and dancing like mad persons to the sound of the pipe.... We fortuned to come to a certain rich man's house, where at our first entry they began to howl all out of tune and hurl themselves hither and thither, as though they were mad. They made a thousand gests with their feet and their heads; they would bend down their necks and spin round so that their hair flew out in a circle; they would bite their own flesh; finally, every one took his twy-edged weapon and wounded his arms in divers places....so that you might see the ground to be wet and defiled with the womanish blood that issued out abundantly with the cutting of the swords and the blows of the scourge. (8.27-30)

Apuleius goes on to relate how the dancers entered trances and uttered prophecies. Later he describes a salacious scene in which *galli* perform oral sex on a "lusty young man."

In ancient times, the *galli* were equated with the Kouretes and Corybantes because all three groups performed a dance with swords. The poet Lucretius describes the appearance of the *galli* in religious processions in Rome in the mid-first century B.C.E.:

> Palms pound the parchment drumhead, rounded brasses
> ring, and the horn makes hoarse, hair-raising howls,
> while rhythmic Phrygian flutes drive men insane....
> Here men at arms perform a weapon-dance
> shouting with joy at the blood, and in a frenzy
> convulsively shaking their fearsome, feathered caps.
> [a trademark of the Corybantes] (2.618-31)

As Arthur Darby Nock noted, the Corybantes, Kouretes, and related figures are all concerned in one way or another with deliverance. Like the pantheon of saints in Catholicism, they represent less remote figures than the gods on Olympus, and they could be beseeched to intercede with them. The performances of the *galli* may have been intended to have an effect similar to the Corybantic rites Plato describes — the production of catharsis among participants and bystanders — "as if they had received medicinal treatment and taken a purge," in Aristotle's words (*Politics* 8.7.5-6).

Christianity and Paganism: Conflict and Synthesis

In late antiquity, the worship of Cybele and Attis was one of Christianity's chief sources of competition. It is not surprising, therefore, that Christian authors were venomous in denouncing the goddess and her priests. Around 340 C.E., Firmicus Maternus wrote:

> In their very temples can be seen deplorable mockery before a moaning crowd, men taking the part of women, revealing with boastful ostentation this ignominy of impure and unchaste bodies. They broadcast their crimes and confess with superlative delight the stain of their polluted bodies. (*De errore profanarum religionum* 4.2)

The cult of Attis had begun competing directly with Christianity with the introduction of a rite called the *hilaria* in the mid-third century. This annual, springtime festival celebrated Attis's rebirth and incorporated themes of death, salvation, and resurrection quite similar to those of Christianity. In fact, the *hilaria* was often held at the same time that Christians observed Easter, leading to street battles between the two groups in some cities.

The relationship between the religion of Jesus and that of Cybele resulted in more than just antagonism, however. Evidence suggests that the two religions influenced each other, as well. In the mid-second century, for example, Montanism, the so-called Phrygian heresy, arose in the traditional homeland of Cybele. Its leaders included two female prophets, Maximilla and Priscilla, one of whom had visions of Christ as a woman. According to Epiphanius, the sect ordained women as priests. Both Montanism and the cult of Attis featured sacramental meals, blood offerings, and baptisms.

The Roman bishop Hippolytus, writing in the first half of the third century, described at length the cult of the Naasenes in which Christianity and Attis worship appear to have been thoroughly merged. According to Hippolytus, the Naasenes:

...constantly attend the mysteries called those of the "Great Mother," supposing especially that they behold by means of the ceremonies performed there the entire mystery. For these having nothing more than the ceremonies that are performed there, except that they are not emasculated: they merely complete the work of the emasculated. For with the utmost severity and vigilance they enjoin (on their votaries) to abstain, as if they were emasculated, from intercourse with a woman. The rest, however, of the proceeding (observed in these mysteries), as we have declared at some length, (they follow) just as (if they were) emasculated persons. (5.9.74-81)

This revealing passage provides evidence not only of contact between the cult of Attis and Christianity, but precisely how this contact occurred.

In many respects, Attis worship was the pagan cult most like Christianity. The key difference was that in Christian mythology Jesus is sacrificed and then revived through the agency of a father god, while Attis' transubstantiation is effected by a mother goddess. Even so, the ascetic practices of the *galli*, which included not only emasculation but blood-letting and self-flagellation, were not unrelated to the forms of self-abnegation practiced by some Christians. Indeed, for men of a certain disposition, both religions may have had equal and similar appeal.

Consider the statement attributed to Jesus in Matthew: "For there are eunuchs who have been so from birth, and there are eunuchs who have been made eunuchs by others, and there are eunuchs who have made themselves eunuchs for the sake of the kingdom of heaven. Let anyone accept this who can" (19:12). The phrase "kingdom of heaven" links this passage to mystical ascents and the Secret Gospel. Indeed, self-castration would be a practical if crude means of achieving what the Gospel of Thomas recommends as a means for entering heaven: making "the male and the female one and the same, so that the male not be male nor the female female" (22). Hetero-androgyny, asceticism, and sexual transformation all lead to similar ends—becoming spiritual by shedding gender and sexual desire and thereby entering the kingdom of heaven.

Basilides, a Gnostic Christian in Alexandria sometime between 125 and 150, gave Matthew 19:12 a suggestive interpretation. Jesus, he argued, was referring to three types of male celibates: those with a natural revulsion to women; those who practice asceticism out of a desire for glory from their peers; and those who remain unmarried to better do the work of the kingdom (quoted in Clement of Alexandria, *Miscellanies* 3.1.1-4). Basilides' first category would include individuals who are not necessarily castrated but are classified as eunuchs because they lack heterosexual desire—or preferred same-sex relations.

Long after pagan temples throughout the Mediterranean stood in ruins (the last observance of the rites of Cybele and Attis in Rome occurred in 394), Church authorities found it necessary to pass canon laws against the practice of self-castration. This appears to have been a particular problem in the very areas where eunuch priesthoods originated—ancient Turkey and Syria.

In Syria, uneven conversion resulted in a long period of pagan and Christian coexistence. It was also home to some of the most ascetical versions of Christianity to arise. The sanctuary of Dea Syria (the Syrian Goddess) in Hierapolis existed up to 384, and the semipagan tendencies found in the writings of the Christian Bardaisanes (154-222 C.E.) continued as late as 579. In Bardaisanes there are signs of an attempt to adapt Atargatis, another name for the Dea Syria, to Christianity. To this evidence might be added the exposition on the sexual exploits of eunuchs and their misdeeds in Christian circles by Basil of Ancyra—a picture reminiscent of Apuleius' account of *galli* in *The Golden Ass*.

In the early fifth century, Bishop Rabbula of Edessa finally destroyed the pagan shrines in that Syrian city, but at the end of the fifth century pagan spring festivals were still being observed. And long after the temples of the Mother of the Gods stood in ruins, Christian councils were still issuing edicts against self-castration. As late as Islamic times, the Sabians, members of a semipagan cult in the northern Syrian city of Harran, were reputed to "make themselves eunuchs for the sake of the kingdom of heaven."

Saint Twin-Twin

Given the imagery of twinning that has been a recurring theme in this book, early traditions of Jesus having a twin brother are intriguing. In the Gospel of John, the disciple Thomas is referred to as "Thomas called Didymus." "Didymus" means "twin" in Greek, as does "Thomas" in Aramaic, so that his name literally means "Twin-Twin." (Robert Eisenman links him to other figures in various writings called Thomas, Judas Thomas, Judas, Theudas, Thaddaeus, Judas of James, and "Judas the brother of James.")

Saint "Twin-Twin" appears in all the gospels, but only the Gospel of John relates details about him. According to John, Thomas offers to accompany Jesus on the potentially dangerous journey to Bethany, undertaken at the news of Lazarus's illness. Later, during the last supper, Thomas interrupts Jesus to ask him to clarify his instructions to the disciples. He appears a third time in the famous "doubting Thomas" episode, when he refuses to believe reports of Jesus' resurrection. His doubts are resolved when he touches the scars of Jesus' crucifixion and declares, "My Lord and my God!" In his fourth appearance in John, Thomas is present at the Sea of Galilee during a postresurrection appearance of Jesus.

Traditions concerning the apostle Thomas had a long history in Syria. The apocryphal Gospel of Thomas is credited to "Judas Thomas the Twin." Thomas was also believed to have traveled to India. According to a late legend, he was Jesus' twin, born shortly after him. They grew up together, alike outwardly in every respect, but while Thomas was human, Jesus was divine. The story appears to draw on myths about the Dioscuri, the twin sons of Zeus, who were also culture bearers; in astrology they are represented by the constellation Gemini. The Christian heretic, Mani, who founded the movement known as Manicheism which spread throughout the Near East in the third century, claimed to have had a twin self in the heavens, who descended to unite with him and convey revelations — again we see the intimate connection between the twin archetype and mystical union with spirits or gods.

In fact, one early compendium of Gnostic writings known as the Pistis Sophia, roughly belonging to the third century, credits Jesus with performing something quite similar. In words attributed to Mary:

> When thou wast small, before the Spirit came upon thee, while thou was in a vineyard with Joseph, the Spirit came forth from the height,…he came to me into my house, he resembled thee. And I did not recognize him and I thought that he was thou. And the spirit said to me: "Where is Jesus, my brother, that I may meet him?"

Afraid that the spirit was "a phantom to tempt me," Mary grabs it and ties it to the leg of her bed (!), and goes to get Joseph and Jesus from the field. When they all return, she and Joseph observe Jesus and the Spirit together.

> And we looked at thee with him, we found thee like him. And he that was bound to the bed was released, he embraced thee, he kissed thee. And thou also, thou didst kiss him and you became one. (1.61.11)

Here, in language that recalls Aristophanes' account of lovers who desire "to be made one out of two," the connection of the Twin archetype and the mystical tradition of same-sex love becomes apparent. Union with the same sex is ultimately a union with oneself — a purified, perfect self — a spirit twin. Further, in the absence of difference, love is instantaneous, unrestrained, and, most importantly, unconditional.

The twin archetype survived in Christian tradition in the figures of Saints Cosmas and Damian. Twin brothers from Syria, they were reputed to be great healers, especially knowledgeable in the use of plants and herbs, who refused payment for their services. They were martyred during the reign of the Emperor Diocletian (284-305 C.E.). Their cult eventually spread throughout the Mediterranean, replacing in some cases worship of the Dioscuri. Believers slept in churches and sanctuaries devoted to them to receive healing dreams. As late as the eighteenth century, Saints Cosmas and Damian were honored in remote Italian towns on their feast day with votive wax offerings in the shape of phalluses, a remnant of pre-Christian fertility magic.

Repression and Revival in Siberia

Repression of native Siberian religion and its alternative gender roles began under the tsars and continued unabated through the Soviet regime. Indeed, the Marxist-Leninist view of shamanism hardly differed from that of tsarist officials and Orthodox Christian missionaries. Shamans were charlatans who foisted superstitious beliefs on their followers. As a result, shamans and their ceremonies were forced underground. Gender-different shamans were singled out for persecution. According to Marjorie Balzer, "Transformed men and women were doubly reviled in the Soviet period, just as they were doubly powerful before intense Russian contact. In the 1920s and 1930s, they were persecuted as both shamans and sexual deviants."

Held in secret, some shamanic ceremonies survived. With the dissolution of the Soviet empire at the end of the 1980s, a revival of native traditions began. In her 1996 article, "Shamans, Bear Festivals, and Androgyny," Balzer reports:

> When I was in the Khanty region in 1976, people were very secretive about the continued existence of bear ceremonies [a rite performed throughout Siberia featuring gender role reversals and sexual mimicry], claiming they had been nearly eliminated or homogenized (made less sexy) by the Soviets. But when I returned in 1991, I learned of the emergence from underground, and the resurgence of both the seven-year periodic ceremony and the more impromptu bear festivals. Some of the more publicized festivals were sponsored by the newly formed Association for the Salvation of the Ugrian People. Several of the leaders in the revival movement were women, and several women had become hunters.... In the many hours of videotaped bear ceremony that I studied,

from a festival held in winter 1991 in the sacred Khanty village of Iuilsk, it was clear that both the spirit of raucous play and pious belief were still wedded in sacred revelry.

Balzer concludes:

The possibility certainly remains for a reemergence of transformed shamans, given the renewed interest through Siberia in all forms of spiritual healing....Among the postmodern, post-Soviet Sakha [Yakut], many of the most talented artists, musicians, poets, and actors are those who are exploring themes of gender tensions and ambiguity. Some are people who are not afraid to be slightly effeminate males and masculine females. In 1992, I was given a recently made drum embellished with old Sakha motifs: a dancing shaman wore female dress, through which was a clearly drawn penis. In the *fin-de*-Soviet 1990s, the Sakha and other Siberians are looking to their spiritual past for the cultural future.

Jesus the Shaman/Plato the Magician

And when Jesus had been baptized, just as he came up from the water, suddenly the heavens were opened to him and he saw the Spirit of God descending like a dove and alighting on him. And a voice from heaven said, "This is my Son, the Beloved, with whom I am well pleased."

Then Jesus was led up by the Spirit into the wilderness to be tempted by the devil. (Matt. 3:16-4:1)

Many characteristics of Jesus' career are similar to that of a shaman. His ministry starts with a spiritual crisis. Voices instruct him to enter the wilderness where he is attacked by demons. Surviving this trial, he returns to his community with powers of healing and prophecy and the ability to control spirits. His subsequent suffering, death, and resurrection are all typical patterns of shamanic initiation. Like a shaman, Jesus backed up his claims with convincing demonstrations of his powers. In the Gospel of Thomas and other early Christian writings, he is credited with preaching the negation of gender — spiritual androgyny — another common element of shamanism.

As Eliade notes:

Shamans are persons who stand out in their respective

societies by virtue of characteristics that, in the societies of modern Europe, represent the signs of a vocation or at least of a religious crisis. They are separated from the rest of the community by the intensity of their own religious experience. In other words, it would be more correct to class shamanism among the mysticisms than with what is commonly called a religion. We shall find shamanism within a considerable number of religions, for shamanism always remains an ecstatic technique at the disposal of a particular elite and represents, as it were, the mysticism of the particular religion.

Of course, Jesus was a philosopher, a teacher, and the founder of a social and religious movement as well as a spiritual adept. He could not have had direct contact with any form of tribal shamanism, but he was a mystic in Eliade's terms, and the religion he inaugurated generated and transmitted shamanic ideas and practices to the spiritual heritage of Western civilization.

Recent scholarship has given us a different view of Plato as well. As Peter Kingsley shows, Pythagoreanism and Orphism were both rooted in magic—the kind of ideas and practices found in the Greek magical papyri. The reputed founders of both schools, Orpheus and Pythagoras, were credited with magical powers and with instituting rites that employed magical techniques. Even the theories they developed, such as Empedocles' account of the forces of Love and Strife, relied on ideas typical of magic.

In the past, scholars have downplayed the role of magic in Pythagoreanism and derided neoplatonism for "degenerating" into such practices. Kingsley, however, argues that when the neoplatonists drew on magical ideas and practices they were, in fact, returning to the wellsprings of Western philosophy. This being the case, we need to adjust our image of the founder of Western philosophy. To the extent that Plato was influenced by Pythagoreanism and Orphism—and the consensus of classical scholars is that he drew extensively from both traditions—then he was influenced by magic. Indeed, at least two Platos emerge from his dialogues, as represented by Socrates: the rational, sober, authoritarian Plato of the *Republic*, and the ecstatic initiate into the mysteries of love that we find in the *Symposium* and *Phaedrus*; the moralist who advocates moderation in all things and the philosopher-shaman who seeks to unite with the spirit of his beloved and ascend to heaven.

Say What?

> Basing itself on Sacred Scripture, which presents homosexual acts as acts of grave depravity, tradition has always declared that "homosexual acts are intrinsically disordered." They are contrary to the natural law. They close the sexual act to the gift of life. They do not proceed from a genuine affective and sexual complementarity. Under no circumstances can they be approved. (*Catechism of the Catholic Church* §2357)

It would seem hard to argue that the Bible does *not* condemn homosexuality, but, in fact, a closer look reveals that its attitude is not nearly as clear-cut as today's churches would have it. As pointed out earlier, there are no Hebrew or Greek words that have a meaning equivalent to "homosexual" or "homosexuality." What this means practically is that any connection between what the Bible says and those who call themselves "gay" today is a matter of interpretation.

Let's take a closer look at the passage from the Catholic catechism quoted above. It fairly represents the position of most Christian denominations today. The first thing to note is that while it begins by mentioning scripture it quickly turns to nonscriptural authority, citing something called "natural law" (not to be confused with the actual natural world, where homosexual behavior and pair bonding are widely documented) and then proceeds to make assertions without citing any authority at all: that love for the same sex is not love (it is not "affective") and that it is to be condemned because it is not based on "complementarity"—which amounts to saying that homosexuality should be condemned because it is not heterosexuality.

As authoritative as all this sounds, it rests on a house of cards. Its superstructure (nonbiblical concepts such as "natural law" and "sexual complementarity") is flimsy enough, but its foundation, the biblical authority it is based on, is even weaker. Specifically, the catechism cites Genesis 19:1-29 (the story of Sodom) and three verses from the letters of Paul (Rom. 1:24-27; 1 Cor. 6:10; and 1 Tim. 1:10).

The first observation to be made about these citations is that none come from the foundational texts of Christianity, the gospels. The fact is, there is almost nothing in the statements and teachings attributed to Jesus that can be construed as a comment on homosexuality. In Matthew, in response to a question from the Pharisees, Jesus endorses heterosexual marriage, quoting Genesis that God "made them male and female," but he does not say that everyone must marry or be heterosexual (19:3-12). In fact, he goes on to endorse chastity, as represented by three categories of "eunuchs"—those who were born so, those who were castrated by others, and those "who have made

199

themselves eunuchs for the sake of the kingdom of heaven."

An exception to Jesus' silence on homosexuality might be his comment in the course of the Sermon on the Mount as reported in Matthew. Jesus says, "Whoever says to his brother, Racha, shall be liable to the sanhedrin [the Jewish council of priests]" (5:22; KJV). The meaning of the non-Greek word *racha* remained a mystery to translators until 1934, when a papyrus from Egypt was published with the term used in reference to a particular individual. The context suggests that the term *racha* was equivalent to *malakos* in Greek, "effeminate." If so, then Jesus' single comment on the subject of homosexuality is an admonition against what, in modern terms, might be called "fag-baiting."

The only New Testament verses that seem to refer to homosexuality are in Paul's letters. In the First Letter to the Corinthians, Paul lists several categories of "unjust ones" who will not inherit the kingdom of God (6:9). Two of the terms he uses, *malakoi* and *arsenokoitai*, have been taken to refer to homosexuals, but as pointed out above neither really correspond to the modern concept of individuals with a preference for same-sex relations. Paul may be referring to *some* homosexuals, but not homosexuals as a group and not only homosexuals. In any case, Paul's attitude toward these sinners is revealed in the next verse. They are not to be ostracized as evil-doers; rather, they are members of the church that Paul himself founded. As he tells the Corinthians, "You were washed, you were sanctified, you were justified in the name of the Lord Jesus Christ and in the Spirit of our God" (1 Cor. 6:11).

Then, there is the passage in the Letter to the Romans where Paul claims that God, in his wrath against pagans, "gave them up [or handed them over] to degrading passions" such that "their women exchanged natural intercourse for unnatural, and in the same way also, the men, giving up natural intercourse with women, were consumed with passion for one another. Men committed shameless acts with men and received in their own persons the due penalty for their error" (1:26-27). Paul's diatribe continues with a laundry list of sins, crimes, and other bad behavior, sexual and nonsexual, that God "gave them up to."

Although Paul is undoubtedly referring to homosexual acts in this passage, there is some ambiguity in the wording. Does he mean to condemn all people who desire their own sex and every instance of same-sex intimacy? The context here is a denunciation of pagans who have willfully rejected God. Homosexuality is just one of the sins they commit, which, in fact, they engage in not by choice, but because God has imposed such desires on them as punishment for their idolatry. What if one formed a committed, long-term sexual relationship with a member of his or her own sex, and was *not* an idolater, gossip, murderer, or fool (some of the other sins Paul lists)? Is every sexual act between men "shameless" or is it possible that some are not? John Boswell concluded that in this passage Paul had in mind heterosexuals who gave up their "natural" or normal sexual orientation to engage in homosexuality, not homosexuals for whom same-sex love was natural: "The whole point of Romans I, in fact, is to stigmatize persons who have rejected their calling, gotten off the true path they were once on."

Ultimately, it is the Old Testament, not the New, that churches must turn to in justifying their antihomosexual stance. The Old Testament story cited most often for this purpose is, of course, that of the city of Sodom in Genesis. Its destruction, modern churches claim, was God's punishment on the city after its men tried to have sex with angels who were visiting Lot—in the inscrutable language of Genesis, they wanted to "know" them.

This interpretation, however, hinges on the meaning of the Hebrew word "to know." It is rarely used in the Tanakh in sense of "to have intercourse" (only 10 times out of 943 uses according to Boswell, and of these only its use in the Sodom story possibly refers to homosexual intercourse). The normal meaning of the term is simply "to become familiar, to gain knowledge of." In fact, other Old Testament authors and early Christians, including Jesus himself, understood the crime of the Sodomites as inhospitality toward strangers. "If anyone will not welcome you or listen to your words," he says in Matthew, "shake off the dust from your feet as you leave that house or town. Truly I tell you, it will be more tolerable for the land of Sodom and Gomorrah on the day of judgment than for that town" (10:14-15). This is how most scholars today (in contrast to church dogmatists) interpret the story.

Another term in the Hebrew Bible that is sometimes taken to refer to homosexuals and translated into English as "sodomites" is *kadash* (pl. *kadēshim*), which literally means "consecrated" or "sacred one." The *kadēshim* were pagan temple officials whom the ancient Hebrews accused, along with their female counterparts, of engaging in sacred "prostitution." Following this usage, scholars have imagined that temple functionaries throughout the Near East were sacred prostitutes when, in fact, there is little evidence that sexual acts were actually performed in temples anywhere. The authors of the Old Testament were polemicists, committed to portraying polytheism in the worst possible light. In any case, even if it is conceded that the *kadēshim* engaged in homosexual acts as part of temple worship, we can legitimately ask whether denunciations of them are meant to be applied to every instance of same-sex intimacy, secular as well as sacred, voluntary as well as commercial. Again, the relevance of these references to homosexuals is not at all clear.

Finally, there is Leviticus, the ancient Jewish instruction manual for performing sacrifices and ensuring ritual purity. Two passages—18:22 and 20:13—address same-sex intercourse in similar terms: "Thou shalt not lie with mankind, as with womankind: it is abomination." Clearly, this prohibits Jews from engaging in same-sex intercourse. The larger context of these provisions, however, is the prohibition of idolatry (which Jews had succumbed to as a result of their contact with Egyptians and Canaanites) and instructions for obtaining ritual purity. Verse 21, for example, which immediately proceeds the prohibition of male-male acts, condemns the use of semen in the worship of Molech. It seems likely that verse 22 was written with the practices of the male temple officials, or *kadēshim*, in mind.

Although Levitical laws are interpreted today in moral terms ("lying with mankind" is "wrong"), the Hebrew word translated as "abomination," *toevah*, refers to impurity, not moral wrongdoing. Violations of purity laws disqualified Jews from performing rituals honoring God until they underwent the appropriate purifying procedures. Such laws served to erect a boundary between Jews and other peoples. Further, there is some ambiguity here. Why is lying "with mankind" qualified with the phrase "as with womankind"? Isn't it sufficient to say "don't have sex with other men"? Or is the law only concerned with penetrative intercourse—sex with a man *as if* he were a woman? The wording suggests that the problem is not same-sex intimacy as such, but the fact that such intimacy renders the man who is penetrated into a woman. Are other forms of same-sex intimacy not involving anal intercourse exempted? A more modern and less misogynist reading of Leviticus might be that what it condemns is sexual contact that degrades one person in relation to another. Is this problem unique to homosexuality? Are there no degrading forms of heterosexuality?

But, again, let's concede that Leviticus *does* prohibit same-sex intimacy. The question that arises next is whether Christians are obligated to follow this and other Old Testament laws. Scholars continue to debate whether Jesus himself advocated nonobservance of religious laws—the consensus being that he did not reject the Law of Moses in its entirety the way Paul did. Had he done so, Jewish authorities likely would have acted against him much sooner than they did. Morton Smith, however, suggested the possibility that Jesus preached liberation from the law privately and observance of the law publicly. In Matthew, he says he has come to fulfill the law, not to abolish it. But elsewhere, he indicates that in being fulfilled the law is no longer necessary. In its place, Jesus gives two broad decrees—love God and love one's neighbor as oneself (Matt. 22:39-40).

Jesus' parables downplay observance of traditional laws in relation to a broader evaluation of how individuals lead their lives. In the story of the beggar Lazarus and the rich man, for example, Lazarus is described as eating any morsel of food he can find — thus violating strict dietary laws and being in a state of impurity as a result. In contrast, the rich man obeys the dietary laws even as he lives and eats sumptuously. When the two men die, however, Lazarus is "carried away by the angels" to heaven, while the rich man is tormented in Hades (Luke 16:19-31).

Whereas the gospels attribute Jesus with varying attitudes toward observance of Jewish laws, Paul was unequivocal on the subject: "Christ is the end of the law so that there may be righteousness for everyone who believes" (Rom. 10:4). Having been sanctified through baptism, Paul claimed that the law no longer applied to him: "All things are lawful to me" (1 Cor. 6:12). What caused a traditional Jew to be "unclean" had no effect on him. Other early Christians, like James, remained observant. The debate between Paul and the traditionalists culminated in the so-called Council of Jerusalem around the year 45. Paul's position prevailed. The Council declared that gentile converts were not bound by Jewish laws. They were merely urged to "keep themselves" from "what has been sacrificed to idols and from blood and from what is strangled and from fornication [*porneia*]" (Acts 15:29). If they avoid these things, they "will do well." The language here is surprisingly moderate compared to the harsh dictates and penalties of Leviticus — *porneia* is not abominable, merely inadvisable. Further, in this context *porneia* may not even refer to sexual acts. In both the Old and New Testament, the term is frequently used as a metaphor for the worship of idols and other gods.

Whether or not Jesus advocated the complete abandonment of the law, he consistently rejected the concept of physical purity as applied to food and sex, introducing a new kind of moral system that emphasizes intentions and attitudes over outward conformity. In this system, sexual acts are not the source of impurity or sin in and of themselves; it is the motives that matter. On those occasions when Jesus did use purity language, he did so metaphorically, in reference to the purity of the heart. Jesus and early Christians like Paul were not anarchists, however. The law remains in the background, a point of reference, and with it, institutions like marriage. But instead of turning to the written word to judge sinners, Jesus tells us to turn to the sinner and apprehend his motives and circumstances, and to love him as we love ourselves and as God loves us.

Gays and the Christian Churches: Now What Do You Say?

In Christianity's early days, its advocates frequently wrote treatises, called apologias, defending their religion from its critics. This book, however, is not an apologia for homosexuality. It has not been my goal to answer the claim of many modern Christian churches that loving one's own sex is sinful. Rather, taking advantage of the discovery of the Secret Gospel, I have sought to offer Christians and non-Christians alike an opportunity to find same-sex love not only represented within the Christian heritage but capable of realizing its highest ideals.

A single fragment of text, however, cannot be the basis for changing an entire moral system. Gay and lesbian Christians must respond to the totality of the Bible's teachings, which are not merely antigay, but antisexual and patriarchal as well. It must be shown not only that same-sex love does not have to be condemned in all cases, but that it can fulfill God's will, just as his will is fulfilled when men and women observe Christian marriage vows.

The contribution of this book is not so much in arguing with the Bible, but in raising questions about the way it is applied when contemporary Christians condemn homosexuals. Simply put, are Christians practicing Christian love?

In fact, the Bible's references to homosexuality are not at all as clear as commonly assumed. Questions such as to whom these passages are directed and what behavior they actually refer to have no simple answers. Do Hebrew tirades against pagan religious officials apply to contemporary homosexuals who are not temple prostitutes and who profess love for each other? Does "lying with mankind, as with womankind" encompass all forms of intimacy between men or just penetrative sex?

Uncertainties such as these lead me to conclude that while the Christian Bible is certainly unfriendly to homosexuality, it does not require the condemnation of every instance of same-sex intimacy. Still, its view of sexuality is restrictive. Even opposite-sex intimacy is narrowly limited to marital activities and specific acts. And while the Bible may not prohibit every intimate same-sex relationship, it provides few guidelines for them. The burden falls upon gay and lesbian Christians to show how homosexuals and homosexual relationships can be integrated into a Christian community.

At the same time, Christians who would condemn homosexuals have a burden as well: to formulate their judgment in a Christian way.

If the example of Jesus is to be followed, reading and interpreting texts alone is not enough. In fact, the question of how to judge others is a central issue in the gospels, part of the original Q material that the gospels draw on. Jesus' teaching underscores two points. First, those who would judge ought to be humble and acknowledge their own failings first. As Jesus says in Luke, "Do not judge, and you will not be judged; do not condemn, and you will not be condemned. Forgive, and you will be forgiven" (6:37). A few verses later he repeats this maxim in metaphorical terms: "You hypocrite, first take the log out of your own eye, and then you will see clearly to take the speck out of your neighbor's eye" (6:42).

A second point Jesus makes is that judgments of others should be based on their intentions and dispositions, as well as their acts. This view is illustrated in the story told in chapter 9 of John, where Jesus heals a blind man. Jews (and others) in the ancient world viewed physical imperfections and disease as evidence of religious transgressions, either by the victim or the victim's family. But when Jesus encounters the blind man and his disciples ask, "Rabbi, who sinned, this man or his parents, that he was born blind?" Jesus replies, "Neither this man nor his parents sinned; he was born blind so that God's works might be revealed in him" (9:3). In other words, individuals should be judged on the basis of their lives and works, not by rote application of laws nor by the actions of others that they have no control over. Further, simply being born different (that is, blind) is not a sin. Indeed, as Jesus says, such differences represent a special opportunity to witness God's ways—in particular, his capacity for unconditional love.

As for the Levitical laws and other traditional codes on which contemporary churches base their condemnation of homosexuality, Jesus' attitude is revealed in the story of the adulterous woman. Caught in the act, the "scribes and the Pharisees" bring her before Jesus and remind him that Jewish law requires that she be stoned to death. "Now what do you say?," they ask him. Jesus does not immediately respond. He bends down and doodles in the dust with his finger, apparently in deep reflection. Finally, he speaks, delivering the famous line, "Let anyone among you who is without sin be the first to throw a stone at her." One by one, the woman's accusers leave. When Jesus is alone with the woman, he looks at her directly and asks if no one has condemned her. "No one, sir," she replies. "Neither do I condemn you. Go your way, and from now on do not sin again," he says (John 8:3-11).

Jesus' attitude here could not be more different than that attributed to the Pharisees, who were prepared to brutally kill the woman on the spot in the name of religious law. Jesus engages the woman and addresses her as an equal, not as an authority figure. Following his own admonition to the Pharisees, he does not condemn her—implying that he, too, is a sinner. Finally, he appeals to her conscience to stop sinning.

The woman's sin, it should be noted, is a specific heterosexual act. Jesus does not command her to stop being heterosexual. Similarly, Matthew refers to prostitutes becoming followers of John the Baptist. Most commentators assume that this means they stopped being prostitutes, but neither Matthew nor Luke actually say this, and, as William Countryman asks, how else could they have supported themselves, since ex-prostitutes remained pariahs in Jewish society, and women lacking husbands or fathers had no means of support? Given this, we might imagine Jesus addressing homosexuals similarly—it is specific transgressions, such as adultery, that must be given up, but not homosexuality in and of itself.

Jesus does not reject every traditional law, however. Common codes of morality still applied, and the gospels are at pains to show that he was not an advocate of sexual freedom or countercultural lifestyles. In Matthew, Jesus prohibits divorce (19:6-9). But nowhere in the gospels does he mention, let alone endorse, the Levitical prohibition of male-male intercourse. When he announces in Luke that "the law and the prophets were in effect until John [the Baptist] came" (16:16), there is no reason to doubt that Leviticus 18:22 and 20:13 were not among the laws no longer in effect.

Why, then, do churches hold up isolated provisions of Leviticus to condemn homosexuality, even as they set aside nearly all other Old Testament codes and, indeed, Jesus' own unequivocal prohibition of divorce, opening themselves to the charge of hypocrisy and to ridicule? (One spoof widely circulated on the Internet poses a series of rhetorical questions to Dr. Laura, the conservative television personality, regarding these laws: "Lev. 25:44 states that I may buy slaves from the nations that are around us. A friend of mine claims that this applies to Mexicans but not Canadians. Can you clarify?" and so forth.) As Boswell concluded, "It was not their respect for the law which created their hostility to homosexuality but their hostility to homosexuality which led them to retain a few passages from a law code largely discarded."

Contemporary "fundamentalists" and "literalists" might be better described as "selectivists." They pick and chose among biblical verses according to an agenda based in something other than biblical authority. While treating heterosexual acts on an individual basis—some are approved, others are not—they condemn all homosexual acts regardless of context. By implication, any heterosexual relationship is better than any homosexual one. The commitment and caring between lovers demonstrated so many times in the AIDS epidemic counts for nothing. Of course, the Christian view of sexuality makes even heterosexuality problematic. But it is not condemned; it is held to strict standards. Gays, in contrast, are not even given the chance to meet these standards, even as they are being liberalized in regards to divorce, contraception, and permitted sexual acts. And what are we to make, finally, of the sexual code advocated by a church whose own failure to adhere to it and whose attempts to hide that failure have reached criminal proportions?

Even if homosexual acts are sins, forgiveness, as the story of the adulterous woman dramatizes, is one of Jesus' most important teachings. Indeed, he says that a repentant sinner is better than one who never sinned at all! In the parable of the Pharisee and the tax collector, the tax collector is "justified" because he is humble before God and admits his sins. The Pharisee, in contrast, is not justified, even though he observes the laws, because he considers himself better than others. (This story would have had a dramatic impact in Jesus' time, since Jews who served as tax collectors were considered ritually impure.)

Christian forgiveness of sins is not only redeeming, giving individuals a "second chance" at a moral life, it is unconditional. Those who sin repeatedly are to be repeatedly forgiven. As Jesus tells his disciples, "If the same person sins against you seven times a day, and turns back to you seven times and says, 'I repent,' you must forgive" (Luke 17:4). By extension, then, why can't individuals who "sin" by having intimate contact with their own sex also be forgiven, and forgiven again even if they are unable to stop "sinning" — as long as they repent, that is, humbly admit their failings? Given Jesus' teachings on the forgiveness of sin, homosexuals shouldn't have to become sinless heterosexuals or celibate to join a church — any more than heterosexuals should have to give up heterosexuality because they commit the sin of adultery (which men commit, Jesus teaches, every time they look at women with lust in their hearts [Matt. 5:28]).

In the gospel narratives, Jesus' teachings concerning sin, forgiveness, and the judgment of others are part of a lengthy response to charges by the Pharisees that he ate with tax collectors and sinners. This was scandalous because it involved contact with people defined as "unclean." In fact, these two elements of Jesus' ministry — his outreach to marginal people and his rejection of a moral code based on outward conformance to the law — are directly connected. As he declares in Mark, "I have come to call not the righteous but sinners" (2:17).

The dogma of contemporary Christian churches regarding gays, lesbians, and other sexual minorities is at odds with Jesus' teachings. Casting themselves as modern Pharisees, churches are clinging to Old Testament attitudes, upholding laws that Jesus set aside, harshly and arbitrarily condemning gays as the Pharisees condemned the adulterous woman. In practice, if not by official policy, churches have silenced or banished gay members of their communities without genuinely encountering them, as Jesus encountered and engaged the marginal members of his society.

In Luke, Jesus tells his followers, "When you give a luncheon or a dinner, do not invite your friends or your brothers or your relatives or rich neighbors, in case they may invite you in return, and you would be repaid. But when you give a banquet, invite the poor, the crippled, the lame, and the blind. And you will be blessed, because they cannot repay you" (14:12). This is a radical commandment because, in Jesus' time, these people were normally feared and contact with them avoided. Today, gay people are among those whom society fears and avoids. Is it far-fetched to imagine that a modern Jesus would include them among the untouchables that true Christians should reach out to?

If modern Christians were to follow Jesus' example they might decline to condemn gay people or participate in stigmatizing them, as Jesus refused to condemn the adulterous woman. They might come to view differences, such as the desire for same-sex intimacy, not as sins but, as in the case of the man born blind, special opportunities to witness God's work. If they followed Jesus' admonitions concerning the judgment of others, they might recall their own sins and how they were forgiven, and acknowledge the complexity of human beings who can sin and yet still perform good works. Then, even if they still believed that homosexual acts were sins ("intrinsically disordered" in the purple language of the Catholic church), they might still be able to acknowledge the truth that some of those who commit such sins still earn glory in God's eyes, and, when they do, like the beggar Lazarus and the humble tax collector, they are superior to the observant Pharisee.

Laws and social conventions are not discarded, but they are set aside long enough to allow a genuine encounter with those accused of sinning. We are to treat others as we treat ourselves. Aren't we sinners, too? In fact, we are commanded to love sinners without conditions, even if the law says they are polluted and dangerous, even if society deems them despicable. We are to eat at their tables and look them in the eye before we judge them. Having had that encounter, we are likely to have discovered something of ourselves in them and realized that they, too, are fallible humans with a divine spark. If we seek forgiveness for our own sins, surely we ought to be ready to forgive the sins of others. Suspension of the law means we no longer live in a world of moral certainty. Jesus' teachings show us how to live in a culturally relative world, whether that of first-century Palestine or today.

This is what has been missing in the modern Christian response to gay people—a genuine encounter. In such an encounter, Christians would find, indeed, that homosexuals are sinners, sometimes depraved ones. But they would also witness acts of compassion, commitment, and selflessness such as those that occurred between lovers and friends in the AIDS epidemic. Admitting that gay people can love others and perform good works—even if Leviticus abominates them—would be a crack in the facade of Christian intransigence toward gays.

For the facade to be breached, however, a second, more intimate truth about queer lives must be witnessed as well. The sexual desires of homosexuals are intertwined with their capacity for altruism. For many Christians this will be an unfamiliar and uncomfortable realization, and yet it is a truism of human nature: that we first experience feelings of love and care in relationships with specific others and then later learn to transfer these feelings to others in general. This is what we saw in the life and poetry of Walt Whitman. It is true for heterosexuals and homosexuals. Love for mother and father (whether or not covertly sexual as Freud believed) is the first love of the infant and from there the individual's circle of loved ones grows, until, crossing the threshold of adulthood, it extends beyond the family. The emergence of desire for intimacy with others is not a break from the love learned and practiced in familial relationships, but an addition to it.

What this means is that if society wishes to benefit from the altruistic potential of those who are gay, then gay sexuality needs to be affirmed. This is not to say all homosexual acts are to be condoned, anymore than Christianity can condone all heterosexual acts. But the love that same-sex partners express in their sexual relationships can be condoned when it is subject-subject, when it is agape.

While the churches hesitate, society at large has begun such an encounter with gays and other sexual minorities, due in no small part to the AIDS epidemic. As the virus took lives, it has shattered closet doors. Millions of Americans have become aware that gay men were among their friends, relatives, coworkers, neighbors. In my lifetime, I've seen the logjam of prejudice against gays begin to break. Even if fear and dislike of homosexuality remain entrenched in many quarters, it is being offset by an equal distaste for the more rabid forms of homophobic hatred.

When will the churches catch up with the rest of society? The obstacles to equality for sexual minorities are substantial. In the final analysis, there really are no counterparts to contemporary gays, lesbians, and bisexuals in the Bible—people who seek voluntary and reciprocal intimate relationships, who profess their love for each other, who demonstrate that love in times of trial. Nonetheless, those of us who are gay must insist that the truth of our lives be witnessed, by Christians and by society as whole, the good and the bad. If you see a speck in our eyes, remember what speck we might see in yours.

BIBLIOGRAPHIC NOTES

Preface

Terrence McNally, *Corpus Christi: A Play* (New York: Grove Press, 1998). The controversy was widely covered in the popular media—see *Variety*, June 1, 1998 and October 19, 1998; and *Post-Gazette*, November 16, 1998. Robert Graves' comment on Plato is in *The White Goddess: A Historical Grammar of Poetic Myth*, rev. ed. (New York: Farrar, Straus and Giroux, 1966), p. 12. Jennings' book was published by Pilgrim Press in 2003. For Morton Smith's comment, see "Ascent to the Heavens and the Beginning of Christianity," *Eranos-Jahrbuch* 50 (1981): 403-29, p. 403.

There is now an extensive literature on the subject of the social construction and historical emergence of homosexual identity in Western societies. Key proponents, to name a few, include Michel Foucault, Jeffrey Weeks, Kenneth Plummer, David Halperin, David Greenberg, and John D'Emilio. A useful introduction is Edward Stein, ed., *Forms of Desire: Sexual Orientation and the Social Constructionist Controversy* (New York: Routledge, 1992). Social constructionism's most trenchant critic is Stephen O. Murray—see, for example, *Homosexualities* (Chicago: Chicago University Press, 2000).

Prologue

Knud Rasmussen, *Intellectual Culture of the Iglulik Eskimos*, Report of the Fifth Thule Expedition 1921-24, vol. 7, no. 1 (Copenhagen: Gyldendalske Boghandel, Nordisk Forlag, 1929), pp. 111-13.

Chapter One

Unless otherwise noted, New Testament passages are from the New Revised Standard Version Bible and those from the Old Testament from *Tanakh: The Holy Scriptures* (Philadelphia: Jewish Publication Society, 1988).

The discovery of Clement's letter is related in Morton Smith, *The Secret Gospel: The Discovery and Interpretation of the Secret Gospel According to Mark* (Clearlake, CA: Dawn Horse Press, 1982). Smith's publication and analysis of Clement's letter is in *Clement of Alexandria and a Secret Gospel of Mark* (Cambridge: Harvard University Press, 1973).

In writing this and subsequent chapters, I found the following studies of early Christianity useful: John D. Crossan, *The Birth of Christianity: Discovering What Happened in the Years Immediately After the Execution of Jesus* (San Francisco: HarperSanFrancisco, 1998); Helmut

Koester, *History and Literature of Early Christianity*, vol. 2 of *Introduction to the New Testament* (New York: Walter De Gruyter, 1982); Robert Eisenman, *James the Brother of Jesus: The Key to Unlocking the Secrets of Early Christianity and the Dead Sea Scrolls* (New York: Penguin Books, 1998); Geza Vermes, *The Changing Faces of Jesus* (New York: Viking Compass, 2000); Paula Fredriksen, *Jesus of Nazareth: King of the Jews* (New York: Alfred A. Knopf, 1999); Raymond E. Brown, *The Community of the Beloved Disciple* (New York: Paulist Press, 1979); Rudolf Bultmann, *Primitive Christianity in its Contemporary Setting* (Thames and Hudson, 1983 [1956]); J. G. Davies, *The Early Christian Church* (New York: Barnes and Noble, 1995 [1965]); and the several articles in Bruce Corley, ed., *Colloquy on New Testament Studies: A Time for Reappraisal and Fresh Approaches* (Macon, GA: Mercer University Press, 1983).

The comment on Jesus as a "possibly homosexual baptizer" appears in John D. Crossan, *Four Other Gospels: Shadows on the Contours of Canon* (Minneapolis, MN: Winston Press, 1985), p. 102. Helmut Koester discusses the Secret Gospel in "History and Development of Mark's Gospel (from Mark to Secret Mark and 'Canonical' Mark)," in Corley, ed., *Colloquy on New Testament Studies*, pp. 35-57. Guy G. Strousma has recently published an account of his examination of the book in which Clement's letter is inscribed at the Mar Saba monastery in 1976. It was subsequently removed to Jerusalem by church officials and has since disappeared. Strousma confirms both the existence of the manuscript and the genuineness of the photographs Smith published. He is, however, the last living person who has seen this precious document. See "Comments on Charles Hedrick's Article: A Testimony," *Journal of Early Christian Studies* 11(2) (summer 2003): 147-53.

Chapter Two

For the uses and significance of the *sindōn*, see Smith, *Clement of Alexandria*, pp. 175-78.

On Paul's mission and the controversy over gentile conversion see the studies of early Christianity cited above and E. Earle Ellis, *Prophecy and Hermeneutic in Early Christianity* (Grand Rapids, MI: William B. Eerdmans Publishing, 1978). The classic study of rites of passage is Arnold van Gennep, *The Rites of Passage*, trans. Monika B. Vizedom and Gabrielle L. Caffee (Chicago: University of Chicago Press, 1960); see also Victor W. Turner, *The Ritual Process: Structure and Anti-structure* (Chicago: Aldine Publishing Co., 1969).

The history of ancient Near Eastern concepts of heaven is the subject of J. Edward Wright, *The Early History of Heaven* (New York: Oxford University Press, 2000). Peter Kingsley's useful study is *Ancient Philosophy, Mystery, and Magic: Empedocles and Pythagorean Tradition*

(Oxford: Oxford University Press, 1995).

On the influence of Greek language and culture on Jews in Palestine see Vermes, *Changing Faces of Jesus*, p. 241; Koester, *History and Literature of Early Christianity*, p. 90; and Saul Lieberman, "How Much Greek in Jewish Palestine?" in *Biblical and Other Studies*, ed. Alexander Altmann *(Philip W. Lown Institute of Advanced Judaic Studies, Studies and Texts 1)*, pp. 123-41 (Cambridge, MA: Harvard University Press, 1963). For E. R. Dodds' comment, see *Pagan and Christian in an Age of Anxiety: Some Aspects of Religious Experience from Marcus Aurelius to Constantine* (Cambridge: Cambridge University Press, 1965), p. 38.

Chapter Three

On the Merkavah and Hekhalot literature, see David J. Halperin, *The Faces of the Chariot: Early Jewish Responses to Ezekiel's Vision*, Texte und Studien zum Antiken Judentum, vol. 16 (Tübigen: J. C. B. Mohr [Paul Siebeck], 1988); "Merkabah" and "Throne of God," in *Encyclopaedia Judaica*; Gershom G. Scholem, *Major Trends in Jewish Mysticism* (New York: Schocken Books, 1961 [1941]) and *Jewish Gnosticism, Merkabah Mysticism, and Talmudic Tradition*, 2nd ed. (New York, 1965); Morton Smith, "Observations on *Hekhalot Rabbati*," in *Biblical and Other Studies*, pp. 142-60; John J. Collins, "A Throne in the Heavens: Apotheosis in pre-Christian Judaism," in *Death, Ecstasy, and Other Worldly Journeys*, ed. John J. Collins and Michael Fishbane (Albany, N.Y.: State University of New York Press, 1995), pp. 43-58; Adela Yarbro Collins, "The Seven Heavens in Jewish and Christian Apocalypses," in *Death*, pp. 59-93; Alan F. Segal, "Paul and the Beginning of Jewish Mysticism," in *Death*, pp. 95-122; David R. Blumenthal, *Understanding Jewish Mysticism: A Source Reader, vol. 1, The Merkabah Tradition and The Zoharic Tradition* (New York: KTAV Publishing House, 1978); and Peter Schäffer, *Hekhalot-Studien* (Tübigen: J.C.B. Mohr, 1988). For an overview of heavenly ascent in the ancient world, see Martha Himmelfarb, "The Practice of Ascent in the Ancient Mediterranean World," in *Death*, pp. 123-37. A useful overview is Luther H. Martin, *Hellenistic Religions: An Introduction* (New York: Oxford University Press, 1987).

Hekhalot texts are extremely obscure. Scholars are often at a loss to determine which of various manuscripts is the most original or accurate, and it is often difficult to tell where a particular text begins or ends. In some cases, unrelated material has been copied into the middle of a completely separate text. The texts themselves are written in Aramaic and Hebrew with long passages of untranslatable incantations and hymns. Few scholars are able to read, let alone translate them with any confidence. As a result, it has taken until the last few decades for their significance for the history of both Judaism and Christianity to be recognized.

For the hero's journey, see Joseph Campbell, *The Hero with a Thousand Faces*, 2nd ed. (Princeton, NJ: Princeton University Press, 1968).

There is a debate among scholars regarding the extent to which Hekhalot texts can be characterized as instruction manuals for heavenly ascents. Gershom Scholem and Morton Smith believed that they were, and that they grew out of a Jewish esoteric tradition that had already absorbed elements of Hellenistic magic by the time Christianity appeared. Most scholars now believe that Hekhalot texts were all written some centuries after the birth of Christianity. They draw on Jewish apocalyptic traditions, but as these were transmitted by rabbinic Judaism and Christianity. David J. Halperin and others point out that only a few Hekhalot texts really contain explicit instructions for ascending to heaven; nor are the activities related in them necessarily identified as restricted or esoteric. According to Peter Schäffer, the most common element found in these writings are adjurations directed at angels for the purpose of controlling them without having to ascend to heaven to do so. In this regard, they are more like the everyday spells of ancient magic in which practical, not mystical, ends were the goal. One of these practical goals was instantaneous mastery of the Torah. Nonetheless, whatever the final consensus of scholars, ascending to heaven is undeniably the goal in at least some of these texts, and some include rather explicit instructions for achieving it.

On ancient magic, see Fritz Graf, *Magic in the Ancient World* (Cambridge, MA: Harvard University Press, 1997) and the various articles in Christopher A. Faraone and Dirk Obbink, *Magika Hiera: Ancient Greek Magic & Religion* (New York: Oxford University Press, 1991). Most New Testament scholars agree that exorcisms were central to Jesus' mission and the source of his authority as a teacher. See Morton Smith, *Jesus the Magician* (San Francisco: Harper & Row, 1978) and *Secret Gospel*; Koester, *History and Literature of Early Christianity*; Vermes, *Changing Faces*; and Fredriksen, *Jesus of Nazareth*.

Halperin, *Faces of the Chariot*, is the source of the passages quoted from the *Hekhalot Rabbati* (p. 367), Rabbi Ishmael (p. 369), and the *Hekhalot Zutarti* (p. 374).

Chapter Four

See Carol Zaleski, "Death and Near-Death Today," in Collins and Fishbane, eds., *Death*, pp. 383-407. On nudity in early Christian baptism, see M. Smith, *Clement of Alexandria* and Jonathan Z. Smith, "The Garments of Shame," *History of Religions* 5 (1965): 217-38. For an example of a same-sex love spell, see Marvin Meyer and Richard Smith, eds., *Ancient Christian Magic: Coptic Texts of Ritual Power* (San Francisco:

HarperSanFrancisco, 1994), pp. 177-78. The Egyptian references to heavenly ladders are quoted from E. A. Wallis Budge, *The Egyptian Book of the Dead* (New York: Dover, 1967), p. lxxi.

Chapter Five

Koester discusses Mark 10:21 in *History and Literature of Early Christianity*, p. 53.

In *The Man Jesus Loved*, Jennings offers a very different interpretation of the evidence concerning the beloved disciple from that of Brown's, arguing that his role is simply that of a witness to Peter's authority with no evident connection to any theological issue or party. By his own admission, however, the idea that a community of Christians would create a gospel based on this figure's recollections and yet not claim him as a theological authority is "remarkable." Jennings subsequently allows that the Gospel of John indeed may have been "theologically motivated either by the beloved or the writers/editors or both."

Since writing the section on the relationship of the Secret Gospel youth to other figures in Mark and John, I have become aware of Miles Fowler's useful article, "Identification of the Bethany Youth in the Secret Gospel of Mark with other Figures Found in Mark and John," *Journal of Higher Criticism* 5(11) (spring, 1988): 3-22.

Countryman's study is *Dirt, Greed and Sex: Sexual Ethics in the New Testament and their Implications for Today* (Philadelphia: Fortress Press, 1988). Peter Schäffer's remark on the role of love in the Hekhalot tradition is in *Hekhalot-Studien*, p. 298. The comment on Plato's role in Western civilization is from Walter Wili, "The Orphic Mysteries and the Greek Spirit," in *The Mysteries: Papers from the Eranos Yearbooks*, ed. Joseph Campbell, pp. 64-92 (Princeton, NJ: Princeton University Press, 1978), p. 87.

Chapter Six

Quoted passages from the *Symposium* and *Phaedrus* are from William S. Cobb, trans., *Plato's Erotic Dialogues* (Albany, NY: State University of New York Press, 1993). Those from *Lysis* are in W. R. M. Lamb, trans., *Plato*, vol. 3 (Loeb Classical Library, 1925). The definitive study of Greek same-sex relations is still K. J. Dover, *Greek Homosexuality* (Cambridge: Harvard University Press, 1978).

There is ongoing debate on how Plato should be read. The conventional view is that the dialogues are philosophical treatises in which Plato systematically lays out his ideas with Socrates as his mouthpiece. More recently, some scholars have pointed to the nonphilosophical elements of the dialogues—the dramatic devices, the use of humor and irony—and argued that their real point is to show how philosophy is based on facile and contradictory arguments. Socrates, in this view, is being held up for criticism, even ridiculed, and nothing in the dialogues is meant to be taken seriously.

I read the *Symposium* and *Phaedrus* more conventionally, as if they were vehicles for serious ideas. At the same time, it is clear they are meant to be entertaining, too. This is philosophy "lite," if you will. The presentation of ideas, especially in the *Symposium*, is often playful. Thus, the dialogues offer potpourris of ideas, not airtight systems. Their ironic elements serve to deflate Socrates (and the author behind him) without necessarily negating the ideas he expresses. Not every question is definitely answered. In this regard, Plato's dialogues are "indeterminate" in a postmodern sense. As William Cobb concludes, "Their open-ended character and their many-sidedness stimulate the sort of reflexive give-and-take that makes for effective fertilization in living conversation" (p. 167).

Anders Nygren's study was published in English as *Agape and Eros*, trans. Philip S. Watson (Philadelphia: Westminster Press, 1953). For Catherine Osborne, see *Eros Unveiled: Plato and the God of Love* (Oxford: Clarendon Press, 1994). Jung's essay, "Answer to Job," is in *The Portable Jung*, ed. Joseph Campbell, pp. 519-650 (New York: Penguin Books, 1971).

Chapter Seven

The classic albeit outdated study of Orphism is W. K. C. Guthrie, *Orpheus and Greek Religion: A Study of the Orphic Movement* (Princeton, NJ: Princeton University Press, 1993 [1935]). See also M. L. West, *The Orphic Poems* (Oxford: Clarendon Press, 1983) and Wili, "Orphic Mysteries and the Greek Spirit." The passage from the *Rhapsodic Theogony* is from Guthrie, pp. 137-38. The reference to double sex organs is in fragment 80, part of the Hieronymus-Hellanicus theogony. See Luc Brisson, *Sexual Ambivalence: Androgyny and Hermaphroditism in Graeco-Roman Antiquity*, trans. Janet Lloyd (Berkeley: University of California Press, 2002). On Plato and Orphism, see Guthrie, *Orpheus and Greek Religion*, and Kingsley, *Ancient Philosophy, Mystery, and Magic*.

On the role of *mania* and the Corybantic rites in Plato, see Ivan M. Linforth's articles, "Telestic Madness in Plato, Phaedrus 244DE," University of California Publications in Classical Philology 13(6): 163-72 and "The Corybantic Rites in Plato," *University of California Publications in Classical Philology* 13(6): 121-62. See also, Arthur Darby Nock, "A Cabiric Rite," *American Journal of Archaeology* 45(4) (1941): 57-81 and Walter Burkert, *Ancient Mystery Cults* (Cambridge, MA: Harvard University Press, 1987).

The text of the Orphic gold plate is from Guthrie, p. 173. Quoted lines of Orphic hymns are from Wili, "Orphic Mysteries and the Greek Spirit," p. 71 and West, *Orphic Poems*, pp. 214-15.

On Salmoxis, see Mircea Eliade, "Zalmoxis," *History of Religions* 11 (1972): 257-302. For recent research on the Scythians, see the essays in Ellen D. Reeder, ed., *Scythian Gold* (New York: Henry N. Abrams, 1999). For archaeological findings suggesting alternative gender roles among the Scythians and Samartians, see Jeannine Davis-Kimball, *Women Warriors: An Archaeologist's Search for History's Hidden Heroines* (New York: Warner Books, 2002). Georges Dumézil discusses the parallels between Scythian traditions and Ossete folklore in "Les 'Énarées' scythiques et la grossesse du Narte Hamyc," *Latomus* (Brussels) 5 (July-December, 1946): 249-55. On parallels between the Corybantes, Cabeiri/Kabeiroi, Dactyli, and others, see Nock, "A Cabiric Rite," and C. [K.] Kerényi, "The Mysteries of the Kabeiroi," in Campbell, ed., *The Mysteries*, pp. 32-63.

Chapter Eight

For the controversy over the Secret Gospel, see Shawn Eyer, "The Strange Case of the Secret Gospel According to Mark," *Alexandria: The Journal for the Western Cosmological Traditions* 3 (1995): 103-29; Morton Smith, "Clement of Alexandria and Secret Mark: The Score at the End of the First Decade," *Harvard Theological Review* 75(4) (1982): 449-61; Charles W. Hedrick, "The Secret Gospel of Mark: Stalemate in the Academy," *Journal of Early Christian Studies* 11(2) (summer 2003): 133-45; and the Secret Gospel of Mark home page at http://alf.zfn.uni-bremen.de/~wie/Secret/secmark_home.html. On anthropology's silence concerning cross-cultural homosexuality and gender diversity, see Will Roscoe, "'Strange Craft, Strange History, Strange Folks': Cultural Amnesia and the Case for Lesbian/Gay Studies," *American Anthropologist* 97(3) (1995): 448-53.

The exchange between Bogoraz and Boas is in Stanley A. Freed, Ruth S. Freed, and Lalia Williamson, "Capitalist Philanthropy and Russian Revolutionaries: The Jesup North Pacific Expedition (1897-1902)," *American Anthropologist* 90 (1988): 7-24. On Bogoraz, see also Lawrence Krader, "Bogoraz, Vladimir G.; Sternberg, Lev Y.; and Jochelson, Vladimir," in *International Encyclopedia of the Social Sciences*, vol., 2, pp. 116-19 (New York: Free Press, 1968). Quoted passages of Bogoraz are from Waldemar G. Bogoraz, "The Chukchi of Northeastern Asia," *American Anthropologist* 3 (1901): 80-108 and *The Chukchee, Memoirs of the American Museum of Natural History*, vol. 11 (Leiden: E. J. Brill, 1909).

For reports on related practices throughout Siberia and Central

Asia, see M. A. Czaplicka, *Aboriginal Siberia: A Study in Social Anthropology* (Oxford: Clarendon Press, 1914); Vladimir N. Basilov, "Vestiges of Transvestism in Central-Asian Shamanism," in *Shamanism in Siberia*, ed. Vilmos Diószegi and Mihály Hoppál, pp. 281-90 (Budapest: Akademiai Kiado, 1978); A. Johansons, "The Shamaness of the Abkhazians," *History of Religions* 11 (1972): 251-56; Å. Hultkrantz, "Ecological and Phenomenological Aspects of Shamanism," in *Shamanism in Siberia*, pp. 27-58; Marjorie M. Balzer, "Sacred Genders in Siberia: Shamans, Bear Festivals, and Androgyny," in *Gender Reversals and Gender Cultures: Anthropological and Historical Perspectives*, ed. Sabrina P. Ramet, pp. 164-82 (London and New York: Routledge, 1996); and Bernard Saladin d'Anglure, "Rethinking Inuit Shamanism through the Concept of 'Third Gender,'" in *Northern Religions and Shamanism [Ethnologica Uralica 3]*, ed. Mihály Hoppál and Juha Pentikäinen, pp. 146-50 (Budapest and Helsinki: Akadémiai Kiadó and Finish Literature Society, 1992).

Marcel Mauss is quoted in Kingsley, *Ancient Philosophy, Mystery, and Magic*, p. 229.

Chapter Nine

The key works cited in this chapter are Mircea Eliade, *Shamanism: Archaic Techniques of Ecstasy* (Princeton, NJ: Princeton University Press, 1972); Claude Lévi-Strauss, *Structural Anthropology* (New York: Basic Books, 1963); and C. G. Jung, *Mandala Symbolism*, trans. R. F. C. Hull (Princeton, NJ: Princeton University Press, 1972). On Korean shamanism, see Laurel Kendall, *Shamans, Housewives, and Other Restless Spirits: Women in Korean Ritual Life* (Honolulu: University of Hawaii Press, 1985). The Gold shaman's account is from Leo Sternberg, "Divine Election in Primitive Religion," in *Congrès International des Américanistes, Compte-Rendu de la XXIᵉ session*, Pt. 2 (1924), pp. 472-512 (Göteborg: Göteborg Museum, 1925).

Chapter Ten

For a fuller account of Klah's life, see Will Roscoe, *Changing Ones: Third and Fourth Genders in Native North America* (New York: St. Martin's Press, 1998).

The findings from the archaeological site of Monte Verde, Chile were published in T. D. Dillehay, ed., *Monte Verde, A Late Pleistocene Settlement in Chile*, 2 vols. (Washington, D.C.: Smithsonian Institution Press, 1989, 1997). For the subsequent controversy see the special report of *Scientific American Discovering Archaeology*, November/December 1999.

Jesus and the Shamanic Tradition of Same-Sex Love

On the Navajo deity Begochídíín, see Karl W. Luckert, *The Navajo Hunter Tradition* (Tucson: University of Arizona Press, 1975) and Donald Sandner, *Navaho Symbols of Healing* (New York: Harcourt Brace Jovanovich, 1979). Klah's comment on Begochídíín is in *Hail Chant and Water Chant*, ed. Mary C. Wheelwright, Navajo Religion Series 2 (Santa Fe: Museum of Navajo Ceremonial Art, 1946).

On religious and alternative gender status in the ancient Near East and Mediterranean, see Will Roscoe, "Priests of the Goddess: Gender Transgression in Ancient Religion," *History of Religions* 35(3) (1996): 295-330. The passage quoted from "Descent of Inanna" is translated in Diane Wolkstein and Samuel N. Kramer, *Inanna, Queen of Heaven and Earth: Her Stories and Hymns from Sumer* (New York: Harper & Row, 1983), pp. 65-66.

Chapter Eleven

For Hay, see Stuart Timmons' biography, *The Trouble with Harry Hay: Founder of the Modern Gay Movement* (Boston: Alyson Publications, 1990). Hay's own writings appear in Will Roscoe, ed., *Radically Gay: Gay Liberation in the Words of Its Founder* (Boston: Beacon Press, 1996). "A Separate People Whose Time Has Come" is in *Gay Spirit: Myth and Meaning*, ed. Mark Thompson (New York: St. Martin's Press, 1987), pp. 279-91 (the extended quote is from p. 286). Harold Norse, Dennis Altman, and the London Gay Liberation Front manifesto are all in Len Richmond and Gary Noguera, eds., *The Gay Liberation Book* (San Francisco: Ramparts Press, 1973), pp. 171, 16, and 126.

Quotes of Whitman's poetry are from *The Complete Poems*, ed. Francis Murphy (Harmondsworth: Penguin Education, 1975). Other passages quoted are from Rictor Norton, "Walt Whitman: Prophet of Gay Liberation," *The Great Queens of History*, updated Nov. 18, 1999, http://www.infopt.demon.co.uk/whitman.htm. See also Robert K. Martin, *The Homosexual Tradition in American Poetry* (University of Texas Press, 1979); Roy Morris, Jr., *The Better Angel: Walt Whitman in the Civil War* (New York: Oxford University Press, 2000); and Charley Shively, ed., *Calamus Lovers: Walt Whitman's Working Class Camerados* (San Francisco: Gay Sunshine Press, 1987), p. 101.

Edward Carpenter's comment on Whitman is in *My Days and Dreams*, 3rd ed. (London: George Allen & Unwin, 1921), p. 86. "Desperate Living" was first published in *RFD* 10(1) (1983): 21-27. For Andrew Sullivan's comments on gay friendship, see *Love Undetectable: Notes on Friendship, Sex, and Survival* (New York: Alfred A. Knopf, 1998), p. 175. Kath Weston's study is *Families We Choose: Lesbian, Gays, Kinship* (New York: Columbia University Press, 1991).

C. G. Jung's comments on homosexuality and friendship are from

"Psychological Aspects of the Mother Archetype," in *The Archetypes and the Collective Unconscious*, 2nd ed., trans. R.F.C. Hull, *Collected Works of C. G. Jung*, vol. 9, part 1 (New York: Bollingen Series XX, Pantheon Books, 1968), pp. 75-112 (extended quote on pp. 86-87).

Chapter Twelve

The passage from "Democratic Vistas" is in *Walt Whitman, Complete Prose Works* (New York: Mitchell Kennerley, 1914), pp. 197-250. Robert Hopcke discusses archetypal patterns in the psychology of contemporary gay men in *Jung, Jungians, and Homosexuality* (Boston: Shambala, 1989). See also Mitch Walker, *Visionary Love: A Spirit Book of Gay Mythology* (San Francisco: Treeroots Press, 1980), p. 23.

The closing lines from Whitman are in Shively, ed., *Calamus Lovers*, p. 101.

Appendices

Spell-Checking the Word of God

Catechism of the Catholic Church (Liguori, MO: Liguori Publications, 1994).

Useful works on the origin and development of early Christian literature include Koester, *History and Literature of Early Christianity* and "History and Development of Mark's Gospel"; Burton L. Mack, *Who Wrote the New Testament: The Making of the Christian Myth* (San Francisco: HarperSanFrancisco, 1995); Arthur G. Patzia, *The Making of the New Testament: Origin, Collection, Text & Canon* (Downers Grove: IL: InterVarsity Press, 1995); Robert M. Grant, *The Formation of the New Testament* (New York: Harper & Row, 1965); and F. F. Bruce, *The Books and the Parchments: Some Chapters on the Transmission of the Bible*, rev. ed. (Westwood, N.J.: Fleming H. Revell, 1963). The quote regarding New Testament editing is from Patzia, *Making of the New Testament*, p. 132.

Morton Smith's comment is in "Clement of Alexandria and Secret Mark," p. 458.

The attestation of the gospels in papyri is summarized by Crossan in *Birth of Christianity*, pp. 124-26. A useful cross-reference table indicating the knowledge and opinion of various early Church Fathers concerning New Testament texts can be found at http://ntcanon.org/table.shtml

Jesus and the Shamanic Tradition of Same-Sex Love

Sex and Spirit in Corinth

Regarding Paul's opponents, see Ellis, *Prophecy and Hermeneutic*.

For discussions of the terms *malakos* and *arsenokoitai*, see Countryman, *Dirt, Greed, and Sex*, pp. 117-18, 202 and Boswell, *Christianity, Social Tolerance, and Homosexuality: Gay People in Western Europe from the Beginning of the Christian Era to the Fourteenth Century* (Chicago: University of Chicago Press, 1980), pp. 338-53. For recent studies of ancient sexuality see John J. Winkler, *The Constraints of Desire: The Anthropology of Sex and Gender in Ancient Greece* (New York: Routledge, 1990); David M. Halperin, *One Hundred Years of Homosexuality and Other Essays on Greek Love* (New York: Routledge, 1990); and Craig A. Williams, *Roman Homosexuality: Ideologies of Masculinity in Classical Antiquity* (New York: Oxford University Press, 1999).

The comment regarding unattractive characters in Jesus' mission is quoted in Crossan, *Birth of Christianity*, p. 281.

On the significance of women uncovering their heads, see Wayne A. Meeks, "The Image of the Androgyne: Some Uses of a Symbol in Earliest Christianity," *History of Religions* 13(3) (1974): 165-208.

For recent studies emphasizing Jesus' Jewish background, see Fredrickson, *Jesus of Nazareth* and Vermes, *Changing Faces of Jesus*. On early Christianity as a form of zealotry, see Eisenman, *James the Brother of Jesus*. On Paul's opponents, see E. Earle Ellis, *Prophecy and Hermeneutic*.

Hetero-androgyny in Early Christianity

For the "baptismal reunification formula," see Meeks, "Image of the Androgyne"; see also Jonathan Z. Smith, "The Garments of Shame." For cross-dressing female monks and holy women, see Marie Delcourt, *Hermaphrodite: Myths and Rites of the Bisexual Figure in Classical Antiquity*, trans. Jennifer Nicholson (London: Studio, 1961), pp. 84-102; John Anson, "The Female Transvestite in Early Monasticism: The Origin and Development of a Motif," *Viator 5* (1974): 1-32; Aline Rousselle, *Porneia: On Desire and the Body in Antiquity*, trans. Felicia Pheasant (New York: Blackwell, 1988); Peter Brown, *The Body and Society: Men, Women, and Sexual Renunciation in Early Christianity* (New York: Columbia University Press, 1988); and Joyce E. Salisbury, *Church Fathers, Independent Virgins* (London: Verso, 1991).

Paul's Ascent to the Garden

On the number of heavens in Jewish tradition, see P. Alexander in James H. Charlesworth, ed., *The Old Testament Pseudepigrapha,* vol. 1,

Apocalyptic Literature and Testaments (Doubleday & Company, 1983); see also Peter Schäffer, "New Testament and Hekhalot Literature: The Journey into Heaven in Paul and in Merkavah Mysticism," in *Hekhalot-Studien*, pp. 234-47; and Himmelfarb, "The Practice of Ascent in the Ancient Mediterranean World," in *Death*.

Uprising to Heaven

Quoted passages are from David J. Halperin, *The Faces of the Chariot*, p. 407 and Schäffer, *Hekhalot-Studien*, p. 289.

Why Was Diotima a Woman?

See David M. Halperin, *One Hundred Years of Homosexuality*, pp. 113-51.

The Boy Who Became a God

Robert Koehl, "Ephoros and Initiatory Homosexuality in Bronze Age Crete," paper delivered at "At the Frontier: Homosexuality and the Social Sciences," City University of New York, December 2, 1993. See also, James M. Saslow, *Ganymede in the Renaissance: Homosexuality in Art and Society* (New Haven: Yale University Press, 1986).

The *Galli* and Their Kind

For a fuller discussion of the *galli* and their counterparts, see Roscoe, "Priests of the Goddess," and Randy P. Conner, *Blossom of Bone: Reclaiming the Connections between Homoeroticism and the Sacred* (San Francisco: HarperSanFrancisco, 1993). Other works referred to are Kerényi, "The Mysteries of the Kabeiroi," and Nock, "A Cabiric Rite."

Christianity and Paganism

See Robert Murray, "The Characteristics of the Earliest Syriac Christianity," in *East of Byzantium: Syria and Armenia in the Formative Period*, ed. Nina G. Garsoïan, Thomas F. Mathews, and Robert W. Thomson, pp. 3-16 (Washington, DC: Dumbarton Oaks, 1982); Th. Nöldeke, "Die Selbstentmannung bei den Syrern," *Archiv fur Religionswissenshaft* 10(1) [1907]: 150-52; and H. J. W. Drijvers, *Cults and Beliefs at Edessa* (Leiden: E. J. Brill, 1980).

Jesus and the Shamanic Tradition of Same-Sex Love

Saint Twin-Twin

On Cosmas and Damian, see William Smith and Samuel Cheetham, eds., *A Dictionary of Christian Antiquities* (London: John Murray, 1875), p. 473, and Richard P. Knight, *A Discourse on the Worship of Priapus* (Secaucus, NJ: University Books, 1974), pp. 5-7.

Repression and Revival in Siberia

See Balzer, "Sacred Genders in Siberia," p. 172.

Jesus the Shaman

See Eliade, *Shamanism*, p. 8.

Say What?

For useful reviews, see Daniel A. Helminiak, *What the Bible Really Says about Homosexuality*, rev. ed. (New Mexico: Alamo Square Press, 2000) and Martin S. Cohen, "The Biblical Prohibition of Homosexual Intercourse," *Journal of Homosexuality* 19(4) (1990): 3-20. See also Boswell, *Christianity, Social Tolerance, and Homosexuality*—the quote is from p. 109—and Countryman, *Dirt, Greed, and Sex*, pp. 110-17.

Gays and the Churches

Boswell's remark on the source of hostility to homosexuality is in *Christianity*, p. 105.

Will Roscoe received his PhD in Historical Consciousness/Anthropology from the University of California, Santa Cruz. His first book, *The Zuni Man-Woman* (University of New Mexico Press) received the Margaret Mead Award of the American Anthropological Association and a Lambda Literary Award. He has since published *Queer Spirits: A Gay Men's Myth Book* (Beacon) and *Radically Gay: Gay Liberation in the Words of its Founder* (Beacon) by Harry Hay. He is also co-editor of *Islamic Homosexualities* (New York University Press) and *Boy-Wives and Female Husbands: Studies of African Homosexualities* (St. Martin's). In 1998, he published *Changing Ones: Third and Fourth Genders in Native North America* (St. Martin's), a comprehensive study of the lives and cultures of Native American berdache, or two-spirit, people.

Roscoe has taught at UC/Berkeley, UC/Santa Cruz, San Francisco State University, the California Institute of Integral Studies, and Dominican College. From 1991-1995, he was an affiliated scholar at Stanford University's Institute for Research on Women and Gender at Stanford University. In 2003, he received a Monette-Horowitz Award for lifetime achievement in combatting homophobia.